Key Concepts in
Critical Management Studies

Recent volumes include:

Key Concepts in Work
Paul Blyton & Jean Jenkins

Key Concepts in Governance
Mark Bevir

Key Concepts in Marketing
Jim Blythe

Key Concepts in Public Relations
Bob Franklin, Mike Hogan, Quentin
Langley, Nick Mosdell & Elliott Pill

**Key Concepts in Human Resource
Management**
John Martin

**Key Concepts in Operations
Management**
Michel Leseure

**Key Concepts in Corporate Social
Responsibility**
Suzanne Benn & Dianne Bolton

The SAGE Key Concepts series provides students with accessible and authoritative knowledge of the essential topics in a variety of disciplines. Cross-referenced throughout, the format encourages critical evaluation through understanding. Written by experienced and respected academics, the books are indispensable study aids and guides to comprehension.

MARK TADAJEWSKI, PAULINE MACLARAN,
ELIZABETH PARSONS AND MARTIN PARKER

Key Concepts in
Critical Management
Studies

Los Angeles | London | New Delhi
Singapore | Washington DC

SAGE Publications Ltd
1 Oliver's Yard
55 City Road
London EC1Y 1SP

SAGE Publications Inc.
2455 Teller Road
Thousand Oaks, California 91320

SAGE Publications India Pvt Ltd
B 1/I 1 Mohan Cooperative Industrial Area
Mathura Road
New Delhi 110 044

SAGE Publications Asia-Pacific Pte Ltd
33 Pekin Street #02-01
Far East Square
Singapore 048763

Library of Congress Control Number: 2010930472

British Library Cataloguing in Publication data

A catalogue record for this book is available from the
British Library

ISBN 978-1-84920-568-9
ISBN 978-1-84920-569-6 (pbk)

Typeset by C&M Digitals (P) Ltd, Chennai, India
Printed in India at Replika Press Pvt Ltd
Printed on paper from sustainable resources

contents

contents

v

key concepts in
critical management studies

notes on contributors

EDITORS

Prof. Pauline Maclaran is Professor of Marketing and Consumer Research at Royal Holloway, University of London.

Prof. Martin Parker is Professor of Organisation and Culture at the University of Warwick.

Dr. Elizabeth Parsons is Senior Lecturer in Marketing at Keele Management School.

Prof. Mark Tadajewski is Professor of Marketing at the University of Strathclyde.

AUTHORS

Prof. Paul Adler is Harold Quinton Chair in Business Policy and Professor of Management and Organization at the University of Southern California.

Peter Armstrong is Emeritus Professor at the Management School of the University of Leicester.

Prof. Bobby Banerjee is Associate Dean (Research), College of Business at the University of Western Sydney.

Dr. Armin Beverungen is Lecturer in Organisation Studies at the University of the West of England.

Prof. Sharon C. Bolton is Professor of Organisational Analysis at the University of Strathclyde.

Prof. Janet Borgerson is Associate Professor in Philosophy and Management at the University of Exeter.

Dr. Michèle Bowring is Assistant Professor at the University of Guelph.

Dr. Alan Bradshaw is Senior Lecturer in Marketing at Royal Holloway, University of London.

Prof. Joanna Brewis is Professor of Organisation and Consumption at the University of Leicester.

Prof. Steven D. Brown is Professor of Social and Organisational Psychology at the University of Leicester.

Prof. Alan Bryman is Professor of Organisational and Social Research at the University of Leicester.

Dr. Nick Butler is Lecturer in Organisation Studies at the University of St Andrews.

Prof. Stewart Clegg is at the University of Technology, Sydney.

Dr. Robert Cluley is at the University of Leicester.

Dr. Stephen Dunne is Lecturer in Social Theory and Consumption at the University of Leicester.

Prof. Geoff Easton is Professor of Marketing at Lancaster University Management School.

Prof. Paul du Gay is Globaliseringsprofessor at the Copenhagen Business School.

Jo Grady is Lecturer in HRM and Industrial Relations at the University of Leicester.

Dr. Philip Hancock is Professor of Management at the University of Essex.

Prof. Nancy Harding is Professor of Organisation Theory at Bradford University School of Management.

Prof. Stefano Harney is Chair in Strategy, Culture and Society at Queen Mary, University of London.

Dr. David Harvie is Lecturer in Finance and Political Economy at the University of Leicester.

Prof. Eduardo Ibarra-Colado is Professor of Management and Organization Studies at the Universidad Autónoma Metropolitana-Cuajimalpa.

Prof. Rick Iedema is at the University of Technology, Sydney.

Prof. Gavin Jack is Professor of Management at La Trobe University.

Dr. Campbell Jones is Senior Lecturer in Critical Theory and Business Ethics at the University of Leicester.

Prof. Mihaela Kelemen is Professor of Management Studies at Keele Management School.

Robin Klimecki is at Cardiff Business School.

Prof. David L. Levy is Professor of Management at the University of Massachusetts, Boston.

Dr. Geoffrey Lightfoot is Senior Lecturer in Entrepreneurship and Accounting at the University of Leicester.

Prof. Stephen Linstead is Professor of Critical Management at the University of York.

Dr. Keir Milburn has just completed a PhD at the University of Leeds.

Dr. Albert J. Mills is Professor of Management and Director of the Sobey PhD (Management) at Saint Mary's University.

Prof. Carl Rhodes is Professor of Organisation Studies at Swansea University.

Prof. Rolland Munro is Professor of Organisational Theory at Keele Management School.

John O'Shaughnessy is at Columbia University.

Prof. Cliff Oswick is Professor of Organisation Theory and Discourse at Queen Mary, University of London.

Prof. Jeffrey Unerman is Professor of Accounting and Accountability at Manchester Business School.

Jeroen Veldman is at the University of Leicester and Assistant Professor at the University of Utrecht.

Dr. Kaspar Villadsen is Associate Professor at the Copenhagen Business School.

Dr. Robert Westwood is Professor of Organisation Studies at the University of Technology, Sydney.

Prof. Hugh Willmott is Research Professor in Organisational Studies at the Cardiff Business School.

Dr. Edward Wray-Bliss is Senior Lecturer at the University of Technology, Sydney.

Introduction: What is Critical Management Studies?

Mark Tadajewski, Pauline Maclaran, Elizabeth Parsons
and Martin Parker

Critical management studies (CMS) as a distinctive brand name is usually traced to the publication of Mats Alvesson and Hugh Willmott's edited collection of the same name (1992). Falling under this banner are a range of perspectives including Marxism, critical theory, poststructuralism, postcolonialism and feminist approaches to name but a few. What perhaps unites such a disparate group when they are mobilised by CMS scholars is their role in contesting the traditional imperatives of mainstream management research and practice (Fournier and Grey, 2000; Parker, 2002).

Put simply, the plurality of perspectives that constitute CMS are not used by CMS activists to help managers run their businesses more efficiently, nor to render employees more docile or customers more amenable to the constellations of products and services offered by business enterprises. Rather, there is a belief amongst the CMS community that something is wrong with the narrowly instrumental way in which management, marketing and accounting are taught to each new generation of students (Brownlie et al., 1999). Each discipline, so we are told, offers a set of ostensibly neutral techniques that supposedly enable us to rationally manage, predict and control a variety of organisational and social phenomena. Yet, from politics to popular culture, there is a widespread suspicion about the effectiveness of management techniques, and the ideologies that they sustain.

The concerns of CMS with the way profit-motivated goals structure organisational practice and how this affects the wider social environment are not, it must be said, a new phenomenon. Religious texts have long bemoaned the credit practices that oil the gears of the economy

(Crane, 2000). The Romans and Greeks were extremely aware of the problems that accompanied one faction gaining monopoly power in the marketplace (Dickson and Wells, 2001). And with the onset of the industrial revolution, criticism of business continued apace. Parker (2009), for example, draws attention to the various forms of critique that have been levelled at managerial and bureaucratic practices for at least the last 250 years. The nineteenth and twentieth centuries, moreover, were characterised by the massive growth in industrial power that was exerted by a small number of individuals. This economic power was a worry precisely because the so-called 'Robber Barons' managed to translate it into political influence that was believed to corrupt government policy and legislative intent (Dickson and Wells, 2001). In the early twentieth century, business people were labelled 'Babbitts', following Sinclair Lewis' (1932/2003) popular book, and their conservatism, self-promotion and commitment to consumer culture varyingly satirised or grudging praised (Gramsci, 1985).

But it was not just academics writing about these subjects. Similar ideas and calls for action were articulated by union leaders, journalists, feminists and others who had experienced or witnessed marginalisation in the economic and social order. They highlighted discrepancies between what advocates for capitalism claimed it provided for workers (e.g. fulfilling employment; freedom; a vast range of products) and what many felt the political-economic system really offered (deskilled and precarious employment; alienation from family and social relations).

Frequently, there were gestures made to the fact that business education and practice served the needs of the industrial system and some vague 'power elite' (Mills, 1956), rather than improving the general quality of life experienced by many, or offering opportunities for meaning and community, but this did not develop into a consistent body of work critical of managerialism and the business school. However, by the late 1960s, groups of academics and practitioners in the business school and related disciplines (e.g. sociology, heterodox economics, political economy) were devoting considerable energy to questioning a largely uncritical mainstream of business theory or practice. They offered their own critiques of the industrial system and the values and theoretical positions that worked to structure free-market capitalism, leading to inequitable distributions of wealth and marketplace access, as well as status and reward distinctions which stretched from the skyscraper's corner office to the industrial 'accidents' on the shop floor (Braverman, 1974).

Very broadly speaking, then, we can say that people writing and thinking about CMS tend to agree with a number of key ideas. Along the lines articulated by Fournier and Grey (2000), CMS is dedicated to some type of 'denaturalisation', which might involve questioning the taken-for-granted nature of work, the value of job enrichment schemes, the ethics of employing cheap labour in export processing zones, or the use of financial statements to represent organisational 'reality'. Put simply, CMS supporters argue that we must register the power relations that structure and reaffirm the social, political and economic environment.

Complementing this commitment to denaturalisation is the 'epistemological reflexivity' that CMS advocates adopt. What this means is that they believe scholars should fully appreciate and document how their own interests and those of influential funding organisations such as universities, corporations and the government drive the production of knowledge in certain ways and not others (Whittle and Spicer, 2008). This has implications for the types of research that are conducted, the questions that are deemed appropriate for study, and often the methods that we utilise in producing research, textbooks and other materials. Because scholars are involved with the production of knowledge, then it can be argued that they should also be responsible for its influence in and on the social world beyond their ivory towers.

The above ways of thinking about CMS are quite widely supported. More contentious is the notion that CMS research and teaching should be 'non-performative'. This term is used to indicate that management research and teaching should not necessarily be driven by the narrow needs of business or current government demands for efficiency (Fournier and Grey, 2000). Neither must it be undertaken in the interests of making practice more efficient and effective unless, and this is the problem, it concerns the governance of 'alternative' organisations – such as worker co-operatives, local mutuals and so on. The key political and ethical issue here is perhaps not performativity as such, but the question of 'performative for whom?'.

Another comment that is often made about CMS research is that it is undeservedly critical of management or business practice. The majority of managers are not all nefarious characters who actively seek to affect the world in detrimental ways. Popular culture and the news media notwithstanding, many managers have to work within the constraints imposed by the existing political-economic system which holds maximising shareholder returns, or some other notion of efficiency, as its central goal. This has an impact on everyday business practice in that middle managers may lack substantive power, and are often deeply focused on trying to perform their own organisational role effectively which, in turn, limits critical reflection on corporate practices (e.g. the operation of sweatshops) that may be cognitively and spatially far removed from the managers' own corporate and social existence (Desmond, 1998). Such factors are all too easily forgotten and can lead to the unfair representation of managers, accountants, marketers and so forth, who are subject to blanket critique, rather than actually spoken to and made active participants in CMS research. This has led to calls for CMS to be more critically, but affirmatively, performative. This means listening to practitioners, as well as all other groups affected by management practices, rather than dismissing their concerns or motives outright (Spicer et al., 2009; Voronov et al., 2009).

Indeed, CMS and the various concepts that are found in this book are directly relevant to most practising managers (Grey, 2004). The world of business practice is shot through with power relations: between staff members inside an organisation seeking to control resources, between the organisation and its customer base, or between the organisation and government (Svensson, 2007). Most employees and managers already know this, and CMS could provide a way of voicing what they know, rather than assuming that they are dupes suffering from 'false consciousness'. CMS is not merely an academic project. The Key Concepts found in the pages that follow can help us all make sense of the complex social world we inhabit, offering the promise of allowing us to question the way the world is structured, and why certain ways of thinking are taken-for-granted, thereby enabling us to move beyond the conventional limits of business education and management practice.

USING THIS BOOK

We have edited this text in the hope of encouraging others to examine the growing body of research associated with CMS. What we would like to make clear at the outset is that we do not feel that this book is a replacement for exploration of the primary texts associated with CMS. In short, this book should not be considered an easy way of avoiding reading the academic articles, books and textbooks that the contributors to this volume draw upon.

Nevertheless, we recognise that students and teachers alike often need more information than textbooks alone can provide, at the same time as they would like pointers to the appropriate intellectual resources associated with a given research speciality. It is all too easy for academics to forget how difficult it can be to orient oneself to a completely new programme of study. We realise this and fully appreciate that intellectual signposting is necessary and useful, and that is what this book seeks to achieve. We have tried to pick what we believe to be the fifty or so most important ideas within the area, though this inevitably means that we will have omitted certain issues in order to produce a useable text.

Moreover, like other specialist academic subjects, the language of 'paradigms', 'ideology' and 'neoliberalism' used in this text is quite difficult to understand. With this in mind, the contributors of Key Concepts in this collection have been tasked with making the ideas, theoretical traditions and concepts that they discuss comprehensible to any motivated person confronting CMS and its sister disciplines of Critical Marketing Studies and Critical Accounting for the first time.

Our contributors have tried to avoid impenetrable jargon (Grey and Sinclair, 2005) in anticipation that the ideas discussed will reach the largest possible audience. These Key Concepts and the further readings that the contributors provide should therefore be especially useful when students are starting a new course. In much the same way, the discussions found here will be useful for revision purposes and in the preparation of coursework. Finally, we would just add that the resources provided on the CMS (http://www.criticalmanagement.org/) and the CMS Division of the Academy of Management (http://group.aomonline.org/cms/) webpages will also provide useful supporting resources.

REFERENCES

Alvesson, M. and Willmott, H. (eds) (1992) *Critical Management Studies*. London: Sage.

Braverman, H. (1974) *Labor and Monopoly Capital*. New York: Monthly Review Press.

Brownlie, D., Saren, M., Wensley, R. and Whittington, R. (1999) 'Marketing Disequilibrium: On Redress and Restoration', in Brownlie, Saren, Wensley and Whittington (eds) *Rethinking Marketing: Towards Critical Marketing Accountings*, pp. 1–22. London: Sage.

Crane, A. (2000) *Marketing, Morality and the Natural Environment*. London: Routledge.

Desmond, J. (1998) 'Marketing and Moral Indifference', in M. Parker (ed.) *Ethics & Organizations*, pp. 173–96. London: Sage.

Dickson, P.R. and Wells, P.K. (2001) 'The Dubious Origins of the Sherman Antitrust Act: The Mouse that Roared', *Journal of Public Policy & Marketing* 20(1): 3–14.

Fournier, V. and Grey, C. (2000) 'At the Critical Moment: Conditions and Prospects for Critical Management Studies', *Human Relations* 53(1): 7–32.

Gramsci, A. (1985) *Selections from Cultural Writings*, eds D. Forgacs and G. Nowell-Smith, tr. W. Boelhower. London: Lawrence and Wishart.

Grey, C. (2004) 'Reinventing Business Schools: The Contribution of Critical Management Education', *Academy of Management Learning and Education* 3(2): 178–86.

Grey, C. and Sinclair, A. (2005) 'Writing Differently', *Organization* 13(3): 443–53.

Lewis, S. (1932/2003) *Babbitt*. Mineola: Dover Publications.

Mills, C.W. (1956) *The Power Elite*. London: Oxford University Press.

Parker, M. (2002) *Against Management*. Oxford: Polity.

Parker, M. (2009) 'Managerialism and its Discontents', in S. Clegg and C. Cooper (eds) *The Sage Handbook of Organizational Behaviour, Volume II: Macro Approaches*, pp. 85–98. London: Sage.

Spicer, A., Alvesson, M. and Kärreman, D. (2009) 'Critical Performativity: The Unfinished Business of Critical Management Studies', *Human Relations* 62(4): 537–60.

Svensson, P. (2007) 'Producing Marketing: Towards a Socio-Phenomenology of Marketing Work', *Marketing Theory* 7(3): 271–90.

Voronov, M., Cox, J.W., LeTrent-Jones, T. and Weir, D. (2009) 'Introduction: Intersections of Critical Management Research and Practice: A Multi-Domain Perspective', in Cox, LeTrent-Jones, Voronov and Weir (eds) *Critical Management Studies at Work: Negotiating Tensions Between Theory and Practice*, pp. 1–16. Cheltenham: Edward Elgar.

Whittle, A. and Spicer, A. (2008) 'Is Actor Network Theory Critique?', *Organization Studies* 29(4): 611–29.

key concepts in
critical management studies

Accountability

Rolland Munro

> **Definition:** Accounts are the explanations we offer each other as we go about our everyday lives.

Accountability is one of the mainstays of civilisation and has been since the dawn of the first cities (Ezzamel, 1997). To state this is no exaggeration, but it is important to emphasise how the idea of accountability is only beginning to be given due prominence, primarily in the worlds of government and business. For the most part the giving and receiving of accounts remains a pervasive, little noticed feature of society, and I open with this theme before going on to deal with more formal and technical aspects.

An account might be anything we say to one another, from an aside about the weather to an intimate admission about what it is like at home or at work. Accounts thus range from phatic utterances, such as 'Wow!', to conversational remarks, including explanations such as 'I am tired' and 'this seems to be the way to go'. Accounts also cover speech acts such as promises, as well as theoretical propositions and statements about life and beliefs.

Defining accounts in this all-embracing way reflects sociological understandings of social order and takes us well beyond Scott and Lyman's (1968) version of accounts as 'statements made by a social actor to explain unanticipated or untoward behavior'. Their contribution is to show how accounts in the form of excuses and justifications act as a kind of 'repair work', healing or covering up perceived breaches in conduct. Valuable though this insight is, a more critical approach might extend this focus and identify, instead, a lack of reciprocity in the practices of giving and receiving accounts. These can take a numerical as well as a narrative form.

Where excuses and justifications flow in one direction only, they reveal *asymmetries* in power. For example, hierarchy is a mechanism for sucking credit upwards and divesting blame downwards (Munro, 2001). Thus it is normal for employees to account for their actions and to offer solutions to problems, but unusual to find bosses returning these favours. Gender studies suggest a tendency for women to be more prone to explain and justify themselves than are men. So too older people can find it hard to justify their existence within a work-oriented economy. Within what is called identity politics, minorities typically lobby as a group by way of refusing this perceived need to account for themselves.

This wider understanding of accountability is now key to explanation of social orderings. In part this is due to Garfinkel's (1967) seminal work, in which he points to how members of groups have *methods* for making themselves 'visible and accountable'. Against Kant's stated focus to explore the 'universe within' – treating self as if it were the source of ethics – Garfinkel's ambition is to explore what he calls the 'moral universe without'. His focus is on ways in which members use accounts to help 'pass' *as* members. This continual sanctioning of each other, from moment to moment, helps align accounts and so accomplish social order in members' everyday worlds (Munro, 1996).

A consequence of these wider notions – and the sanctions of inclusion and exclusion accountability practices carry – is that organisational arrangements can no longer be understood to be primarily a matter of design. Attempts to formalise reporting structures within institutions are parasitic on these taken-for-granted forms of account giving. Whereas the common assumption in theories of bureaucracy has been that authority is something that can be delegated, this convention elides the institutional arrangements in which *discretion* also has to be abrogated prior to any redistribution of accountabilities.

As already indicated, the critical issue is one of establishing asymmetries of power. This entails tracing the *direction* in which accounts flow; for example by identifying constraints on how and when members can exercise their discretion, if any. Germane also may be the *rationale* within which accounts are permitted: for instance whether responses need to be 'logical' or 'original' or 'incidental' or 'factual' and so on. To whom should we account? Over what? And when? The rule for investigation is *cui bono*: who benefits from accountability being formalised? Who profits from lines of reporting being established that require one particular person must account to another? Who gains from there being set formats in which accounts may be given? Who has the discretion to interpret whether or not an account 'passes'?

Under feudal arrangements forms of accountability were aligned with notions of sovereignty. In disputes over property one could be called to account in the name of the king; that is by whomever stood in the place of the king, such as a judge or an overlord. So early notions of 'steward-ship' entailed that property was accounted for by virtue of its having been kept more or less intact. The tally stick was one such device whereby the stick was marked up and then split in two, with the over-lord keeping one part and the steward the other until the two could be matched up once again on the overlord's return.

Capitalism, with its emphasis on exchange value, requires the incentive of a regular return on its investments, usually in the form of profit. Likewise the modern state depends greatly on this focus on accumulating assets for the expansion of its own institutions. There are two points here that are conjoined. The first, like the fabled talents in the Biblical story, is that property today must be continually *enhanced*; and second, in a kind of commodity fetishism, that everything gets turned into property. So in the drive for enhancement through exchange and accumulation, ideas become intellectual property and values and taste become part of one's cultural capital.

In all this accountability has come to be seen as key to the good running of democracy. Society expands, as the sociologist Talcott Parsons suggests, by power being 'invested' in others – much as money as a system helps the economy expand. Equally, in return, reciprocity implies that those appointed should then be held accountable for the actions they take by those investing power in them. However, the contemporary fetish for enhancement, and the ubiquity of exchange, means it is no longer sufficient for those running institutions simply to discharge their duties faithfully. The consensus of the modern state suggests problems arise wherever accountabilities are left inward looking. Policy now demands greater institutional 'transparency'; particularly, in the light of neoliberal discourse, to what is understood to be their 'markets'. Action is not only to be done well today; it has to be *seen* to be done well. It should be noted, however, that this market emphasis on making public institutions 'visible and accountable' has led to many unanticipated consequences and potentially disastrous outcomes.

A principal effect is the creation of what Strathern (2000) has called 'audit cultures'. In ways that define the twentieth-century transition from 'administration' to 'management', accountabilities today are *personified*. This is usually accomplished by the device of attaching so-called 'agreed' targets to managers and holding each to be 'responsible' for delivery of these outcomes. This individuating of institutional accountabilities – the good running of a hospital or a school – has over time disseminated responsibility onto those least able to effect change and, unfortunately, away from those holding ultimate authority. Commensurately, these managerial agendas have also been argued to have greatly increased the impact of 'panoptican' power into official and professional life, heightening a tendency towards self-audit (Power, 1999).

In terms of the prevailing tendency to look for *financial* measures, business corporations in the US led the way, with their management control procedures drawing principally upon 'accounting numbers' derived from market transactions. In this way accountability for managers in both the public and private sectors has strayed far from earlier ethical concerns and surveillance now frequently narrows to variance in budgeting (Munro, 1999; 2001). Cost budgets become cash limits that are not to be exceeded, with variances in spending closely watched. Profit budgets, in contrast, are regarded as superior; provided the target profit is met, fewer questions get asked!

In summary, issues of accountability appear more prevalent than ever. This is due in part to improved understandings of social order as well as to a 'governmentality' effect (Foucault, 1991) that stems from greater regulation of society. To counter the neoliberal dogmas in circulation here, more grounded understandings of how accountability works in everyday practice are badly needed. The individuation of community projects and purposes into personal targets seems irreversible but – in that measures conceal as much as they reveal – it should be noted how much such changes merely reinforce interpretive discretion for the bosses. And these managerial agendas have to reckon also with a tendency to destroy pride in our belonging to institutions such as hospitals, schools and universities. More too has yet to be said about how the coterie of managers that appoint each other set goals for themselves that are highly remunerated, but too easily achievable through outsourcing and downsizing the labour force. Transparency, the fashion of the day, remains a will o' the wisp.

FURTHER READING

Garfinkel's (1967) *Studies in Ethnomethodology* is an important background text for understanding theories of accountability. Munro's (1996) book chapter, 'Alignment and Identity Work: The Study of Accounts and Accountability', is a useful exposition of these theories in the organisational context.

See also: *Bureaucracy, Critical Accounting, Governmentality, Identity, Neoliberalism, Subjectivity and Subjectivation*

REFERENCES

Ezzamel, M. (1997) 'Accounting, Control and Accountability: Preliminary Evidence from Ancient Egypt', *Critical Perspectives on Accounting* 8(6): 563–601.

Foucault, M. (1991) 'Governmentality', in G. Burchell, C. Gordon and P. Miller (eds) *The Foucault Effect: Studies in Governmentality*, pp. 87–104. London: Harvester Wheatsheaf.

Garfinkel, H. (1967) *Studies in Ethnomethodology*. Engelwood Cliffs, NJ: Prentice-Hall.

Munro, R. (1996) 'Alignment and Identity Work: The Study of Accounts and Accountability', in R. Munro and J. Mouritsen (eds) *Accountability: Power, Ethos and the Technologies of Managing*, pp. 1–19. London: Thomson International Business Press.

Munro, R. (1999) 'Power and Discretion: Membership Work in the Time of Technology', *Organization* 6(3): 429–50.

Munro, R. (2001) 'Calling for Accounts: Numbers, Monsters and Membership', *The Sociological Review* 49(4): 473–93.

Power, M. (1999) *The Audit Society: Rituals of Verification*. Oxford: Oxford University Press.

Scott, M.B. and Lyman, S.M. (1968) 'Accounts', *American Sociological Review* 33(1): 46–62.

Strathern, M. (2000) 'New Accountabilities: Anthropological Studies in Audit, Ethics and the Academy', in M. Strathern (ed.) *Audit Cultures: Anthropological Studies in Accountability, Ethics and the Academy*, pp. 1–18. London: Routledge.

Aesthetics

Philip Hancock

Definition: Aesthetics is the philosophical investigation of sensuality, traditionally concerned with questions of beauty, taste and the nature of art.

While relatively straightforward to define, aesthetics remains a rich and multifaceted concept. Most commonly it refers to the search for criteria by which phenomena, both natural and fabricated, might be defined as beautiful, sublime, ugly or even repulsive. It is also used to describe a concern with providing objective criteria by which art might be evaluated and deemed to be of aesthetic value. While its origins can be found in the philosophies of antiquity, its contemporary meaning derives largely from the work of eighteenth-century figures such as Francis Hutcheson (1694–1746) and, more notably, Alexander Gottlieb Baumgarten (1714–1762). In his two-volume work entitled *Aesthetica* (1750 and 1758), Baumgarten in particular focused on developing what might be termed a *science of sensuality*, a legacy perhaps best encapsulated in Eagleton's (1990: 13) assertion that, at its core, aesthetics is concerned with 'the business of affections and aversions, of how the world strikes the body on its sensory surfaces, of what takes root in the gaze and the guts and all that arises from our banal, biological insertion into the world'.

As such, the question of modern aesthetics can be understood as closely related to that of epistemology in that it asks how we might both acquire and communicate knowledge of sensuality, particularly as it pertains to the experience of art. For Immanuel Kant (1724–1804), perhaps the most important figure in the development of modern philosophical aesthetics, this problem rested on the proposition that while the experience of aesthetic qualities – such as beauty – is apparently subjective in nature (and, as such, does not reside in the object of apprehension), at the same time it is also able to elicit common agreements or disagreements amongst individuals suggesting grounds for objective evaluation. Kant responded to this problem through the idea of *aesthetic judgement*, a fusing of the sensuality of individual experience with what he claimed was the rational – and therefore universal – faculty of taste.

THE AESTHETICS OF MANAGEMENT AND THE MANAGEMENT OF AESTHETICS

Within management studies the concept of aesthetics has tended to follow one of several trajectories. One is that the values of art and conceptions of the beautiful might, in one form or another, be incorporated into the management of contemporary work organisations. This has proven popular amongst those looking to transpose the sensibility of art into the workplace in order to produce organisations that are more creative, innovative and, arguably, humane (cf. de Monthoux, 2004).

Closer to the epistemological concerns of say Baumgarten and Kant, however, is a critical concern with how one might actually research the embodied and often ineffable characteristics of aesthetic experience within organisations. While more traditional approaches to visual analysis, such as semiotics (Hancock, 2005), have been employed in order to examine the ways in which existent organisational artefacts are rendered aesthetically meaningful, an emergent concern is with how we might attune our own aesthetic faculties to the needs of the research process. Hence, Warren (2008), for example, argues for a sensual methodology that focuses on the aesthetic experiences of both organisational members and researchers. This is in order to pursue what, in the terms of the philosopher Gadamer, might be understood as a sensual fusion of horizons; one directed towards establishing a hermeneutics of aesthetic experience as a means by which it might be possible to establish a deeper understanding of the aesthetic character of everyday organisational life.

A third, more structural concern amongst critical scholars, is with what Gagliardi (1990) describes as the *landscaping* of organisational environments. By this he is referring to the ways in which organisational artefacts, ranging from furniture to lighting, through to spatial layout and buildings themselves, are designed and manipulated in order to promote, as Witken (1990: 332) describes it, 'the suppression of those sensuous values which realise elements of the life process of the members that are excluded from the business of organisational life [and] the positive cultivation of certain sensuous values that directly express or realise the organisational presence demanded'. One of the most notable examples of such an approach is Strati's (1999) consideration of the humble chair: an artefact present in nearly all organisations. As Strati observes, a chair can stimulate many, if not all of, our senses. We can see its design and colour, feel its texture and shape, smell the materials it is constructed from and hear its movement. All of these potential stimuli tell us not only about the chair itself, however, but also about the organisation it inhabits and the people who might or might not use it, such as the status of its owner, the political and cultural values of the organisation, or its attitudes towards clients, customers and suppliers.

A related term, *aesthetic labour* (Hancock and Tyler, 2000), has emerged to describe the landscaping carried out by organisational employees on their own bodies in order to present a prescribed organisational aesthetic through the self-management of embodied attributes such as poise and deportment, as well as the maintenance of required standards of personal grooming and dress. While largely concerned with the management of employees concentrated in what one might term interactive service roles – such as flight attendants, shop assistants and bar staff – research into aesthetic labour also focuses on more traditionally performative occupations such as fashion modelling and acting. At the heart of such critical work into organisational aesthetics, therefore, resides a concern with how the materiality of organisational life is subject to certain structuring interventions in order to render it amenable to the pursuit of predominantly managerial aspirations. For some this process is contributory to what Böhme (2003: 82) has described as the rise of the aesthetic economy. This is an economy based on the emergence of *staging value*; namely economic value derived from goods and services orientated towards the capacity to 'stage, costume and intensify life'.

By way of a conclusion it is probably important to emphasise that the study of organisational aesthetics, especially from a CMS perspective, remains in its infancy. What is presented here, therefore, represents a brief overview of a relatively underdeveloped body of work. Nonetheless, along with related areas such as employee embodiment, organisational spatiality and architecture, and workplace emotionality, a concern with aesthetics offers an important corrective to the over-rationalised understanding of management and organisation that continues to permeate the field. Furthermore, through an exploration of how things come to have aesthetic meaning within organisations it also has the potential to challenge the equally over-simplistic, and rather romantic, proposition that sensuality represents a fundamentally untainted dimension of human experience; one somehow shorn of organisational power relations. In doing so, aesthetics might add not only to our understanding of how organisational management currently functions, but equally, how it might be made to function differently in the future..

FURTHER READING

For a critical and philosophically rich introduction to the concept of the aesthetic, Terry Eagleton's (1990) *The Ideology of the Aesthetic* is an important, if somewhat challenging, starting point. For an introduction to the relationship between aesthetics and organisational analysis one can still do no better than Gagliardi (1990) and Strati (1999).

See also: Hermeneutics, Materiality, Postmodernism

REFERENCES

Böhme, G. (2003) 'Contribution to the Critique of the Aesthetic Economy', *Thesis Eleven* 73: 71–82.

De Monthoux, P.G. (2004) *The Art Firm: Aesthetic Management and Metaphysical Marketing, From Waaner to Wilson*. Stanford: Stanford University Press.

Eagleton, T. (1990) *The Ideology of the Aesthetic*. Oxford: Blackwell.

Gagliardi, P. (1990) 'Artifacts as Pathways and Remains of Organizational Life', in P. Gagliardi (ed.) *Symbols and Artifacts: Views of the Corporate Landscape*, pp. 3–38. Berlin: de Gruyter.

Hancock, P. (2005) 'Uncovering the Semiotic in Organizational Aesthetics', *Organization* 12(1): 29–60.

Hancock, P. and Tyler, M. (2000) '"The Look of Love": Gender, Work and The Organization of Aesthetics', in J. Hassard, R. Holliday and H. Willmott (eds) *Body and Organisation*, pp. 108–29. London: Sage.

Strati, A. (1999) *Organisation and Aesthetics*. London: Sage.

Warren, S. (2008) 'Empirical Challenges in Organizational Aesthetics Research: Towards a Sensual Methodology', *Organisation Studies* 29(4): 559–80.

Witkin, R.W. (1990) 'The Aesthetic Imperative of Rational-Technical Machinery: A Study in Organizational Control Through the Design of Artifacts', in P. Gagliardi (ed.) *Symbols and Artifacts: Views of the Corporate Landscape*, pp. 325–38. Berlin: de Gruyter.

Alternative Organisation

Martin Parker

Definition: An institution arranged on principals which differ from the mainstream, whether in terms of democratic decision-making, equity of reward, ownership and membership, or economic and political values.

What counts as an alternative depends on what counts as mainstream, but in the present context, we will assume the mainstream to be a form of hierarchical managerialism which assumes market efficiency as the key criterion of success. In that sense, an alternative is any organisational form that places democracy, non-hierarchical organisation, feminist, environmentalist or localist politics at the core of its organising processes. This is not the same as saying that, for example, a company that manufactures organic bread is necessarily alternative, because it might be organised according to the dominant principals of market managerialism. Where institutional structures are concerned, organising is politics made durable, even though many people might commonly assume that there are no alternatives to the growing global dominance of forms of managerialism.

It is often said of 'critical management studies' that it spends most effort in criticism, and little on positive proposals. Like much academic work perhaps, it is stronger on theory than practice, and hence often invites the accusation of ivory-tower irrelevance. In that regard, it might be said that (in the global North) activists and practitioners of alternative organising were there first. Ever since the industrial revolution reshaped relations between the city and the country, and employer and employee, a wide variety of groups have attempted to organise themselves differently. Building on previous traditions of resistance to feudalism, and of religious non-conformism, communities were established which attempted to share wealth, decision-making, work and so on. If we describe this as a sort of practical utopianism, then it combined a perfectionist account of human beings with a sense that social organisation needed to be reformed if people were to become both good and happy. By the nineteenth century in the global North, entrepreneurs like Robert Owen, various Christian groups, and pioneers of the co-operative movement were beginning to identify the combination of capitalism, urbanism and deskilling as a threat to social order. Though the motives and ends differ widely, since then there have been many attempts to found communities and organisations which challenge the orthodoxy.

It seems that there are at least four basic ways in which alternative organisation has been imagined. The first is anarchism, an organisation theory in the truest sense. Rather than assuming, as many more conservative organisational theorists do, the existence of the division of labour, capitalism, hierarchy and so on, all these 'facts' become questions. No 'natural order' is assumed, and issues of governance, control, decision-making, production and so on are all assumed to be matters that the autonomous individual can make intelligent choices about.

Management, in anything other than the role of a temporary coordinating function, is simply superfluous since people are largely assumed to be able to organise themselves. Unsurprisingly, given that anarchists are not keen on being told what to do, there is little agreement on any other guiding principles. Some anarchists stress forms of association at the local level, others that autonomy is a value that should not be compromised by any constraints at all. Most would assume that certain constraints are acceptable in order to maintain minimal forms of organisation, but there would be considerable debate about the nature and force of collective sanctions. Whatever the view, the privileges of management would certainly be questioned in most forms of anarchist thought.

However, when we move towards socialist versions of anarchism, and then on to communism, the importance of more elaborate organisational forms becomes apparent. Since the aim of socialism is primarily large-scale political change then the use of industrial action is often seen to be a means of defending the interests of workers against management and of overthrowing the present order. The central issue for socialists and communists is usually ownership, with the original hierarchy being conceived as based around class. However, in order to achieve effective worker control, labour organisations need to develop workplace democracy and worker self-management. It is here that more centralised forms of authority might become tolerated for tactical reasons, something that we also see in many co-operatively run organisations. There is a considerable continuum of work and practice here, ranging from forms of minimal involvement and ownership that retain most managerial privileges (such as organisations run as trusts, employee share ownership, and versions of empowerment), through to fully fledged co-operative forms of ownership and control. The latter are particularly vibrant today in Italian workerism, combined with a variety of forms of anticorporate protest and attempts to unionise precarious workers.

Another current of alternative organisational thought is rather more recent, and is associated with versions of radical feminism, echoed weakly in managerial ideas about women having a more collaborative leadership style. Patriarchy is here argued to be the original form of oppressive authority from which all others develop. Feminists should thus struggle against all forms of hierarchy, and perhaps towards ways of being that are more collective and supportive. However, as with anarchism and socialism, there are many inflections within this feminist resistance to authority. Feminists might take their principal problem to be men, leading to separatist forms of organisation. Or they might articulate the problem as patriarchal relations, or capitalist relations, or some combination of both. The connections between feminism and forms of environmentalism are also particularly strong. However, whatever the differences, the general point would be that radical feminists are suspicious about the naturalisation of authority, the sexual division of labour, and any separation between impartial public action and passionate private action, such as that embodied in a Weberian description of bureaucracy. If the personal is political, as most feminists would argue, then organising is certainly political too.

We find a similar diversity of anti-authoritarian positions within green or environmentalist thought. In this case, it is very often the human relationship to nature that is articulated as an original hierarchy, though ecofeminist positions would also argue that this is a peculiarly male way of relating to the natural world. So if positions of dominance and exploitation are problematic, then it is obvious enough that more collective and co-operative relations should be encouraged within our work and our communities. Of crucial importance here is the trend to localisation, to the grassroots, both for reasons of responsible economics, but also to allow for face to face senses of responsibility. As Ernst Schumacher said, 'small is beautiful', and the sorts of organisational relations sponsored by green activists and writers would tend to be based on ideas of the eco-village, and the sustainable community. Coordination may require a limited division of labour, but the general principal would usually be that hierarchy should be minimised, and forms of collective decision-making would be the norm. Again, it needs to be noted that there is no 'one' environmental position. Variants of collectivism and individualism, as well as diagnoses of the source of the problem, shade over into feminist, socialist and anarchist positions. Uniting these varieties of green thought and practice would be metaphors of 'working with' and being 'close to', which would tend to refuse the physical or intellectual separations that managerialism must rely on.

All these alternative forms of organisation share a deep distrust of the notion of the expert organiser. The idea of the MBA qualified manager, as someone with more status and reward who is not involved in day-to-day organising, is entirely antithetical to most anarchist, socialist, feminist and environmentalist practices. Whether we look at the long history of intentional communities, co-operatives, alternative economic practices or contemporary attempts to resist the hegemony of the capitalist work organisation, these are all alternatives to managerialism. All of these forms of thought are also now given contemporary resonance by the possibilities of virtual organising, which appears to provide space for democratic consultation and practical organising, but without the constraints (and environmental costs) of time and space. And these are not temporary, minor or historical alternatives, but a continual stream of practical opposition that is as vibrant now as it has ever been.

FURTHER READING

The dictionary provided by Parker, Fournier and Reedy (2007) attempts to cover this area, but really only scratches the surface. For overviews of anarchism see Marshall (1993), of feminism see Ferree and Martin (1995), and of environmentalism see Scott Cato (2009). For worker participation and control, see Harley, Hyman and Thompson (2005) and Pannekoek (2002). For contemporary listings see the publications and websites of the Fellowship for Intentional Community (www.fic.org) in the USA and Eurotopia (www.eurotopia.de) in Europe.

See also: Environmentalism, Feminism, Managerialism, Utopia and Utopianism

REFERENCES

Ferree, M. and Martin, P. (1995) *Feminist Organisations*. Philadelphia: Temple University Press.
Harley, B., Hyman, J. and Thompson, P. (eds) (2005) *Democracy and Participation at Work*. Basingstoke: Palgrave.
Marshall, P. (1993) *Demanding the Impossible*. London: Fontana.
Pannekoek, A. (2002) *Worker Councils*. Oakland, CA: AK Press.
Parker, M., Fournier, V. and Reedy, P. (2007) *The Dictionary of Alternatives*. London: Zed Books.
Scott Cato, M. (2009) *Green Economics*. London: Earthscan.

alternative organisation

American Pragmatism

Mihaela Kelemen

> **Definition:** American Pragmatism is a philosophical tradition that challenges the dichotomy 'knowledge/experience' and positions practical action at the heart of theoretical inquiry.

American Pragmatism was developed by three American philosophers, Charles Peirce, William James and John Dewey, as an alternative to dominant forms of Western rationalism. The three founding fathers of American Pragmatism held various and loosely connected concerns about philosophy, truth, human experience and meaning. For example, Charles Peirce (1839–1914) trained as a scientist and, as such, was keen to apply scientific principles to philosophical problems. For Peirce, meaning was established by direct interaction with the sensible effects of one's actions. On a slightly different tack, William James (1842–1910) was troubled by the precarious place of humans in the new scientific world. His scholarly interests shifted from logic to moral and psychological matters. The pursuit of truth was less a matter of scientific endeavour and more to do with the 'here and now'; in other words, the context and the individual. John Dewey (1859–1952) affirmed Peirce's inquiring critical spirit and logical methods but, like James, his interests were moral, aesthetic, and educational, and his notion of the truth was pluralistic and tolerant of diversity.

KEY TENETS

American Pragmatism has had a significant influence on public administration, policy development, education, philosophy and politics, but has received relatively little attention in management and marketing studies. Notwithstanding existing disagreements amongst the early theorists, there are some commonalities across their ontological, epistemological, methodological and ethical perspectives.

Ontology. Pragmatism favours a processual and relational view of the world, where reality is always in the making, on its way to be constituted but never quite finalised. Pragmatism is mostly interested in the interrelationships between social entities rather than the essence of these social entities. These interrelationships are seen as contingent on the specific context; grasping them allows one to better understand the changing nature of the world, its paradoxes, complexities and general messiness. In Dewey's words, the world exhibits an 'impressive and irresistible mixture of sufficiencies, tight completedness, order, recurrences which make possible prediction and control, and singularities, ambiguities, uncertain possibilities, processes going on to consequences yet indeterminate' (1958: 47).

Epistemology. Pragmatists claim that there are many ways of interpreting the world and some are better than others. The researcher can recognise the superiority of one theory over another thanks to practical experience and dialogue. For the pragmatists, the meaning of an idea is the practical consequences of the idea and 'truth' is only attainable through practice. Knowledge and human action are intertwined, for what people know about the world is influenced by what they do, can do and want to do, not only as individuals but more importantly as collectivities. As such, knowledge is not an individual achievement, but a social one, and the validity of a theory is assured when the theory makes sense and is useful to a certain community of practice.

The pragmatist interest in what works, and how and why it works (or doesn't), translates into a notion of knowledge which is antifoundational and directed towards problem-solving using the data and understandings available at the time. Pragmatism does not reject the concept of rationality and its role in theorising, rather it advocates the need to accept that rationality is embodied. This embodied rationality allows the individual (be it researcher or subject of research) to cope effectively with the perennial indeterminacy and contingency inherent in everyday existence. According to the pragmatists, to think means to experience the world in one way or another, and not accounting for this experience means escaping into abstract and useless theory. Experience means not only what had happened in the past but encapsulates one's visceral and embodied response to the immediate context.

Pragmatist *methodology* upholds a reality that does not always lend itself to clear-cut judgements. The researcher is allowed (indeed encouraged) to use indeterminate truth values in the attempt to handle situational indeterminacy. The quest for pragmatic certainty sensitises the researcher to fuzzy things, multiple realities, paradox and ambiguity. Participant observation, and other hands-on ethnographic methods of data collection and analysis, are seen to be the most effective ways to comprehend uncertainty and provide tentative yet workable solutions to problems.

Ethics. Pragmatism has an acute interest in action, not for its own sake, but as a way to change existence. Researchers have a moral responsibility to present knowledge that has consequences for future applications. The research endeavour is aimed towards knowledge that makes a positive difference and contributes to better practice. Pragmatism counsels tolerance to ambiguity and calls for personal responsibility on the part of the researcher. Personal effort in one's immediate community of practice is more important than following universal codes of ethics, for every moral situation is a unique situation (Campbell, 1995). Resulting theories therefore are never neutral for they have ethical and political implications.

AMERICAN PRAGMATISM AND ORGANISATIONAL KNOWLEDGE

Many organisational theorists owe an intellectual debt to pragmatism – a debt often unacknowledged. The neglect of pragmatism within organisational and marketing studies is a rather curious state of affairs because pragmatism seems more than capable of helping scholars to explore the interrelationship between rationality, knowledge and everyday practices/experiences. What is more, pragmatism may find points of reference in critical and postmodern thought, especially regarding its antifoundational view of knowledge. There are also possible points of connection with Feminism, Actor–Network Theory and Practice Studies though such interdisciplinary explorations remain largely underdeveloped.

Pragmatism goes beyond the shortcomings of positivism and certain versions of postmodernism by insisting that there is a reality out there (however fragile and disputed it might be). Further to this, pragmatism suggests that reality can be changed for the better by applying reason. While subjective interpretations are important in this endeavour, not all of them are equally useful. Usefulness becomes a central concern for pragmatists, which is defined primarily in two ways. First, epistemologically, in terms of whether the information or knowledge is credible, well founded, reliable and relevant. Second, normatively, in terms of whether knowledge/theory helps to advance one's cause/project and improve one's immediate circumstances (Wicks and Freeman, 1998). This strikes a chord with the emphasis currently placed on relevance, and/or the impact of organisational knowledge on practice.

Studying practical problems of everyday organisational life is a process situated within a particular social formation, which Dewey calls *the community of inquiry*. People belonging to *communities of inquiry* are connected by three elements – the practical problem, the scientific methods needed to resolve that problem, and the democratic values to be upheld in coming up with a practical solution (Shield, 2003). According to Dewey, the focus on a problematic situation is essential because it helps a community to form around the issue requiring resolution. Second, members of a community of inquiry must bring a scientific attitude to the problem situation and view both theory and method as tools to address it. Third, communities of inquiry must be democratic as they must take into account values and ideals such as freedom and equality, as well as efficiency, in pursuing their goals (Evans, 2000).

The members of a community of inquiry proceed with a sense of critical optimism and a belief that there are practical solutions to practical problems. Dewey was a strong believer in the capacity of humanity to progress while accepting that there is uncertainty and doubt in the world. Although Dewey applauded science for offering rigorous methods for solving problems and acquiring information about how the world works, science was not regarded as the ultimate or the only way to know the world. Dewey maintained that the process of inquiry began with and ended in experience. Inquiry, as a contingent, open-ended process relied on the positive or negative feedback from the community of inquiry. The conclusions of the process of inquiry are not truth, but the best available solution at the time, and are always subject to revision. Thus scientific inquiry is not a means or method to discover the truth: it is merely the means and method to reduce doubt and restore balance to a problematic situation. Moreover, knowing the world through experience is instrumental to rearranging it, and giving it a form that is more useful to one's purposes.

FURTHER READING

Kelemen and Rumens (2008) *An Introduction to Critical Management Research* provides a detailed overview of American Pragmatism.

american pragmatism

Wicks and Freeman's (1998) article, 'Organization Studies and the New Pragmatism: Positivism, Anti-Positivism and the Search for Ethics', gives a useful discussion of its application to organisational studies.

See also: Actor–Network Theory, Business Ethics, Feminism, Postmodernism

REFERENCES

Campbell, J. (1995) *Understanding John Dewey: Nature and Cooperative Intelligence*. Chicago: Open Court.

Dewey, J. (1958) *Experience and Nature*. New York: Dover.

Evans, K. (2000) 'Reclaiming John Dewey: Democracy, Inquiry, Pragmatism and Public Management', *Administration and Society* 32(3): 308–28.

Kelemen, M. and Rumens, N. (2008) *An Introduction to Critical Management Research*. London: Sage.

Shield, P. (2003) 'The Community of Inquiry: Classical Pragmatism and Public Administration', *Administration and Society* 35(5): 510–38.

Wicks, A.C. and Freeman, R.E. (1998) 'Organization Studies and the New Pragmatism: Positivism, Anti-Positivism and the Search for Ethics', *Organization Science* 9(2): 123–40.

Actor–Network Theory (ANT)

Steven D. Brown

Definition: ANT is an approach to the study of mediated relationships between people and things. Its central proposition is that there is nothing outside of what it terms 'heterogeneous' or 'hybrid' networks of human and non-human materials.

INTRODUCTION

According to ANT theorists, the distinctions that we routinely make between subjects and objects, humans and non-humans, and ultimately society and nature, are effects which are produced as networks trace relations within themselves. This levelling of *a priori* dualisms is sometimes referred to as 'generalized symmetry' (Callon, 1986). For instance, the distinction between the human and the technical side of an organisation is not a fundamental ontological given since human interactions are mediated by techniques, and relations between technical components are shaped and respecified by communities of human users. From this point of view, there is no stable distinction between people and things, since both make each other. Distinctions of this type are instead continuously reconstituted within the organisation and subject to reformulation and transformation. It is the activity of making and breaking such contingent relations within networks which is the main object of study for ANT scholars.

A corollary of generalised symmetry is that knowledge and meaning are not seen as the sole property of humans. Drawing on the semiotics of A.J. Greimas, ANT authors such as Bruno Latour and Madeleine Akrich argue that if meaning is a relational effect of the ordering of terms within a network, then heterogeneous networks make their own meanings as part of the material process of ordering their own relations (Akrich and Latour, 1992). Ordering involves selection, discernment, association and juxtaposition. The conceptual is merely a higher-order abstraction which emerges from this material process – it has no other referent. Rather, abstraction has its own material effects, since it acts back on the network by according identities which may serve as a basis for transforming relations, setting the work of ordering off in new directions (or 'path building'). This argument is sometimes referred to as 'material-semiotics' – signs made with things and things made with signs.

Within the approach, the identities/entities which emerge within a heterogeneous network are referred to as 'actants' irrespective of whether they are human or non-human. Actants are in fact not singular entities, but rather portions of the network which have achieved a particular degree of topological complexity such that the myriad relations of which it consists are practically recognised within the network as a single object. This occurs through a process of 'translation' (the term comes from the work of the philosopher Michel Serres), where proto-actants are drawn (and sometimes forced) into relations to create new relational properties. The actants which are taken to emerge are treated as 'simplified' or 'punctualised'. For

example, a manager is in actuality a summation of a range of social, technical and legal relations drawn from across the organisation. Hence any of
the powers which are commonly attributed to managers are, strictly speaking, 'borrowed' from elsewhere (see Latour, 1987; Law, 1994). But as such
it is always possible for this punctualisation to fall apart, and for the stability to become disputed or difficult to recognise. Within ANT, power is
always a shorthand term for following the ongoing interactional dynamics
of network transformation.

HISTORY

The earliest work in ANT emerged from Science & Technology Studies
scholars based at or visiting the Centre for the Sociology of Innovation,
Ecole des Mines, Paris (i.e. Michel Callon, Bruno Latour, John Law). This
'classical' phase of ANT was mostly concerned with scientific and technological innovation (e.g. Renault's electric car, the British TSR2 military
plane, the laboratory work of the Salk Institute). However, the unique
approach to organisational processes defined by the approach drew ANT
towards something which resembled more traditional ethnographies of
managing innovation, such as Law's (1994) study of the Daresbury laboratory or Latour's study of the Aramis transport system. This period of
ANT remains of particular significance for management studies because
it provides an exemplary demonstration of how to combine detailed
empirical work with high-level theorising (see Czarniawska and Hernes,
2005). However, from the early 1990s onwards a series of critiques
emerged which argued that ANT had seriously overestimated the extent
to which punctualisation could secure durable identities and the longer-
term processes to which networks might be subject (Lee and Brown,
1994). A particular concern here is with the effects of generalised symmetry – is the levelling of the difference between the human and the
technological not precisely the dream of certain kinds of retrograde
managerial and work-intensification processes? Ought there not be a
clear ethical commitment to maintaining the status and the dignity of the
'human side' of organisations?

The next generation of work within ANT recognised the potential
'managerialism' of early work and redefined ANT as a way of engaging
in social theory and hence promoted its relevance to all areas of social
science (this can in fact by traced back to earlier work by Callon, Latour
and Law). During this phase, ANT became adopted and reworked across
a range of disciplines, notably geography, information studies, and
organisation studies. The attraction of ANT for the latter, particularly

the epistemologically critical versions of CMS, is that it redefines organisations as assemblages of ordering practices in perpetual transformation (see Law and Hassard, 1999). Hence issues such as the effect of organisational structure on performance, the impact of leadership or organisational change become reframed. It is change which is primary, with stability and durability as transient secondary effects, or 'pools of order' as John Law calls them. For example, in Robert Cooper's adoption of ANT, the topological complexity of organising – how relations between inside/outside, distal/proximal, before/after are constituted – becomes the central puzzle. This demonstrates the potential of the process ontology derived from the philosophers A.N. Whitehead and Gilles Deleuze which is the historical tradition to which ANT properly belongs.

In recent years a third phase of 'post-ANT' work has emerged. This work typically draws upon some of the basic tenets of ANT but reflexively turns its insights back on itself to argue that as a heterogeneous network of activity, the practice of 'doing' ANT is itself in transformation (see Latour, 2005). One of the most interesting developments here has been the application of ANT to the study of markets and economics – or 'performative economics'. Beginning with Callon's (1998) studies of how markets can be punctualised as economic actants, this approach has been particularly successful in empirically demonstrating how new economic devices, instruments and procedures (e.g. derivatives; screen-based trading; short selling) have been rendered durable in the production of modern financial markets. Once again, the fundamental move of viewing the object of study as a heterogeneous network of relations in transformation, wherein the social, the technological and the economic are produced, pays dividends in terms of developing new ways of seeing things that we thought we already knew.

See also: Materiality, Postmodernism, Power, Reflexivity

FURTHER READING

Latour (2005) is a good starting point for students interested in ANT. This could then be followed by Latour (1987).

REFERENCES

Akrich, M. and Latour, B. (1992) 'A Summary of a Convenient Vocabulary for the Semiotics of Human and Nonhuman Assemblies', in W. Bijker and J. Law (eds) *Shaping Technology, Building Society: Studies in Sociotechnical Change*, pp. 259–64. Cambridge, MA: MIT Press.

actor–network theory (ant)

Callon, M. (1986) 'Some Elements of a Sociology of Translation: Domestication of the Scallops and the Fishermen of Saint Brieuc Bay', in J. Law (ed.) *Power, Action and Belief: A New Sociology of Knowledge?*, pp. 196–233. London: Routledge and Kegan Paul.

Callon, M. (ed.) (1998) *The Laws of the Markets*. Oxford: Blackwell.

Czarniawska, B. and Hernes, T. (eds) (2005) *Actor–Network Theory and Organizing*. Copenhagen: Copenhagen Business School.

Law, J. (1994) *Organizing Modernity*. Oxford: Blackwell.

Law, J. and Hassard, J. (eds) (1999) *Actor Network Theory and After*. Oxford: Blackwell.

Latour, B. (1987) *Science in Action: How to Follow Scientists and Engineers Through Society*. Milton Keynes: Open University Press.

Latour, B. (2005) *Reassembling the Social: An Introduction to Actor–Network Theory*. Oxford: Oxford University Press.

Lee, N. and Brown, S. (1994) 'Otherness and the Actor Network', *American Behavioral Scientist*, 37(6): 772–90.

Lee, N. and Hassard, J. (1999) 'Organization Unbound', *Organization* 6(3): 391–404.

Bureaucracy

Paul du Gay

Definition: A distinctive form of organisation marked by a clear hierarchy of authority, and staffed by full-time, salaried officials functioning under impersonal, uniform written rules and procedures.

INTRODUCTION

Bureaucracy is a term that brings together under one heading a wide variety of concepts and ideas. It often functions as a loose cover for a diverse and frequently paradoxical range of complaints about the inequities of central government, of the inherent dysfunctions of formal organisations applying rules to particular cases, and the ceaseless instrumental rationalisation of all forms of human conduct. However, it also carries a specific, technical meaning referring to a body of officials and the procedures, tasks and ethos regulating their conduct within a particular system of administration. It is often difficult to separate out the popular pejorative and technical meanings of the term. As early as 1764, for instance, Baron de Grimm, a French Philosopher, refers to 'an illness in France which bids fair to play havoc with us; this illness is called bureaumania'. John Stuart Mill writing in 1837 referred to 'that vast network of administrative tyranny ... that system of bureaucracy'.

The word is generally considered to derive from the French 'bureau' meaning a 'writing desk' (more specifically, the cloth covering such a desk) but also a place where officials worked. The addition of a suffix, derived from the Greek word for 'rule', resulted in a term with a remarkable capacity for cultural mobility. Greek concepts of government having long been domesticated in the European languages, and the new term quite easily underwent the same transliterations as 'democracy' and 'aristocracy', quickly becoming a central feature of international political discourse (Albrow, 1970). The French *bureaucratie* rapidly translated into the German *Bureaukratie*, the Italian *burocrazia*, and the English and North American *bureaucracy*. Furthermore, in keeping with the derivatives of democracy, accompanying bureaucracy were: *bureaucrat, bureaucratic*, and *bureaucratisation*. It is not surprising, therefore, that early dictionary definitions of bureaucracy were remarkably consistent (Albrow, 1970). The Dictionary of the French Academy accepted the word in its 1789 supplement defining it as 'Power, influence of the heads and staff of governmental bureaux'. An 1813 edition of a German dictionary of foreign expressions defines it as 'the authority or power which various government departments and their branches arrogate to themselves over fellow citizens'. An Italian technical dictionary of 1828 refers to it thus: 'Neologism, signifying the power of officials in public administration'. From its earliest deployment, then, the term bureaucracy refers not only to a form of governance (public and private) where an important governing role is in the hands of administrative officials; it also functions as a collective designation for those officials.

Within management and organisation studies, the systematic study of bureaucracy is usually considered to begin with the classic work of Max Weber at the beginning of the twentieth century (1978). It is Weber more than any other scholar who has provided the definitive analysis of both the technical and ethico-cultural characteristics of bureaucracy – an analysis that also has the significant explanatory advantage of not sliding into simple stereotyping. While Weber's work has called forth many critics, his analysis has yet to be dispensed with.

MAX WEBER: BUREAUCRACY AS AN ETHICAL VOCATION

According to Weber, a bureaucracy establishes a relation between legally instituted authorities and their subordinate officials which is characterised by the following: defined rights and duties, prescribed in written rules that are preserved in files; authority relations between positions which are organised hierarchically; appointment and promotion based on fixed criteria such as merit or seniority; expertise in a given area, normally certified by examination, as a formal condition of employment; fixed monetary salaries; a strict separation of incumbent from office in the sense that officials do not own and cannot appropriate the position they occupy. Bureaucratic administration is thus a full-time job, a career, and bureaucratic office-holding is also a vocation. It constitutes a focus of ethical commitment and duty that is both autonomous of, and superior to, the office-holder's ties to kin, class, or indeed conscience. For Weber, then, the hierarchical, procedural and technical organisation of the bureau, in addition to providing the conditions for a distinctive organisational apparatus, also provide the ethical conditions for a special comportment of the person. Key among these ethical attributes are that bureaucrats are not moved by personal moral enthusiasm but conduct themselves '*sine iro et studiium*', without hatred or passion, and hence without affection or enthusiasm. As Weber (1994: 160) puts it, bureaucrats take 'pride in preserving their impartiality, overcoming their own inclinations and opinions, so as to execute in a conscientious and meaningful way what is required of them by the general definition of their duties or by some particular instruction, even – and particularly – when they do *not* coincide with their own political views'. Without this ethical discipline and self-denial, Weber stresses, the whole apparatus of the state would disintegrate.

The resulting 'impersonality' has been represented by critics as one of the key pathologies to which all bureaucracies are presumed to be subject. In effect, the bureaucratic form of organisation is assumed to require humans to act in ways that are regarded as inherently inhuman (Bauman, 1989; Ritzer, 2007). This though, as Weber pointed out, underplays the ways in which individuals are implicated in bureaucracies as roles, duties and purposes rather than as human beings *per se*. Furthermore, it is to occlude the ways in which in modern and highly specialised societies, bureaucratic impersonality – precisely because of its procedural imperviousness to overriding moral imperatives – is capable of forming a check against the arbitrary exercise of power. In particular, Weber stresses the ways in which the ethos of bureaucratic office-holding constitutes an important political resource because it serves to divorce the administration of public life from private moral absolutisms. Without the historical emergence of the ethos of bureaucratic office-holding the construction of a buffer between civic comportment and personal principles – a crucial feature of liberal government – would never have been possible. Indeed, without the 'art of separation' (Walzer, 1984) that the state bureau effected and continues to effect, many of the qualitative features of government, such as reliability and procedural fairness in the treatment of cases, would not exist. For Weber, the very 'formalistic impersonality' of bureaucratic administration – its blindness to inherited differences in status and prestige – was the source of democratic, equalising effects. The point then is that through their very operation, formally rational bureaucratic practices of administration give rise to and facilitate the production and reproduction of substantive ethical and political goals, including many of the goals – equality, accountability, fairness, security – that are deemed the cornerstones of liberal democratic governance.

BUREAUCRACY, POLITICS AND MANAGERIALISM

Most governmental, or state, bureaucracies, exhibit a great deal of concern with jurisdiction, fixed rules, and record-keeping. This, in turn, has made them susceptible to the sorts of criticisms levelled at Weber's so-called 'ideal type': 'red tape', conservatism, and inflexibility. Because public institutions have come to be seen as the epitome of Weberian bureaucracy, understood pejoratively as a portmanteau term for the defects of large organisations, they have continually been subject to calls for the radical reform or 'modernisation'. Indeed, not only has the idea that public bureaucracies need reforming gained a somewhat axiomatic status, there has often been extensive, though by no means complete, agreement concerning the nature and direction of the required change. Over the last three decades, similar problematisations of public bureaucracies and of the core ingredients for their reform have emerged from a variety of locales, and these have over time come to be known collectively as New Public Management or Entrepreneurial Governance (Osborne and Gaebler, 1992). Central to this programme of reform has been an attempt to improve the efficiency and effectiveness of public bureaucracies through exposing them to the vicissitudes of a govern-mentally constituted set of quasi-market relations. These market-type mechanisms have been designed to change the conduct of public busi-ness, by 'incentivising' public bureaucracies to mimic the perceived competitive behaviour of private-sector enterprises. Such developments have at their core an antipathy to bureaucracy, and are represented as the means through which its presumed rigidities and inflexibilities are to be overcome through an infusion of market-based entrepreneurial-ism. They are also generally held to have presided over a vast, expensive, and expanding network of audit regimes that is now regularly (and mis-takenly) referred to as 'bureaucratic' (Power, 1997; Strathern, 2000), but which arguably lacks the integrality, flexibility, and suppleness of the classic Weberian bureaucracy (du Gay, 2000).

FURTHER READING

Weber's work (1978; 1994) should be the starting point for students interested in the concept. Useful commentaries and discussions can be found in Albrow (1970) and in the first chapter of Perrow (1986). In the light of managerial and social theoretical critiques of bureaucracy, new interpretations of Weber's work and defences of the bureaucratic form have appeared. These can be traced in du Gay (2000) and Kallinikos (2004), for example.

See also: *Accountability*

REFERENCES

Albrow, M. (1970) *Bureaucracy*. London: Pall Mall Press.
Bauman, Z. (1989) *Modernity and the Holocaust*. Cambridge: Polity.
Du Gay, P. (2000) *In Praise of Bureaucracy*. London: Sage.
Kallinikos, Y. (2004) 'The Social Foundations of the Bureaucratic Order', *Organization* 11(1): 13–36.
Osborne, D. and Gaebler, T. (1992) *Reinventing Government: How the Entrepreneurial Spirit is Transforming the Public Sector*. Reading, MA: Addison-Wesley.
Perrow, C. (1986) *Complex Organizations*, 3rd edn. London: McGraw-Hill.
Power, M. (1997) *The Audit Society*. Oxford: Oxford University Press.
Ritzer, G. (2007) *The McDonaldization of Society*. London: Sage.
Strathern, M. (ed.) (2000) *Audit Cultures*. London: Routledge.
Walzer, M. (1984) 'Liberalism and the Art of Separation', *Political Theory* 12(3): 315–30.

key concepts in critical management studies

Weber, M. (1978) *Economy & Society* (2 vols). Los Angeles: University of California Press.

Weber, M. (1994) 'The Profession and Vocation of Politics', in P. Lassman and R. Speirs (eds) *Weber: Political Writings*, pp. 309–69. Cambridge: Cambridge University Press.

Business Ethics

Edward Wray-Bliss

Definition: 'Business ethics' may be understood as the conceptualisation, critique, and promotion, of ethics as it relates to business and organisational behaviour.

The academic field of business ethics is typically presented as arising out of an ongoing, and recurring, crisis of confidence in the ability of capital to self-regulate. We can see a correspondence between interest in business ethics and certain periods of 'crisis'. For instance, a surge in interest in business ethics during the 1980s (including the launch of the *Journal of Business Ethics* in 1982) coincided with a period when the consequences of deregulation, free-market economics, and the changing balance in industrial relations strongly in favour of management control began to be felt. The journals *Business Ethics Quarterly*, and *Business Ethics: A European Review* both published their first papers in 1991, in the shadow of the Savings and Loans crisis (to which the inaugural editorial of *Business Ethics Quarterly* refers) and Enron, Lehman Brothers, and the accompanying 'global financial crisis' have each precipitated further examination within the field.

On the surface it would appear that there is considerable confluence between business ethics and the concerns of CMS. Attempting to dethrone the sovereignty of the 'economic' in business through the introduction of the 'ethical', and questioning the adequacy of managerial self-regulation to produce wider social goods, both accord strongly with what we can broadly assume to be the politics of CMS. For CMS writers, however, the field of business ethics has not lived up to its promise. Rather than heralding a thoroughgoing critique of self-regulation, of managerialism, or indeed free-market capitalism, business ethics is understood to be in a symbiotic and parasitic relationship with them. Managerialism and self-regulation are legitimised through the field's support for voluntaristic, organisationally codified and managed ethical policies, and capitalism is supported through the field's failure to seriously consider whether 'ethics' and capitalist 'business' can actually reside together at all. At best, business ethics is seen as a well-meaning but essentially misguided and toothless development, too easily incorporated into the business realm which it wished to hold to account. More searchingly, some CMS texts view business ethics as complicit in deception, serving to contain and deflect criticism from the institutions of capitalism, enabling business to bluff ethical, to present a caring front while carrying on exploitative and unethical practices as usual behind its back.

Jones, Parker and ten Bos' (2005) *For Business Ethics* has, despite its title, presented one of the more impassioned critiques of the field – and their critique can stand in here for CMS scholars' disquiet about business ethics more generally. In the opening chapter to their text they list six problems or 'foreclosures' reproduced by the field. For the authors, business ethics has *foreclosed philosophy*, clipping the radical wings of classical philosophy to make it non-threatening for business and almost completely ignoring the major contributions of twentieth-century philosophy and social theory. It has *foreclosed society*, individualising matters of ethics without due consideration to the economic and organisational structures that influence and constrain behaviour. Business ethics has *foreclosed 'the ethical'*, naturalising many, ethically questionable, aspects of business such as the employment relationship, the profit motive, or the authority of managers. It has *foreclosed the meaning of 'ethics'*, reducing it to an apparently straightforward process of using classical philosophy to codify ethical rules that individuals then merely have to follow. Business ethics is charged with *foreclosing politics*, casting ethics as the task of investigating micro and local practices in specific business contexts, while leaving the wider ethico-political questions about the ethics of business, of capitalism, of globalisation, of modern large-scale bureaucratic organisations untouched. Finally business ethics forecloses the *goal of ethics*, rather than understanding ethics as the permanent problematisation of where we are, how we live and how we might live better, ethics is reduced to raising only those problems in business that can be 'solved' within the relatively small space of a journal article.

The main contributions that CMS has made to business ethics are threefold. First, CMS has, as in the work of Jones, Parker and ten Bos (2005), presented what we might regard as an 'ideology' critique of the core assumptions and unexamined politics of business ethics. Second, CMS authors have introduced a broader range of philosophical and social theory to the field. Derridian, existentialist, feminist, Marxist, poststructuralist, posthumanist and postmodernist theory have each been explored. Within each of these approaches, scholars have tended toward an ethics that is questioning of taken-for-granted notions of natural or good practices, that provokes uncertainty rather than complacent moralism, and one which refuses an individualistic notion of the sovereign moral agent whose ethical conduct is divorced from her or his participation in wider power relations. Willmott's (1998) contribution to Parker's edited text *Ethics and Organizations* presents a perceptive, conceptual exploration of such an antifoundational, non-essentialist ethics. Recently, a number of CMS scholars have drawn the ideas of Emmanuel Levinas into the field of business ethics, arguing that this presents a radical critique of core assumptions regarding such things as the primacy of the organisation over the Other, and the idea of boundaries being placed on the notion of the social responsibilities of corporations. Roberts (2001) shows what can be achieved through such Levinasian informed critiques of business ethics. Rather than rendering Business and Management 'vulnerable' to the infinite moral responsibility to the Other, Roberts argues that business ethics as currently conceived and practised is an ethics of narcissus, concerned with the corporation's *image* of itself as good. Such a preoccupation makes the corporation *less* vulnerable to the Other, as an ethical image is projected which the corporation can use to deflect critique, meaning, in Roberts' view, that 'this new regime of ethical business is no ethics at all' (2001: 110).

The third contribution that CMS has made is an engagement with ethics as a concept not for normative pronouncement or philosophical critique, but for empirical investigation. Clegg, Kornberger and Rhodes (2007) have argued that critical research on business ethics needs to now move away from a conceptual critique of the 'static nature' (113) of ethical codes of conduct and such, and instead now begin to consider how these and other moral discourses are used in practice by organisational members in their local, situated, organisational contexts: contexts that are invariably saturated with uncertainty, ethical pluralism and the multiple constituting and conflicting webs of power. Watson is one of the few authors who have begun to engage with ethics in this way as an empirical concern. In his 2003 *Human Relations* article, for example, he explores empirically the latitude available, and carved out, for what he terms 'ethically assertive' individuals to bring to bear their personal ethical considerations upon their professional roles. He demonstrates how it is necessary to appreciate how individuals draw upon numerous situated, competing, ethical discourses in their strivings and struggles to organise their professional activities in ways that they can find morally acceptable.

These sorts of empirical examinations of ethics in practice are, however, the least developed of CMS's contributions. In a recent review of ethics in CMS, Wray-Bliss (2009) has argued that scholars seem to have succumbed to a problematic privileging of politics *over* ethics – where distanced denouncements of the ethics of the abstract entity 'business', the category 'management', or the field 'Business Ethics', takes precedence over proximate encounters with real organisational others and their encounters and difficulties with ethics. This, he suggests, needs to be redressed if CMS is to make the kind of contribution to the field of business ethics that *it* promises.

FURTHER READING

Though not a self-consciously CMS text, Jackall's (1988) ethnographic critique of the amorality of corporate managers should still be the starting point for those wishing to critically examine the ethics of management practices. Jones, Parker and ten Bos (2005) provide an extended critique, and reimagining, of business ethics. Contributions to Parker's (1998) edited collection illustrate some of the range of CMS scholars' engagement with ethics, across both theory and practice, and Wray-Bliss (2009) provides an extended critical review of CMS engagement with ethics.

See also: Accountability, Corporate Social Responsibility

REFERENCES

Clegg, S., Kornberger, M. and Rhodes, C. (2007) 'Business Ethics as Practice', *British Journal of Management* 18: 107–22.
Jackall, R. (1988) *Moral Mazes: The World of Corporate Managers.* Oxford: Oxford University Press.
Jones, C., Parker, M. and ten Bos, R. (2005) *For Business Ethics.* Abingdon: Routledge.
Parker, M. (ed.) (1998) *Ethics and Organizations.* London: Sage.

Roberts, J. (2001) 'Corporate Governance and the Ethics of Narcissus', *Business Ethics Quarterly* 11(1): 109–27.

Watson, T. (2003) 'Ethical Choice in Managerial Work: The Scope for Moral Choices in an Ethically Irrational World', *Human Relations* 56: 167–85.

Willmott, H. (1998) 'Towards a New Ethics? The Contributions of Poststructuralism and Posthumanism', in M. Parker (ed.) *Ethics and Organizations*, pp. 76–121. London: Sage.

Wray-Bliss, E. (2009) 'Ethics: Critique, Ambivalence and Infinite Responsibilities (Unmet)', in M. Alvesson, T. Bridgman and H. Willmott (eds) *The Oxford Handbook of Critical Management Studies*, pp. 267–85. Oxford: Oxford University Press.

Capitalism and Anticapitalism

David Harvie and Keir Milburn

Definition: Capitalism is an economic and social system in which the means of production are owned privately (rather than co-operatively or in common) as commodities. Anticapitalism is the set of beliefs and practices that opposes capitalism.

INTRODUCTION

Within the capitalist system individuals own their capacity to labour (which takes the form of a commodity) and commodities (means of production, means of subsistence or consumption goods and the capacity to labour) are freely exchanged on markets. This definition tells us little, it must be said, about how capitalism affects our lives and thus little about its political and social significance. However once we move beyond the definition above, capitalism becomes a more elusive concept. Indeed there is a tendency for both pro- and anti-capitalists to avoid the term – and capitalism seems to have inbuilt effects that tend to make it disappear as an identifiable and analysable phenomenon.

When people talk about the 'market economy', they are talking about capitalism. Markets have existed in one form or another for at least two thousand years and therefore the euphemism naturalises and ahistoricises capitalism. In fact markets did not start to develop into the market *economy* or capitalism until the sixteenth century and then only in northern Europe. Conversely, in order to emphasise capitalism's historical and spatial specificity – the fact that it does not and has not existed always and everywhere, nor even now in all spheres of life – some thinkers prefer the term capitalist mode of production to capitalism. Karl Marx, for example, only used the word 'capitalism' a handful of times.

We can only understand the capitalist mode of production – or capitalism – by understanding capital. But this, in turn, involves a refusal to understand capital in its more everyday meaning, as factories, stocks of raw materials or sums of money. Capital is a social relation, which includes and to a large extent determines labour. As a social relation it is, by definition, abstract and, as such, hard to grasp. This does not mean that it is not real. Capital's effects on our lives are all too real, concrete and persistent. Marx calls this a real abstraction. So we can think of capital as a diagram of abstract dynamics, but while this definition is accurate we might again ask if it is useful. Here we run into a longstanding problem in anticapitalist thought of how capital can be represented in a way that illuminates anticapitalist practice.

A common mistake – and an enormous problem for anticapitalists – is to personify capital, that is, to identify individuals who stand in for the social relation. This strategy leads to a partial anticapitalism. It is, for example, paradigmatic of populism, which bases its critique not on the ordinary functioning of capital, but on some foreign element or malfunctioning part that interrupts its otherwise-benign operation. 'Greedy' bankers, for instance. On the other hand, naming the problem as capital, and so defining yourself as 'anticapitalist', is not sufficient either. Such words can be easily hollowed of meaning. Profiled by the *Guardian* newspaper in 2002, Zac Goldsmith – then editor of the *Ecologist*, now a Conservative MP – was described as Britain's leading anticapitalist, yet the next line informed us that he was not against business or growth. The operative definition of capitalism employed here is stretched to breaking point.

The most concrete way to define capital is to map the abstract dynamics that comprise it. We cannot provide a full diagram here so we will examine just three aspects: separation, the imposition of work, and the ceaseless search for profit.

First, separation. The capital relation is an alienating one. Humans in capitalist society are separated from the resources necessary to fulfil our needs. We are separated from them because these resources – raw materials, land, food, increasingly water – take the form of private property or commodities. To reproduce ourselves, we must buy these resources, for which we need money. To obtain money we must sell the one thing we do possess, our time, our capacity to work. When we have finished working, the product of our labour is not ours, but belongs to our employer. Thus the producer is separated from her product and the cycle begins anew. This is not the only separation associated with capital. Because our work-for-money-to-live is commanded by someone else, we feel separated – or alienated – from that very activity and also from our fellow workers and, if we believe Marx, from own species-being, our humanity (Marx, 1959).

Let us now look from the perspective of work (the second aspect). Because we are separated from our environment – both 'natural' and produced – we are forced to sell our capacity to work. We do this freely in capitalism – we are neither slaves nor serfs – but our choice is bleak. Either we sell our capacity to work and labour for another or we go hungry. Thus, although formally we choose to work, in reality this work is imposed. Capitalism is not the only mode of production that has imposed work – slaves and serfs were also forced to labour against their will. What distinguishes capitalism is the way work structures the very fabric of society: work structures our identities, our space and our time. In capitalism work – as opposed to religion, custom or culture – organises life.

But what is work exactly? What is common to concrete activities as diverse as digging coal, washing up, writing an essay or designing software? Or, put another way, if someone asks you what you are doing, why is 'I'm working' an adequate answer? Capitalism is key, for the very catch-all label of work or labour – that is counter-posed to leisure – only arose with the emergence of this mode of production. Earlier, and elsewhere, people milked cows, collected firewood, repaired roofs, and so forth, but it made no sense to equate one activity with any of the others.

The common element – the element that makes it possible to equate diverse concrete activities – is abstract labour. It is abstract labour that makes commensurable and exchangeable the many different types of commodities and diverse concrete forms of labour that produce them. In Marx's words, abstract labour is 'labour-power [the capacity to work] expended without regard to the form of its expenditure' (Marx, 1992: 128). Abstract labour is located where capital's heart would be.

Work and abstract labour are measured by value, or money. Here we come to the third aspect: the ceaseless search for profit. Capitalists are motivated by profit, this is what makes them capitalists. To make profit they must purchase labour-capacity along with some raw materials and then compel those humans to produce some good or service (a commodity in Marxian language), whose value when sold is greater than its cost of production, that is, greater than the capitalist's initial outlay. Note that this process depends upon separation. And note too that there are many ways in which this circuit by which the capitalist expands his capital might be disrupted – any act that does disrupt this circuit might be understood as anticapitalist. But assuming all goes well for the capitalist, as soon as one circuit is complete, she is compelled to start another – else she ceases to be a capitalist.

According to capital's logic, this process can *never* cease. Value must always expand and this is because of its abstract form. Even pharaohs, emperors and kings were limited by the amount of wealth they could accumulate. But value and capital is measured as ones and zeroes on an accounting sheet: it is always possible to conceive of a greater number, a greater value. Thus capital can also be understood as the limitless search for profit. Since profit depends upon both separation and the imposition of work, we could define capital as a social relation that requires limitless separation and the limitless imposition of work.

Capitalism simply names a society in which capital is dominant. Where does this leave anticapitalism? Just as simply – but much harder in practice – anticapitalism is that set of kaleidoscopic activities that set limits to capital's ceaseless expansion: activities that resist separation and instead institute commons, say; activities that refuse work; or activities that try to organise life around other values than economic value.

FURTHER READING

The first volume of Marx's *Capital* (1992) remains essential reading, whilst David Harvey's set of video lectures (available here: http://davidharvey.org/reading-capital/) offers useful commentary. Three recent texts that have made important contributions to our understanding of capitalism and anticapitalism are Hardt and Negri (2001), Holloway (2002) and De Angelis (2007). On anticapitalist movements, see Leeds May Day Group (2008).

See also: Commodity Fetishism, Critical Theory, Dialectics, Ideology, Labour Process Theory, Marxism and Post-Marxism

REFERENCES

De Angelis, M. (2007) *The Beginning of History: Value Struggles and Global Capital.* London: Pluto Press.

Hardt, M. and Negri, A. (2001) *Empire.* Cambridge, MA: Harvard University Press.

Holloway, J. (2002) *Change the World Without Taking Power: The Meaning of Revolution Today.* London: Pluto Press.

Leeds May Day Group (2008) 'Anti-Capitalist Movements', in W. Bonefeld (ed.) *Subverting The Present – Imagining The Future: Insurrection, Movement, Commons*, pp. 127–38. Brooklyn: Autonomedia.

Marx, K. (1959) *Economic and Philosophical Manuscripts of 1844.* Moscow: Progress Publishers. Available online at http://www.marxists.org/archive/marx/works/1844/manuscripts/preface.htm.

Marx, K. (1992 [1867]) *Capital: A Critique of Political Economy.* Harmondsworth: Penguin.

Class

Peter Armstrong

Definition: This is the definition of class from the UK's most popular introduction text in sociology. It is not intended as an invitation to controversy: 'most societies today, including Britain, have stratification systems based almost entirely on economic relationships. Inequalities in material life-chances are fundamental; status differences and differences in political influence follow on from this. Structures where economic relationships are primary we call *class societies*, and in these we refer to the different unequal groups as *classes*' (Bilton et al., 1981: 45, italics in original).

If class is founded in economic inequality, it is heavily entrenched in the modern world. In Britain in 2008, for example, the richest tenth of the population received 30% of the country's total income compared to 1.3% received by the poorest tenth (The Poverty Site, 2009). Wealth distribution is even more skewed. In 2003 the richest 10% owned 53% of all personal wealth (71% of marketable wealth, i.e. that which excludes the value of dwellings) whilst the poorest 10% owned about 7% of all wealth and virtually none of which is marketable (Haggar, 2009).

Whilst these figures include land, investment properties and the income from them, it is clear that the capitalist work organisation is fundamental to the uneven distributions of life chances. Accumulated wealth primarily receives its return through capital's share of the value added whilst labour's share is also distributed in a markedly uneven fashion. The *Guardian* newspaper's 2009 survey of UK boardroom pay found that the average chief executive of a bluechip company earned a basic salary of £791,000, about 30 times the median earnings of £489 per week and over 60 times the national minimum wage of £5.80 per hour, assuming a 40-hour week. Even so, the basic salary massively understates the total remuneration at senior levels. Taking into account the value of bonus payments, share awards and perks, nearly a quarter of FTSE 100 chief executives received over £5m (Finch and Bowers, 2009). The effects of these massive imbalances ripple outwards into the wider society. Whole industries are now predicated on the sense of entitlement capable of consuming on the scale now expected of senior executives. At the other end of the continuum, there are the working poor: those whom managers have chosen to employ at, near or below the minimum wage. Below them, there is a stratum which some analysts are ominously beginning to describe as a 'surplus population' (Bauman, 1998); surplus to managerial requirements, that is. These are the sporadically employed, the long-term unemployed, the unemployable. Again whole industries have grown up in response, this time in an attempt to contain the consequent social problems.

The more urgent problem, naturally, is to find some means of theorising these inequalities. Bilton et al. (1981) offer their readership a choice of two suites of ideas: the 'Weberian' in which 'life chances' are a consequence of 'market capacities' – the different skills and other personal attributes which individuals bring to the marketplace; and the 'Marxist', in which they follow from the social relations of production; the matter of whether one lives primarily off the economic returns to capital or by the sale to capital of one's capacity to work (labour power).

'Market capacities' are undoubtedly relevant, as has been cruelly discovered by those middle-aged office managers who have found that organisational delayering has destroyed the social capital accumulated over a working lifetime. What is lacking in this approach, however, is any conception of *why* the market for particular categories of labour changes as it does, or indeed, where it comes from in the first place. The Marxist answer to these questions goes back to fundamentals: that the organisation of labour in a capitalist economy – including the labour of organisation itself – is driven by the tendency of capital to seek the maximum sustainable return. Where the Weberian theorisation implies no particular dividing lines between classes and no particular relationship between them, the Marxist implies that there are only two basic classes and that the cleavage between them is also a point at which their interests conflict at the societal level. Marxist theory also recognises that economic inequality is more than a matter of quantitative differences. Behind these, and more fundamental, are the inequalities in the distribution of power over economic resources. Capitalism is defined by the ownership by capital of the means of production and, give or take the survivals from earlier social formations, the distribution of wealth and income follows from the rights attaching to that ownership.

The advent of managerial capitalism has created ambiguities in the class structure, ambiguities discussed in Marx's own writings as well as in the extensive subsequent debates on the separation of ownership from control (Nichols, 1969). On the one hand management is simply a particular kind of intellectual labour – a labour of 'superintendance' as Marx called it – complemented by whatever technological expertise might be called for. On the other hand, management is the executive arm of capital itself. As is particularly visible in those companies which are organised into business units, managers are charged with a fiduciary responsibility to act in the interests of their employers and they are legally empowered to do so in virtue of the delegated powers of ownership. Managers are the agents of capital.

As such, managers are not only *in* the class structure; they are *of* it. That is to say, they are complicit in the creation and maintenance of a given pattern of wage and salary differentials, albeit they do so with one eye on what is happening in competitor corporations. If the return on capital is to be sufficient to prevent its flight to more lucrative locations – a condition which has not always been present in the UK since the 1970s – the wage costs of labour – including that of subordinate levels of management – must be held correspondingly below the economic return from its employment. These conditions depend on the ability of

class

managers to resist wage claims from organised labour on the one hand and to recruit from unorganised pools of cheap labour on the other. Since the 1970s (once more) these requirements have been abetted by various forms of state intervention such as the abandonment of full employment as a policy, the enforced privatisation of public services, anti-trade-union legislation and the tacit encouragement of inward economic migration as a means of filling those jobs 'no one else wants to do' (as if the rates of pay had nothing to do with that state of affairs). This ability of management at the collective level to hold in place a conventionalised pattern of wage differentials is the missing idea in Weberian 'market capacities' and by the same token, it is the mark of managerial complicity in the maintenance of the class structure.

Now critical management studies (CMS) declares itself to be an emancipatory project, and if emancipation means anything at all it means the abolition of social inequality. In Fournier and Grey's (2000) assessment, moreover, an ancestry for CMS was claimed in labour process theory, Frankfurt School critical theory and Gramscian hegemony theory. If this had turned out to be an accurate portrayal, and if CMS were genuinely emancipatory in its intent, one would expect the vocabulary of class to figure prominently in its writings, the more so since work organisations and their management figure so prominently in the formation and maintenance of the class structure. In reality one can read through a typical journal of CMS from one end to the other without encountering any mention of the concept. Significantly, the index of the *Oxford Handbook of Critical Management Studies* (Alvesson et al., 2009) contains no entry at all on 'class' or 'capital', whilst the reader is referred to just three of its 550 pages for discussions of 'inequality' or 'social inequality'. This is not credible as a scholarship of emancipation, and if CMS is not to stand accused of the cynical appropriation of a label which once stood for an honourable tradition of principled dissent, it needs to change.

FURTHER READING

Given the lack of engagement of CMS with issues of class, it might be appropriate for the interested student to consult John Scott's *Corporations, Classes and Capitalism* (Hutchinson, 1985), especially chapter 8. Interesting on the manner in which class has been occluded from recent debates is Ellen Meiksins Wood's *The Retreat from Class* (Verso, 1998).

See also: *Capitalism and Anticapitalism, Critical Theory, Hegemony, Ideology, Labour Process Theory, Managerialism, Marxism and Post-Marxism*

REFERENCES

Alvesson, M., Bridgman, T. and Willmott, H. (eds) (2009) *The Oxford Handbook of Critical Management Studies*. Oxford: Oxford University Press.

Haggar, R. (2009) http://www.earlhamsociologypages.co.uk/socclassintro.htmlhttp://www.earlhamsociologypages.co.uk/socclassintro.html. Last Accessed 15/12/2009.

Bauman, Z. (1998) *Work, Consumerism and the New Poor*. Buckingham: Open University Press.

Bilton, T., Bonnett, K., Jones, P., Sheard, K., Stanworth, M. and Webster, A. (1981) *Introductory Sociology*. Basingstoke: Macmillan.

Finch, J. and Bowers, S. (2009) 'Executive Pay Keeps Rising, Guardian Survey Finds', *The Guardian*, 14 Sept. 2009.

Fournier, V. and Grey, C. (2000) 'At the Critical Moment: Conditions and Prospects for Critical Management Studies', *Human Relations* 53: 7–32.

Nichols, T. (1969) *Ownership Control and Ideology: An Enquiry into Certain Aspects of Modern Business Ideology*. London: Allen & Unwin.

Nichols, T. (1979) 'Social Class: Official, Sociological and Marxist', in J. Irvine, I. Miles and J. Evans (eds) *Demystifying Social Statistics*, pp. 152–71. London: Pluto.

The Poverty Site (2009) http://www.poverty.org.uk/09/index.shtml. Last Accessed 15/12/2009.

Colonialism and Postcolonialism

Gavin Jack and Robert Westwood

Definition: Colonialism is the control or rule of a country or territory by another country or territory, usually through direct physical settlement and establishment of a colony, and associated forms of cultural, political and economic governance. Postcolonialism is a broad theoretical perspective for investigating the varied historical effects, contemporary legacies and changing forms of colonialism and imperialism.

COLONIALISM

Despite enormous historical and locational variation, the term 'colonialism' is most often used today in relation to the imperialist expansion of a number of European countries from the fifteenth century onwards. Colonialism typically involved the physical settlement of overseas territories by these countries. However, the variety of colonial regimes, the differing scale and types of colonial settlement, and the changing nature of governance mechanisms used by colonising countries mean that colonialism needs to be understood as a heterogeneous practice with local variations.

Colonialism was closely connected to the historical development of capitalism and industrialisation in Western Europe, and one cannot be understood properly without a clear understanding of the other. That is to say, the emergence of modern forms of trade, business, administration and management is tied to colonialism, and vice versa. The colonies provided their imperial rulers with both a source of raw materials and labour for its burgeoning industries, as well as markets for its finished goods. Colonialism was thus based on an asymmetrical system of economic exchange, of core and peripheral dependencies, in which the colonies became subject to and systematically 'underdeveloped' by Western imperial powers.

Colonialism was also cultural and ideological in nature. Colonising regimes attempted to impose their Western knowledge and belief systems, and other cultural practices, onto non-Western contexts. Such instances of cultural imperialism – enacted by a number of different institutions including politicians and government agencies, the church and its missionaries, scientists and educationalists – simultaneously involved efforts to transform, marginalise and/or destroy local belief systems and cultural practices.

The whole imperial edifice was premised on the assumed cultural, moral and intellectual superiority of the 'Western mind' and its organisational, administrative and trading systems. The 'West' was deemed to be more civilised, cultivated, developed and thus further along the trajectory of human progress. Such a belief became the grounds upon which colonialism was legitimated as necessary for the 'good' of the 'uncivilised Other' by colonisers. The presumptions of superiority on which it is based – and the racial differences it served to organise – took form in a vast assemblage of social technologies aimed at 'governing the native' (in a Foucauldian sense) and creating a colonial subjectivity that could putatively be controlled.

The colonial encounter was, however, never a monolithic, unidirectional or unambiguous process. Literature on the colonial encounter demonstrates that it is better conceived of as a dynamic 'zone of tension', in which the colonised's agency took the form of resistance, subversion or mimicry rather than mere passivity or acceptance of the beliefs and actions of the coloniser. Indeed, the history of anticolonialism – especially through passive and armed struggle, as well as the political campaigning of independence parties – is vital for conceptualising the colonial encounter as one of resistance and ambivalence as well as violence.

The concept of neocolonialism signifies that the economic and cultural manifestations of colonialism and imperialism have been modified but remain constitutive forms in postindependence, postcolonial societies. New vehicles for and forms of colonialism remain in the contemporary global economic system, with the US and other superpowers taking up the mantle of imperialism.

POSTCOLONIALISM

Postcolonialism is a contentious term for at least three reasons. First, the term can carry two different conceptions: 'post-colonialism' (hyphenated) signifying a periodisation conveying the somewhat questionable notion of a period *after* colonialism; and 'postcolonialism' (unhyphenated), signifying an interrogative space and a set of epistemological and ethical resources for a critique of continuing and changing forms of colonialism. Second, postcolonialism is not a homogeneous theoretical terrain – there is no singular postcolonial approach, with key writers influenced *inter alia* by poststructuralism, feminism, psychoanalysis, Marxism, and complex engagements between these. Third, modes of textual analysis that have dominated postcolonial scholarship through the work of Said (see below), Bhabha and Spivak have been criticised, particularly by Marxist-informed scholars, for their lack of a strong political agenda and for their reliance on the very kinds of Western/Eurocentric theoretical frames which they critique.

Whilst there are numerous important predecessors, it is the publication of Edward Said's *Orientalism: Western Conceptions of the Orient* (1978) that is credited as a seminal moment in the academic institutionalisation of postcolonial theory and analysis. Said borrows from Foucault and Gramsci to outline and critique the sets of representations utilised by Western scholars in producing accounts of the Orient (and by extension, the Occident). The discourse of Orientalism worked through a series of binary oppositions that simultaneously constructed and positioned the Occident and the Orient in asymmetrical relation to each other. Though Said's text has been critiqued, it opened the way for the development of future and differently theorised postcolonial textual analyses by Bhabha (drawing upon Lacan and Althusser) and Spivak (drawing upon Derrida and Marx, and in critical engagement with subaltern studies scholars).

A key theme uniting these postcolonial critics is a desire to critique 'Eurocentric' knowledge structures and cultural practices. Eurocentrism is a term that refers to forms of knowledge that 'normalize the idea of Europe as the birthplace of the modern', and 'the theoretical subject of all historical knowledge' (Mufti, 2005). Eurocentric knowledge and practices are not geographically limited to European countries; they have travelled through the practices of colonialism and imperialism, and continue to do so. Consequently, critiques of Eurocentrism can apply to a set of ideas from any location and in any institution, including universities.

IMPLICATIONS FOR CRITICAL MANAGEMENT STUDIES

Interest in the concepts of colonialism, anticolonialism and postcolonialism is growing in the CMS community, though they do not constitute a dominant analytical frame. The implications of postcolonialism for management and organisation studies are potentially profound, offering an interrogation of the field's ontological, epistemological, methodological, ethical and political assumptions and commitments. First, a postcolonial perspective can be used to expose Eurocentrism and to 'provincialise' the management discipline's principal theoretical frames, especially when claims are made about their universal application. This is a task of defamiliarisation – of rereading and rethinking our field – and thus of unpacking our presumptive knowledge from the regime of the same and allowing the difference of the local to re-emerge. This challenge also applies to individual researchers, encouraging us to examine who our research and theorising is for, how it is infused with (our own) interests, and with what consequences.

Previous work in management and organisation studies has drawn selectively upon postcolonialism to address a number of issues. First, the history of management theory and practice has been subject to postcolonial critique, with the aim of unravelling how discourses of business, management and accounting emerged in the colonial encounter – rather than being produced in and by the West.

Second, and inspired by Said and Bhabha, the field has begun to critically examine the processes of its knowledge work. Issues addressed in this regard include: critiques of the persistence of Orientalist and Eurocentric practices in the discourses of management and organisational theory (e.g. Jack and Westwood, 2009), and in business practice; attempts to reinstate and valorise voices from the Global South and in particular from indigenous communities in theory development in the field (e.g. Henry and Pene, 2001); critiques of the transfer of corporate or organisational knowledge by/from multinational corporations and Western contexts into non-Western contexts, and associated processes such as appropriation, resistance, accommodation or subjectivation (Frenkel, 2008). Finally, there is an emergent body of work informed by political economy that addresses more macro-level issues such as the neocolonial underpinnings of the unequal global economic order, and the close relationship between war, the military, natural resources expropriation and oppression (Banerjee, 2008).

FURTHER READING

Moore-Gilbert, B. (1997) *Postcolonial Theory: Contexts, Practices, Politics.* London and New York: Verso.

Prasad, A. (ed.) (2003) *Postcolonial Theory and Organizational Analysis: A Critical Engagement.* New York: Palgrave Macmillan.

Said, E. (1978) *Orientalism: Western Conceptions of the Orient.* London: Penguin.

See also: *Critical International Management, Feminism, Globalisation, Identity, Marxism and Post-Marxism, Power, Subjectivity and Subjectivation*

REFERENCES

Banerjee, S.B. (2008) 'Necrocapitalism', *Organization Studies* 29(12): 1541–63.

Frenkel, M. (2008) 'The Multinational Corporation as a Third Space: Rethinking International Management Discourse on Knowledge Transfer Through Homi Bhabha', *Academy of Management Review* 33(4): 924–42.

Henry, E. and Pene, H. (2001) '*Kaupapa Maori*: Locating Indigenous Ontology, Epistemology and Methodology in the Academy', *Organization* 8(2): 234–42.

Jack, G. and Westwood, R. (2009) *International and Cross-Cultural Management Studies: A Postcolonial Reading.* Basingstoke and New York: Palgrave/Macmillan.

Mufti, A. (2005) 'Global Comparativism', *Critical Inquiry* 31(2): 472–89.

Commodity Fetishism

Stephen Dunne

Definition: To suggest that the value of any given commodity can be isolated at the level of consumption, rather than traced back to the sphere(s) of production, is to succumb to commodity fetishism.

Wherever there is capitalism, there will be commodities. Any analysis of capitalism must therefore engage in an analysis of what the individual commodity is *and* of how this individual commodity fits into the broader capitalist economy. So it was within the classical works of political economy, such as those written by Adam Smith, David Ricardo and John Stuart Mill. So it was also within the work of Karl Marx, who set out to write nothing less than a *critique* of the political economy of his predecessors, that is, a *critique* of the ways in which political economy was being applied, in practice.

Marx's three-volume study of political economy, *Capital* (1976, 1978, 1981) is buttressed by an initial diagnosis of the fact that commodity consumers and political economists *alike* suffer from an inability to properly understand the commodity-form in all of its complexities. In other words, Marx asserts that there is a routinised fetishisation of the commodity-form, in which there is an ascription to it of properties which are not its own, properties borrowed from elsewhere. Indeed, it was precisely an uncovering of the commodity-form's inherent propensity to borrow from elsewhere, *as if it was not doing so*, that Marx reveals in his discussion of commodity fetishism. But just what *is* the commodity? And *why* is it fetishised?

The commodity, for Marx, is something potentially useful, of course. After all, we would not consume commodities if we did not think that we could put them towards some sort of end. Additionally, the commodity is something exchangeable: the value contained within it is not realised until the moment at which another person actually consumes it, that is to say, pays for it. This means that it is dangerous for the capitalist to believe that their wares are worth having, and to covet or hoard them accordingly. No money will change hands within such a scenario: the capitalist must rather want only to sell the commodity s/he brings to market. Marx thus demonstrates that in order for capitalism to thrive, ongoing movement is required: commodities must circulate. And in order for this to happen, would-be consumers have to believe that commodities are valuable to them, and to act accordingly. Consumers are therefore the ones that apparently put the wheels of capitalism in motion – the ones who direct money back to the capitalist who can, in turn, bring more and more commodities to market, so that more and more consumers can consume more and more commodities, and so on. The existence of capitalism consequently presupposes the existence of commodities and, what is more, the existence of commodities presupposes, in turn, the existence of consumers. Capitalism is a system of commodity relationships and consumers initially *appear* to be its active agents.

So it *seems*, anyway. But this is not the complete picture – Marx insists that we have to look more closely at the matter, to approach it from a different angle, as it were. Yes, the commodity appears as capitalism's 'elementary form' (Marx, 1976: 125). And yes, the usefulness of the commodity is established, perhaps even proven, in its exchange, that is to say, in its consumption. But what, after all, *is* the source of the usability and exchangeability of the commodity? What is the source of the commodity's dual value? Is commodity-value simply a product of the mind of the consumer? Is commodity-value a characteristic of the commodity itself? Or does the secret of the source of commodity-value lie elsewhere? According to Marx the source of commodity-value does indeed lie elsewhere, within the sphere of production, a sphere analysed by Marx in great detail in volume 1 of *Capital* (Marx, 1976).

Alongside what has been mentioned so far in the name of the commodity then, we can also say that commodities have been *produced*, that they have been worked upon, that they are the outcome of human labour having transformed nature. So the commodity is usable, exchangeable, and it has been laboured upon. For Marx, it is this third and final characteristic of the commodity, the fact that it has been laboured upon, which is crucial. If we are to understand the commodity, and by extension the consumer, as well as the capitalist mode of production, we need to take account of the labour which goes into the commodity, the labour which causes the commodity to be both useful and exchangeable, *first of all*. This we should do, rather than focusing our attention upon either the commodity or the consumer. For Marx, as the definition above suggests, in order to understand the commodity and, by extension, capitalism, we need to turn away from the sphere of circulation, that is the behaviours and relationships characteristic of the market (Marx, 1978), looking instead towards the sphere of production.

And yet, as has already been mentioned, consumers and political economists alike routinely neglect this seemingly obvious fact. In the case of the consumer, the inanimate commodity is routinely related to as if it had qualities, a personality, and even a life of its own (think of contemporary discussions of phenomena such as brand value). Consumers therefore fetishise the commodity-form by pushing to the background the fact that every single thing about the commodity is nothing but the product of human labour. Political economists, for their part, also fetishise the commodity-form by looking for the source of value elsewhere: within the land, within machinery, or within the entrepreneurial spirit, for example. Fetishism therefore amounts to a lack of knowledge concerning causes, the mal-ascription of cause. And in this sense, for Marx, this fetishistic condition, this notion that commodities have lives apart from the labour which produces them, is analogous to the religiously devout mindset. As he puts it, within religion

> the products of the human brain appear as autonomous figures endowed with a life of their own, which enter into relations both with each other and with the human race. So it is in the world of commodities with the products of men's hands. I call this the fetishism which attaches itself to the products of labour as soon as they are produced as commodities, and is therefore inseparable from the production of commodities. (Marx, 1976: 165)

Given the fact, finally, that commodity fetishism is a characteristic feature of the capitalist mode of production, it is not something that can be simplistically cancelled out or overcome without the very cancelling out or overcoming of the context within which it takes place – capitalism. Commodity fetishism is a structural fact, rather than an individual misapprehension. And in this sense, commodity fetishism is not simply an intellectual or scholarly concern. On the contrary, it is rather a concern with the very way in which society as such is mediated by commodity relationships: an inherently practical concern, in other words.

FURTHER READING

The famous section entitled 'The Fetishism of the Commodity and Its Secret' (Marx, 1976: 163–77) is the foundation for Marx's challenging analysis of the commodity-form (1976: 125–77). In order to properly understand what commodity fetishism means, therefore, the commodity-form must be comprehended first of all. The longer going tradition of theorising in the name of fetishism which Marx is engaging *with*, as well as departing *from*, is expertly outlined within the work of William Pietz (1985, 1987, 1988). For a classical interpretation of the concept of commodity fetishism, see the work of Georg Lukács (1974), particularly his piece entitled 'Reification and the Consciousness of the Proletariat'. For an overview of aspects of the contemporary debate around the concept of commodity fetishism, see Miklitsch (1996).

See also: Consumer Culture, Capitalism and Anticapitalism, Critical Marketing Studies, Dialectics, Ideology, Labour Process Theory, Marxism and Post-Marxism

REFERENCES

Lukács, G. (1974) *History and Class Consciousness: Studies in Marxist Dialectics*. London: Merlin Press.
Marx, K. (1976) *Capital: A Critique of Political Economy, Volume 1*, trans. Ben Fowkes. London: Penguin.
Marx, K. (1978) *Capital: A Critique of Political Economy, Volume 2*, trans. David Fernbach. London: Penguin.
Marx, K. (1981) *Capital: A Critique of Political Economy, Volume 3*, trans. David Fernbach. London: Penguin.
Miklitsch, R. (1996) 'The Commodity-Body-Sign: Towards a General Economy of "Commodity Fetishism"', *Cultural Critique* 33(Spring): 5–40.
Pietz, W. (1985) 'The Problem of the Fetish, Part 1', *Res* 9(Spring): 5–17.
Pietz, W. (1987) 'The Problem of the Fetish, Part 2', *Res* 13(Spring): 23–45.
Pietz, W. (1988) 'The Problem of the Fetish, Part 3a', *Res* 16(Autumn): 105–23.

commodity fetishism

Consumer Culture

Alan Bradshaw

> **Definition:** Consumer culture refers to how the consumption of goods, services and brands structure social actions and interpersonal relations.

Whilst consumption has been classically defined as an end-point in the exchange process, or as a process entailing the acquisition, usage and disposal of goods, to say that we live in a consumer culture implies that our lives and relationships can be understood according to how we engage with the goods and services that we purchase and use. In this sense, a consumer culture is part of the lived experience within capitalism, where our daily needs and desires are both produced and then addressed within the marketplace and where people relate to each other as representatives and owners of those goods and services (Marx, 1993). Whilst authors such as Bauman (2007) systematically distinguish between different terms, consumer culture is generally used interchangeably with 'consumer society' and 'a society of consumers'.

Consumer culture is perhaps best approached in terms of its reproducibility. According to Baudrillard (1998), consumer culture is a complex superobject where each object signifies other objects and together they constitute a superobject that draws the consumer into a series of motivations; or as succinctly put by Žižek (2008) – 'the more you have, the more you want'. Indeed, the prominence of both *want* and *desire* within consumer culture identifies the centrality of the principle of pleasure as consumers are encouraged to pursue pleasurable experiences in the marketplace.

However, as argued by Žižek, consumer culture creates the expectation that we will constantly be pleasured by what we consume, and hence the pursuit of enjoyment within consumer culture does not arise spontaneously, but rather follows a cultural expectation that we *must* constantly experience increased levels of pleasure (as satirised by Jello Biafra: 'THE COMFORTS YOU DEMANDED ARE NOW MANDATORY. BE HAPPY'). Therefore, as Bauman identifies, inasmuch as consumer culture is part of a total system that demands forms of behaviour, it operates not in the form of a sacrifice which we must suffer but rather as pleasure and entertainment.

Predicated as it is on pleasure and desire, consumer culture has been historicised as emerging from the impulses and subjectivities of the romantic period. Consumer culture is grounded in fantasy, yearning, daydreaming and desire. Even so, as a romanticist impulse, consumer desire is never satiated because what is desired is desire itself and this serves the reproducibility of consumer culture (Campbell, 1987). Hence consumer culture reproduces itself through integrating people into a spiral of never-ending and never totally satisfactory consumption; it does so through producing desire and operates at a level that strives to seduce, rather than alienate, its subjects.

As well as its reproducibility, consumer culture is also best understood in terms of an irony which regularly reverses its own logic. For example, consumers are encouraged to differentiate themselves through a strong assertion of an individual identity. They could do this, for example, by wearing fashionable clothes. The irony here is that this is typically made possible via the availability of mass-produced textiles that are worn by huge numbers of other people.

Another example of the irony of consumer culture is that for a consumer culture to exist, consumers must produce themselves as consumer subjects. According to Bauman (2007), a precondition for becoming a subject of consumer culture is that we thereby become an object that can be consumed. Take the case of internet dating, wherein consumers must produce themselves as an object of exchange. We have to provide our bio-data so that a potential purchaser can determine from our information whether they want to purchase 'us', much like a shopper selecting between alternative objects on a shelf. Indeed, the minimising of risk that this form of self-presentation encourages serves the purpose of neutralising a person's subjectivity at the same time as objectifying them; in other words, all of the complex aspects of the person are stripped out and simplified until what remains is a personality that can be easily consumed by their suitor, as quickly and as risk-free as possible.

In producing ourselves as commodities, then, we select goods and services that are loaded with lifestyle values and meanings (i.e. they are cool, sexy or chic) in the process of identity construction. This is a double-play inasmuch as our social relations are determined by the way we deploy objects to produce and legitimise ourselves according to consumer culture values, and by so doing we also add value to the brands we consume (Arvidsson, 2006). For example, if a person succeeds in gaining prestige within a social group by successfully wearing an Armani suit, then he/she has increased the value of Armani within that group.

In its general expression, consumer culture is often deployed pejoratively especially by those writing from a Critical (Theory) perspective. For some authors, consumer culture can be understood as occupied by selfish individuals. Put simply, a polarity might be imagined between a consumer culture, which takes the form of groupings of individualistic, self-centred consumers, and a society of socially oriented and public-minded citizens. In that spirit, the boundaries of a consumer culture continue to expand further and further into the lifeworld of individuals as a function of the diffusion of neoliberal values. Here individuals are responsible for crafting their own sense of self, focusing only on their own lifestyle projects, and this makes the inequalities of neoliberalism more bearable. Consumption, put simply, is our reward for working long hours, in jobs we dislike.

Thus, a major critique of consumer culture and its attendant individualism is the reduction in collective responsibility that is demonstrated as we become increasingly self-focused and egotistical. A particularly forceful critique of the so-called collateral damage of consumer culture is provided by Bauman (2007) who details that those incapable of producing themselves as commodities for a culture of consumption become regarded as useless and are held in contempt. This critique of consumer culture as a form of objective violence is similarly deployed by Žižek (2008) who notes the disappearance of individualised consumers into inauthentic utopias in pursuit of pleasures and lifestyles whilst ignoring the injustices that mount around them.

Running counter to the idea of consumer culture as reifying individualism is the emergence of collectives formed around shared consumption practices and experiences; hence there is a growing body of research stemming from Birmingham School studies of subculture that consider such entities as communities of consumption, brand communities, and consumer tribes. As documented in the collection by Cova, Kozinets and Shankar (2008), occasionally these collective entities are able to exert power over corporations, resist hegemonic practices and redefine the form of consumption. This contestation raises questions about the degree of agency achievable by consumers within a consumer culture and challenges perspectives that deny consumer agency. Arguably, these examples also serve as harbingers of a shift in activism away from the traditional political fields towards sites of consumerism.

FURTHER READING

Sassatelli's overview on *Consumer Culture* is a useful starting point for approaching the area. Baudrillard's *Consumer Society* and Bauman's *Consuming Life* provide seminal texts.

See also: Commodity Fetishism, Critical Theory, Identity, Marxism and Post-Marxism, Neoliberalism, Subjectivity and Subjectivation

REFERENCES

Arvidsson, A. (2006) *Brands: Meaning and Value in Media Culture*. London: Routledge.

Baudrillard, J. (1998) *The Consumer Society: Myths and Structures*. London: Sage.

Bauman, Z. (2007) *Consuming Life*. Cambridge: Polity.

Campbell, C. (1987) *The Romantic Ethic and the Spirit of Modern Consumerism*. Oxford: Blackwell.

Cova, B., Kozinets, R. and Shankar, A. (eds) (2008) *Consumer Tribes*. London: Butterworth Heinemann.

Marx, K. (1993) *Grundrisse*. Trans. M. Nicolaus. London: Penguin.

Sassatelli, R. (2007) *Consumer Culture: History, Theory and Politics*. London: Sage.

Žižek, S. (2008) *For They Know Not What They Do: Enjoyment as a Political Factor*. New York: Verso.

consumer culture

Corporate Social Reporting

Jeffrey Unerman

> **Definition:** Corporate social reporting covers a range of practices whereby organisations provide a report of the social and environmental impacts arising from their operations and of their actions to manage these impacts.

INTRODUCTION

Corporate social reporting as practised by a growing number of large corporations draws upon, and acts as a link between, aspects of two other key concepts in critical management: accountability and corporate social responsibility. From accountability, a basic premise underlying corporate social reporting is that where an individual or entity has a responsibility towards another individual, entity or society, it has an allied duty to provide an account to that other individual, entity or society (the accountee) regarding how it has behaved or performed in relation to this responsibility (Gray et al., 1996). This account is an essential counterpart of the responsibility because it should enable the accountee (to whom the responsibility is owed) to evaluate how well the responsibility has been discharged and, on the basis of this information, to decide whether any action needs to be taken to help ensure the individual or entity that has the responsibility improves its performance to better respect the rights of the accountee.

Where an individual or entity has a responsibility to others who are close to it (for example the responsibilities small community-based organisations have towards the communities they serve, or the responsibilities of a local shop to its customers) then the accounting mechanisms are most effective if they are informal, for example through face-to-face interactions. However, for larger organisations, and with responsibilities that are owed to a larger number of other individuals, entities and/or societies that are at some distance from the organisation, the account needs to be much more formal. This formal account is in the form of corporate reporting.

Over the last 150 years or more, a substantial element of the large and arguably very powerful accountancy profession has developed around the practice of corporate financial reporting, whereby considerable resources have been devoted to the provision of largely quantified information regarding how managers have performed in relation to the legally and contractually enforceable financial and economic responsibilities they have to owners and lenders who have formal property rights over the corporation. In contrast to this legal contractual basis underlying the development of much corporate financial reporting, corporate social reporting is grounded in notions of the social contract. Although the social contract is not a formal or legally binding form of contract, it encapsulates the duties and responsibilities that members of a society expect an entity to abide by. These duties are a significant part of an organisation's corporate social responsibilities and usually cover its impact upon, and actions and strategies towards, a variety of social and environmental factors.

RHETORIC V. REALITY IN CORPORATE SOCIAL REPORTING

Although a key purpose of corporate social reporting is to help organisations provide an account of their social and environmental actions and impacts to a broad range of stakeholders, there is no guarantee that any individual organisation's corporate social reporting will provide a complete, fair or balanced account of its actual impacts on society and the environment, or of its actual strategies to manage these impacts. In this sense, the rhetoric or discourse in corporate social reporting does not necessarily match any underlying physical reality and can be regarded more plausibly as a social construction of reality.

As corporate reports have been demonstrated to be believable forms of communication, they are a powerful tool in corporate attempts at social construction of a positive image. The credibility of corporate social reporting is enhanced by the development and use of reporting standards, such as the Global Reporting Initiative (GRI),[1] and by the prevalent practice of attaching to the corporate social report an assurance (or audit or verification) statement provided by a third-party assuror – although research into such statements indicates the limited scope of issues on which assurance is usually provided (O'Dwyer and Owen, 2007).

In practice, there is a continuum from a highly unlikely extreme position where the issues covered in an organisation's corporate social reporting have absolutely no foundation in physical reality, to the opposite equally implausible extreme where the corporate social reporting wholly reflects all of an organisation's direct and indirect impacts on every stakeholder (present and future, animate and inanimate) upon whom its actions might impact.

MOTIVES UNDERLYING CORPORATE SOCIAL REPORTING

A number of academic studies have examined patterns in the differences between the rhetoric in the discourse of corporate social reporting and underlying realities to help theorise managerial motives for engaging in these largely voluntary reporting practices. These empirical insights have been complemented by other studies that have more directly engaged with those responsible for deciding the content of corporate social reports. Key motives identified from these studies are: a quest to build, maintain and/or repair corporate legitimacy through protecting or enhancing the corporation's social licence to operate as established in its social contract (Deegan, 2002); management of reputation risks arising from potential social or environmental incidents; and responding to the types of isomorphic pressures that organisations can experience, as set out in institutional theory (such as coercive, mimetic and normative isomorphism). Often these motives indicate an economically driven desire to socially construct an image through the rhetoric of corporate social reporting that coheres with the social and environmental values and expectations of those stakeholders who hold the strongest economic power over the reporting organisation.

As the groups who hold the most economic power will vary from organisation to organisation and from society to society, as well as over time, the focus of corporate social reporting will similarly vary. Studies have identified practices consistent with what we would now define as corporate social reporting as early as the nineteenth century (Guthrie and Parker, 1989), focused on the likely social expectations of stakeholders who would then have held economic influence over the reporting organisations. Since then, trends in the content of corporate social reporting have followed trends in social concerns – with a limited focus on social reporting in the 1970s declining in the free-market economic context of the 1980s and reviving in the form of environmental reporting in the 1990s. More recently, corporate social reporting has tended to cover a broader range of social and environmental issues.

Until the late 1990s annual corporate financial reports were the common medium in which much corporate social reporting was undertaken. Although a number of corporations had published more substantial stand-alone corporate social reports for several years, since the late 1990s it has been increasingly common for many corporations to publish such stand-alone reports. Different companies have used a variety of changing titles for these reports, ranging from *Environmental Report* through *Corporate Social Responsibility Report* (more recently dropping the word 'social' from this title) to *Sustainability Report*. The scope and nature of corporate social reporting within annual financial reports is now changing again, with a growing recognition of the connected nature of economic, social and environmental impacts, risks and opportunities inherent in sustainability (Hopwood, Unerman and Fries, 2010).

In the internet age, it has become common practice for corporate social reports to be disseminated via the web, with more innovative companies dispensing with a traditional format report and replacing this with a more interactive corporate social and environmental responsibility website. This enables disclosures to be targeted at specific stakeholders, with the corporate social reporting that is still contained in the annual financial report focusing on the perceived information needs of the main users of the annual financial reports – stakeholders with financial interests such as investors and creditors.

FURTHER READING

For recent coverage of many different aspects of the field see: Unerman, Bebbington and O'Dwyer (2007) and Gray, Bebbington and Gray (2010).

See also: Accountability, Corporate Social Responsibility, Critical Accounting

corporate social reporting

61

NOTE

1 The main purpose of reporting standards such as the GRI is to provide a template or checklist to help organisations develop their reporting practices.

REFERENCES

Deegan, C. (2002) 'Introduction: The Legitimising Effect of Social and Environmental Disclosures – A Theoretical Foundation', *Accounting, Auditing and Accountability Journal* 15(3): 282–311.

Gray, R., Bebbington, J. and Gray, S. (eds) (2010) *Social and Environmental Accounting*, 4 vols. London: Sage.

Gray, R., Owen, D. and Adams, C. (1996) *Accounting and Accountability: Changes and Challenges in Corporate Social and Environmental Reporting*. Hemel Hempstead: Prentice-Hall.

Guthrie, J. and Parker, L.D. (1989) 'Corporate Social Responsibility: A Rebuttal of Legitimacy Theory', *Accounting & Business Research* 19(76): 343–52.

Hopwood, A.G., Unerman, J. and Fries, J. (eds) (2010) *Accounting for Sustainability: Practical Insights*. London: Earthscan.

O'Dwyer, B. and Owen, D. (2007) 'Seeking Stakeholder-Centric Sustainability Assurance', *Journal of Corporate Citizenship* 25: 77–94.

Unerman, J., Bebbington, J. and O'Dwyer, B. (eds) (2007) *Sustainability, Accounting and Accountability*. London: Routledge.

Corporate Social Responsibility

Stephen Dunne

Definition: The concept of corporate social responsibility emerges out of a series of ongoing debates as to whether the corporation has additional responsibilities over and above the responsibility to make a profit, or not.

The most (in)famous thing ever written about corporate social responsibility (CSR) came from the pen of the Nobel Prize winning Chicago School economist Milton Friedman. In a short article published in the

New York Times Magazine, Friedman (1970) notoriously argued, straightforwardly but nonetheless virulently, that the *only* social responsibility of business is to increase its profits. That is to say, for Friedman, corporate representatives should concern themselves with profit maximisation and *nothing* else.

Such a sentiment strikes us as almost apocryphal today. This is because today, it seems that not a moment goes by where we do not hear of some corporation or other engaging in some act of seeming benevolence or other. Indeed, social responsibility is something which we have now largely come to expect of corporations, irrespective of whether this expectation comes from our role as corporate critics, as commodity consumers or even as global citizens. This is no mean feat, for sure. And yet, for Friedman, this was precisely the problem: the very fact that corporate executives *were* taking socio-political matters into their own hands was something which, for him, threatened the very foundations upon which free-market societies are built (see also Friedman, 1962/2002).

So just what is it about CSR that Friedman is so opposed to? Simply put – CSR initiatives are nothing other than a set of scenarios within which corporate executives take the capital invested by the shareholder, who expects the highest possible return from his or her investment, the budget of the customer, who expects the lowest possible prices, and the income of the employee, who expects the highest possible wages, and *wastes* it upon endeavours of his or her own misdirected fancy. In this sense, CSR can be understood as identical to theft or, when it is used for the sake of window dressing, which he argued that it routinely was, it can be understood as identical to fraud. In the pursuit of CSR, Friedman argues that corporate representatives deviate from their obligations to shareholders, customers, and employees alike. Instead of doing what they are contractually and morally bound to do for each of these groups, they self-righteously pursue the ends of their own private fancy in the name of public philanthropy. For Friedman this is of course something which must be condemned, rather than condoned, hence the notorious statement with which his work has become synonymous at least on the part of CSR advocates.

Friedman was not the first to argue against CSR along such lines, of course. But what his work does offer, indeed what it *continues* to offer advocates of CSR, is a hurdle which simply has to be negotiated in one way or another. In this regard, perhaps the most prominent way of attempting to negotiate the hurdle that is Friedman today is to be found in the ongoing attempt to connect CSR with financial performance. That is to say, today there exists an ongoing debate to refute Friedman *empirically* through demonstrating that, in the end, CSR *should* be undertaken by corporate representatives *precisely because* they will be rewarded in the form of financial gain. The work of Orlitzky et al. (2003) offers one of the most elaborate examples of such an argument, insisting, on the basis of an extensive overview of the burgeoning academic literature devoted to the topic of the potential profit worthiness of CSR endeavours, that there is a positive connection between 'corporate social performance' (CSP) initiatives and 'corporate financial performance' (CFP), and subsequently making an argument for CSR on the basis of this connection.

The work of Margolis and Walsh (2003), on the other hand, suggests that there is very weak evidence for such an empirical link, claiming instead that, irrespective of the lack of empirical evidence, CSR should nonetheless be pursued by corporate representatives for moral (deontological) as well as pragmatic reasons (see also Margolis and Elfenbein, 2008). According to Margolis, Walsh and Elfenbein, if CSR is to mean anything worthwhile, it has to be undertaken for reasons beyond instrumentality, that is to say, with the serious underlying intention of actually 'doing good', rather than with the conceited and concealed intention of appearing to do good for the sake of making money. Many contemporary debates in and around the question of CSR continue to oscillate around this series of concerns.

Nevertheless, whilst it is true to say that the contemporary argument for CSR is largely prefigured by the ongoing debate over the extent to which CSR is compatible with CFP, it is also true to say that these apparently antagonistic acronyms have not always been the parameters within which the discussion over the relationship between private action and the public good has been expressed. And it is here that a historical sensitivity toward the question of CSR becomes crucial. Widely renowned CSR scholar Archie Carroll, for example, regularly insists upon Arthur Bowen's work (1953) as an inaugural moment in the evolution of the discussion of CSR, whilst historian Morrell Heald (1961), for his part, refers the CSR origination expedition back further, to the 1920s. Others still refer us as far back as Adam Smith. Prevalent within the work of all of these pre-Friedmanite figures, despite their many obvious differences, is the maintenance of something inherently anti-Friedmanite: the notion that whilst profit maximisation is a crucial indicator of corporate worth, it is not the only barometer by which corporate action can be meaningfully measured. Even Adam Smith's notorious invisible hand, far from being an unqualified argument for unmitigated self-interested behaviour, is offered in the spirit of *enlightened* self-interest.

Friedman's dubious achievement, it seems, is to have narrowed the discussion of the public worth of private activity down to the point where what was historically blurred has become more recently sharpened. For Friedman, CSR threatens free-market societies precisely because, in the place of actions undertaken for the sake of private gain (market-economic activities), it smuggles in actions undertaken for the sake of public benefit (political actions). CSR therefore blurs the distinction between two radically distinct forms of action (economic and political), actions which must, he says, *always* be held apart. Elected governments do politics, private actors do economics, and never the twain should meet: such is the nub of Friedman's argument against CSR. Historically the line was never drawn so sharply. The challenge for the contemporary advocate of CSR is one of moving the line more towards a point at which the understanding of the private comes to incorporate the public more and more. Largely thanks to Friedman, the argument for CSR has thus become an argument for maximising profit with increasing recourse to publicly oriented initiatives.

It is still worth recalling that Friedman's argument is a particular observation concerning CSR from the perspective of a wider advocacy of the capitalist mode of production as such. The difficulty of maintaining such advocacy seems to have been put into sharp relief amidst the wreckage of contemporary financial crises. In this regard, it is certainly worth suggesting that future arguments both for and against CSR will go hand in hand with broader debates as to the relative merits and demerits not just of CSR, but also of capitalism more generally. Time will tell.

FURTHER READING

David Vogel's *Market for Virtue* (2005) steers an informative and intelligent course between advocacy of and criticism of CSR scholarship. The voluminous literature on corporate social performance and its connection to corporate financial performance is surveyed in the papers by Orlitzky et al. (2003) and Margolis and Walsh (2003) respectively, whilst other prominent figures within the contemporary debate concerning CSR include Andrew Crane, Archie Carroll, Dirk Matten, Michael Porter, Diane Swanson and Donna Wood.

corporate social responsibility

See also: *Accountability, Business Ethics, Corporate Social Reporting, Corporation, Environmentalism, Neoliberalism*

REFERENCES

Bowen, H.R. (1953) *Social Responsibilities of the Businessman*. New York: Harper & Row.

Friedman, M. (1970) 'The Social Responsibility of Business is to Increase its Profits', *New York Times Magazine*, 13 Sept. Accessed online on 1Feb. 2007 at http://www.colorado.edu/studentgroups/libertarians/issues/friedman-soc-resp-business.html.

Friedman, M. (1962/2002) *Capitalism and Freedom*. Chicago: University of Chicago Press.

Heald, M. (1961) 'Business Thought in the Twenties: Social Responsibility', *American Quarterly* 13(2): 126–39.

Margolis, J.D. and Elfenbein, H.A. (2008) 'Doing Well by Doing Good? Don't Count On It', *Harvard Business Review* 86(1): 19–20.

Margolis, J.D. and Walsh, J.P. (2003) 'Misery Loves Companies: Rethinking Social Initiatives by Business', *Administrative Science Quarterly* 48(2): 268–305.

Orlitzky, M., Schmidt, F. and Rynes, S. (2003) 'Corporate Social and Financial Performance: A Meta-Analysis', *Organization Studies* 24(3): 403–41.

Vogel, D. (2005) *The Market for Virtue: The Potential and Limits of Corporate Social Responsibility*. Washington: Brookings Institute Press.

Corporation

Jeroen Veldman

Definition: 'An ingenious device for obtaining individual profit without individual responsibility' (Bierce, 1996).

As the definition shows, the modern concept of the corporation has a long tradition of critical interpretations. This critical approach is based on the fact that the legal act of incorporation grants a company some unique features like perpetuity and limited liability. Its separate legal representation enables it to be attributed with agency and ownership in its own name. Twentieth-century legal discourse has attributed amendment protections to the separate legal entity on the basis of its singular legal agency.

The contemporary understanding of the separate legal entity is the result of a long history. The central reference in legal scholarship is the thirteenth-century *universitas*. Until the nineteenth century, the use of incorporation as a *universitas* was reserved for public institutions. The sovereign granted a concession to institutions to enable them to carry forward their work independently of individual caretakers. In the colonisation era, incorporation and limited liability became available for companies like the East India Company, mainly as a result of their collusion with state activities (Neocleous, 2003). After the French Revolution, the concept of incorporation changed. The absence of a sovereign meant that incorporation could no longer be seen as the result of a royal concession. Incorporation therefore became gradually available to individuals for almost all economic purposes through general incorporation during the nineteenth century. Based on other models for legal representation like the corporation sole and the trust (Maitland, 2003), incorporation then became a concept that represented the legal rights and duties of groups through a separate legal entity. Incorporation became a legal representation that was held by a group of individuals, rather than the sovereign.

The modern concept of incorporation therefore differs from the medieval *universitas*. The modern form of incorporation is a distinctly legal entity, while the *universitas* was a political construct. While ownership over the concession in the medieval *universitas* was held by the sovereign, the modern separate legal entity is separate as a legal representation of association, which is formed and held by the incorporators. Also, the medieval *universitas* was not a singular legal subject and could not be attributed with agency.

These attributions of singular agency and ownership in legal and economic scholarship are the result of the emergence of the joint use of the natural entity theory and the artificial entity theory at the end of the nineteenth century. The *natural entity* theory sees the separate legal entity as a natural singular entity, capable of agency and attributable with legal rights, comparable to other natural entities (Horwitz, 1985). The natural entity theory was necessary to deal with the increasing distance between shareholders and management (Ireland, 1999). As a natural entity the separate legal entity could be understood in a modern legal context as a singular legal entity (Mayer, 1989) and in a modern economic context as a singular contracting entity, which can 'act', 'own' and 'contract' as an entity in itself (Bratton, 1988). The understanding of the separate legal entity as a separate entity thus enabled the separation of ownership and control (Berle and Means, 1997), majoritarian shareholding and the holding company (Roy, 1999). The *artificial entity* theory stresses the artificiality of the separate legal entity and relates its agency and ownership to the aggregation of individuals that constitutes the corporation. This theory assumes that the separate legal entity is not a completely different type of entity, but rather a legal and economic representation of individuals. It therefore argues that the separate legal entity is no more than a 'legal fiction', used for its legal and economic convenience, rather than its correspondence to a 'real' entity. Although the artificial entity theory and the natural entity theory seem mutually exclusive, aspects of both theories are needed to explain the modern concept of incorporation (Mayer, 1989). The natural entity theory is needed to explain majoritarian shareholding, the holding company and the attribution of rights and agency to a singular legal and economic agent, while the artificial entity theory is needed to understand the separate legal entity as 'property', rather than a full legal subject. The natural entity theory and the artificial entity theory together therefore create a continuum between which the theory of incorporation can be understood.

The simultaneous acceptance of these mutually exclusive positions imports a number of conflicting assumptions. The natural entity theory understands the separate legal entity as a completely separate entity, but this understanding is countered by the artificial entity theory. As a result, it is not clear in what exact capacity the separate legal entity 'owns' and 'acts'. The artificial entity theory cannot account for the use of majoritarian shareholding and the holding company (Horwitz, 1985) It also cannot account for the intrinsic difference between the corporation and a partnership, nor for the attribution of agency, ownership and amendment rights to the separate legal entity as a singular legal entity. Moreover, the use in the artificial entity theory of constituent groups to attribute agency and ownership does not relate well to a formal legal conferral of ownership to the separate legal entity. The unresolved theory on incorporation and the separate legal entity creates the corporation as a placeholder for a large number of concepts about legal and economic representation as well as the representation of groups. This results in a large number of possibilities to understand the attribution of agency, ownership and amendment rights in relation to shareholders, the board and other constituent groups within the corporate structure (Berle and Means, 1997). The conflicting assumptions behind the theory of incorporation therefore exert great influence on the legal treatment and governance theories of the corporation. For these reasons, the understanding of incorporation and the governance structure of the corporation present an ongoing challenge for critical management studies.

FURTHER READING

For a general introduction into the history of the corporation, Micklethwait and Wooldridge (2005) are a good starting point. A more detailed discussion of developments in the nineteenth century can be found in Roy (1999). For critical reflections on the changing nature of shares, shareholding and the separation of ownership and control see Ireland (1999) and Berle and Means (1997). For a discussion of the matter from a liability point of view, look at Fisse and Braithwaite (1993). For more polemical accounts, look at Bakan (2005), Korten (2001) and Nace (2003).

See also: *Accountability, Business Ethics, Corporate Social Responsibility*

REFERENCES

Bakan, J. (2005) *The Corporation: The Pathological Pursuit of Profit and Power*, rev. and exp. edn. London: Constable.

Berle, A.A. and Means, G.C. (1997) *The Modern Corporation and Private Property*, rev. edn. London: Transaction.

Bierce, A. (1996) *The Devil's Dictionary*. Ware: Wordsworth Editions.

Bratton Jr, W.W. (1988) 'Nexus of Contracts Corporation: A Critical Appraisal', *Cornell Law Review* 74: 407–65.

Fisse, B. and Braithwaite, J. (1993) *Corporations, Crime, and Accountability*. Cambridge: Cambridge Univesity Press.

Horwitz, M.J. (1985) 'Santa Clara Revisited: The Development of Corporate Theory', *West Virginia Law Review* 88: 173–224.

Ireland, P. (1999) 'Company Law and the Myth of Shareholder Ownership', *Modern Law Review* 62(1): 32–57.

Korten, D.C. (2001) *When Corporations Rule the* World. San Francisco: Berrett-Koehler.

Maitland, F.W. (2003) *State, Trust and Corporation*. Cambridge: Cambridge University Press.

Mayer, C.J. (1989) 'Personalizing the Impersonal: Corporations and the Bill of Rights', *Hastings Law Journal* 41(3): 577–667.

corporation

Micklethwait, J. and Wooldridge, A. (2005) *The Company: A Short History of a Revolutionary Idea*. London: Modern Library.

Nace, T. (2003) *Gangs of America*. San Francisco: Berrett-Koehler.

Neocleous, M. (2003) *Imagining the State*. Maidenhead: Open University Press.

Roy, W.G. (1999) *Socializing Capital: The Rise of the Large Industrial Corporation in America*. Princeton: Princeton University Press.

Smith, A. (1998) *An Inquiry into the Nature and Causes of the Wealth of Nations*. Oxford: Oxford University Press.

Critical Accounting

Geoff Lightfoot

> **Definition:** Critical accounting encompasses a broad range of approaches to research with the underlying assumption that accounting is not merely a technical practice providing neutral representations of economic data.

Critical accounting as a discipline (or at least a subdiscipline of accounting) can be traced back to behavioural research in accounting in the late 1960s and early 1970s, not least that developed by Anthony Hopwood who founded the journal *Accounting, Organizations and Society* in 1976. The opening editorial of the journal called for research that 'can provide a basis for seeing accounting as a social and organizational phenomenon' (Hopwood, 1976: 3) and asked for theoretical and empirical contributions to aspects of accounting including 'social accounting for the use of scarce resources' and 'behavioural studies of how accounting information is actually used' (ibid. 4). Despite this break with seeing accounting as 'rather static and purely technical', the identification of the possibilities of critical accounting were further set out in Burchell et al. (1980). This influential paper not only called for further research into the historical development of accounting, a consideration of accounting's intertwining

with other aspects of social life, the role of accounting in political processes and how accounting constitutes organisations, but also pointed out
that this required 'theoretical and methodological innovation' (ibid. 23).
Specifically, the authors suggested that 'appeals would have to be made
to very different frames of reference and bodies of knowledge' (ibid. 23).

Subsequent scholars have indeed plundered different bodies of
knowledge from across the social sciences and beyond to apply a multitude of theories and methods to the study of accounting – so much so
that it is perhaps pointless to try and place a boundary around what
might be considered 'critical accounting', or even what the term should
be. Lodh and Gaffikin (1997: 435) note that labels include 'critical studies in accounting research', 'critical accounting movement', 'critical
accounting', 'critical accounting literature' and 'critical studies' as well
as using 'critical theory' to refer to either German or French critical
theory. We could also add the terms 'interdisciplinary' or 'critical' perspectives on accounting to the mix. Within this indeterminate body,
Lodh and Gaffikin (1997: 437) suggested that some ten different theoretical approaches could be discerned: symbolic interactionism and
ethnomethodology; political-economic (including Marxian) analyses;
Habermasian critical theory; Foucauldian approaches; Giddens' structu-
ration theory; Gramsci's concept of hegemony; Derrida's deconstruc-
tionism; social constructionism; critical structuralism; and actor–network
theory. They suggest that although they might share a rejection of
'positivist' thinking that characterises mainstream accounting research,
there is little homogeneity amongst critical accounting researchers (ibid.
436) except for a greater concern for theoretical underpinnings. Indeed,
as Tinker (2005: 100) suggests, 'often they have little in common, except
a mutual suspicion and distrust'.

There are occasional attempts to try and separate out what might be
considered 'critical' from merely 'interdisciplinary'. Tinker, for example,
writing from a political-economy perspective, suggests that it might be
seen to 'encompass all forms of social praxis that are evaluative, and aim
to engender progressive change within the conceptual, institutional,
practical, and political territories of accounting', with progressive change
challenging the subordination of 'individual and collective development
to the priorities of Capital accumulation' (ibid. 101). As such, it brings
together both Marxist studies and those from 'critical accounting theory'
(working primarily with adaptations of Jürgen Habermas's work) but
excludes most postmodern, poststructural and micro-institutionalist
studies. However, as Arnold (2009) points out, it is the latter, often with

a focus on accounting practices rather than the economic foundations of power, which has come to dominate what is widely seen as critical accounting research since the 1990s.

The areas of study are perhaps less contentious, primarily concentrating on financial accounting, auditing and the accounting profession, management accounting, accounting history and, to a lesser extent, finance. Within all these areas, the role of accounting in producing reality becomes crucial, since it defines questions of profit, loss, efficiency and so on. However, within these general categories, the topics examined have expanded considerably from the previous functionalist paradigm. This is especially noticeable in accounting histories, where interdisciplinary and Foucauldian approaches have combined to produce rigorous and spectacular narratives that completely recast the story of the development of accounting (although not without dissent from scholars working within the traditional paradigm). Even beyond accounting history, the inherent openness of the field to insights from other disciplines has resulted in such an eclectic and inchoate body of work that it is beyond the scope of this article to list (or even categorise) all the themes and approaches that might now fall under the banner of critical accounting research. However, this divergence and lack of a core set of beliefs has led some critics to argue that relevance has indeed been lost. Arnold (2009: 805) points out the failure of critical accounting scholars, uniquely placed to offer meaningful critique, 'to anticipate the [financial] crisis or problematize the relationship between financial accounting, the growth of the shadow banking system, and macroeconomic instability'.

Despite the disparate approaches, critical accounting has become solidly established within the academy, especially within the UK and Australia. There are several highly regarded journals within the field and *Accounting, Organizations and Society* is the only top-ranked accounting journal that British academics consistently publish in. However, critical accounting remains peripheral in many other jurisdictions, particularly in the United States, and other leading mainstream accounting journals (again, from the United States) remain resistant. Critical accounting also remains marginal in accounting education, typically only taught (if at all) as a codicil to traditional positivist and technical courses and making up (where found at all) one of the last chapters in mainstream accounting texts. A similar concern presides over the relationship between critical accounting and accounting in practice, which has led to an enduring debate as to how and where to engage. As an example, Roslender and Dillard (2003: 341) argue that, 'it is necessary for all who are committed to the critical accounting project to become as outward looking as possible, and to engage the various parties and stakeholders who share the accounting space with us.' Despite a few notable exceptions this remains an aspect of the project that is largely unfulfilled.

FURTHER READING

Roslender (1992) provides a useful account of the early development of the different approaches in the field of critical accounting while Napier (2006) gives an excellent summary of developments in accounting history.

See also: *Accountability, Critical Theory, Marxism and Post-Marxism, Poststructuralism*

REFERENCES

Arnold, P.J. (2009) 'Global Financial Crisis: The Challenge to Accounting Research', *Accounting, Organizations and Society* 34: 803–9.

Burchell, S., Clubb, C., Hopwood, A., Hughes, J. and Nahapiet, J. (1980) 'The Roles of Accounting In Organizations And Society', *Accounting, Organizations and Society* 5(1): 5–27.

Hopwood, A. (1976) 'Editorial: The Way Ahead', *Accounting, Organizations and Society* 1(1): 1–4.

Lodh, S.C. and Gaffikin, M.J.R. (1997) 'Critical Studies in Accounting Research, Rationality and Habermas: A Methodological Reflection', *Critical Perspectives on Accounting* 8(5): 433–74.

Napier, C. (2006) 'Accounts of Change: 30 years of Historical Accounting Research', *Accounting, Organizations and Society* 31(4/5): 445–507.

Roslender, R. (1992) *Sociological Perspectives on Modern Accountancy*. London: Routledge.

Roslender, R. and Dillard, J. (2003) 'Reflections on the Interdisciplinary Perspectives on Accounting Project', *Critical Perspectives on Accounting* 14(3): 325–51.

Tinker, T. (2005) 'The Withering of Criticism: A Review of Professional, Foucauldian, Ethnographic, and Epistemic Studies in Accounting', *Accounting, Auditing and Accountability Journal* 18(1): 110–35.

critical accounting

Critical Human Resource Management

Sharon C. Bolton

> **Definition:** A critical assessment of the managerial techniques used to coordinate and focus people's skills and abilities towards organisational ends.

WHAT IS HUMAN RESOURCE MANAGEMENT?

In addition to the common comparisons between Personnel and HRM, there are many who believe that HRM is merely a return to the human relations school of management philosophy. It is certainly worth noting how obviously reminiscent the recent HRM literature is of the human relations school as writers advocate many of the same 'must-dos' and are open to the same criticisms. But HRM is different in some very fundamental ways – the human relations school or personnel management did not have such high expectations of their employees, and they had a limited perception of the capabilities of organisational actors. Most importantly, though managers may have wished to enlist (or at least tame) the energies of the informal work group it was never assumed that such energies would become an integral part of the formal organisation in the way that they have for HRM. Personnel management practice was based on an understanding of a plurality of interests, but it has been noted that HRM is a distinct management approach because of its attempts to appropriate the hands, hearts and minds of employees and utilise people's emotional energies in pursuit of strategic goals (Legge, 2006; Townley, 1994). It is also distinct in its attempts to take the management of personnel to board level, where HRM is integrated into the company's business strategy in the belief that people management can be a key source of competitive advantage (Boxall and Purcell, 2007).

STRATEGIC HRM – THE 'SOFT' AND 'HARD' DIMENSIONS

In the 1980s, scholars attached the prefix 'strategy' to the term HRM and the notion of 'strategic integration' became prominent in the HRM literature. Interest among practitioners in linking the concept of strategy to HRM can be partly explained by the pressure to enhance the status of HRM professionals at a time when corporate re-engineering questioned the need for HRM specialists in flatter organisation structures. HRM is part of what is frequently referred to as a 'functional' strategy and is implemented to facilitate the goals of the higher-level business strategy. However, within HRM itself there are different approaches which are often categorised as either 'soft' (the 'Harvard' model) or 'hard' (the Michigan school) HRM. In simple terms, hard HRM prioritises profit through the direct management of costs, with employees registered merely as headcount and recognised only for their productive potential. Soft HRM places a higher value on the human resource as a valued asset, and emphasises their capacity, motivation and commitment based on an unitarist view of mutuality. Soft HR pays attention to employees' needs for interesting work and involved decision-making. However, the instrumental exchange orientation reveals 'soft' management initiatives as simply more insidious methods of motivation and control. Similarly, a range of 'people'-oriented cultural management practices, appearing under a variety of descriptions such as HCM (high commitment management), are used to manage different motivational contexts, and to heighten employee identification with the organisation. Nevertheless, though the hard and soft aspects of HRM indicate a more plural approach, they are analytically inseparable as HRM in practice is a complex combination of both.

BEST PRACTICE HRM AND PERFORMANCE

Strategic HRM suggests a model approach to the adoption of bundles of best practice, which has become a popular means of linking people and performance in corporate strategy (Pfeffer, 1998). The best practice approach emphasises the need to 'bundle' people management practices in order to achieve maximum effectiveness. For instance, recruitment practices need to be linked to retention issues of learning and development and performance and reward. In isolation each practice may have some effect but its impact on overall performance will be minimal. The adoption of a best practice approach to people management has been widely advocated as a means of increasing innovation and performance. A broad consensus has emerged that investment in various HRM practices will create a high-performance workplace. The focus on best practice draws heavily from the resource-based view of the firm that offers an inside-out version of strategic management. This view is quite different from the contingency view which emphasises people management practices involving learning and development, involvement and empowerment and a strong focus on people as the organisation's most important asset.

Closely associated with a move toward bundles of HRM practices, is the focus on leadership as a defining feature of successful organisations. Strong leadership is represented as a creative force and prime motivator for change and quite different from the functional direction of management. In line with the resource-based view of the firm, leadership is portrayed as strategic but with a gentle touch as charismatic leaders create and espouse organisational vision and values within a unitary framework of what good leadership might be. In essence, leadership is seen as an essential prerequisite for the implementation of innovative people management practices leading to best practice and increased performance. The concentration on transformational, rather than transactional, leadership, and softer management practices that focus more on the intrinsic rather than extrinsic needs of employees, clearly reflects the broader move toward changing organisational forms, flatter hierarchies, networked organisations and knowledge-intensive industries where more traditional 'macho management' techniques are deemed no longer applicable.

THE CRITIQUE OF HRM

Despite the intuitive appeal of bundles of HRM practice, the attempted integration of people management with business strategy and charismatic leadership suffers from a number of problematic assumptions. Of particular note is the way HRM accepts an overly simplistic, almost naïve, view of both human nature and a market economy. It assumes that human resource strategy can be shaped to fit the business strategy. This runs counter to the reality that strategy tends to emerge around a battlefield of competing interests and the constraints of externally defined economic pressures (Thompson, 2003). By viewing the employee as an individual resource unit to be optimally configured and managed, these practices conceptually divorce employees from their social context – that is, other relations, other shaping forces and other commitments (even within the workplace) (Bolton and Houlihan, 2007). Often this myopic view is related to concerns over the reach and extent of a range of normative control strategies inherent in HRM practice. Attempts to more fully integrate people into the organisation are said to render human 'subjects as objects' in terms of Foucault's ideas of governmentality and subjectivation (Townley, 1994). In other words, contemporary organisations rely on innovation, entrepreneurship and voluntary compliance, hence soft HRM is used as a means of activating loyalty and commitment to organisational ends (Sewell, 2005). But does it work – do HRM techniques enable organisations to capture the hearts and minds of employees? And in so doing, is performance and productivity enhanced?

It seems that for many, the answer is that HRM has failed to deliver on many of its early promises and has been unsuccessful in its attempts to achieve status as either management's strategic partner or employee champion. In HR's desperate attempts to legitimise its existence we observe an increasingly economic approach to practice with greater and greater emphasis on providing empirical links between people management practice and company performance. This is a move that confirms HR as a product of prevailing political ideology and new economic orders, as well as part of a general move toward a more flexible capitalism. Most clearly of all, this is represented in the observation that over the past three decades, despite economic growth in most developed countries and huge investments in the development of HR practice, we have seen reported increases in job dissatisfaction, work intensification, hours worked, job insecurity and economic and social inequality. When contextualising the practice of HRM in this way, we can see more clearly both the constraints and opportunities it faces, and why it will continue to be a focus of critical inquiry.

FURTHER READING

Two important introductory readings are Townley's (1994) *Reframing Human Resource Management* and Thompson's (2003) 'Disconnected Capitalism: Or, Why Employers Can't Keep Their Side of the Bargain'.

See also: *Governmentality, Identity, Labour Process Theory, Managerialism, Subjectivity and Subjectivation*

REFERENCES

Bolton, S. and Houlihan, M. (2007) 'Beginning the Search', in Bolton, S. and Houlihan, M. (eds) *Searching for the H in HRM*, pp. 1–18. London: Palgrave.

Boxall, P. and Purcell, J. (2007) *Strategy and Human Resource Management*, 2nd edn. London: Palgrave.

Legge, K. (2006) 'Human Resource Management', in S. Ackroyd, R. Batt, P. Thompson and P. Tolbert (eds) *The Oxford Handbook of Work and Organisation*. Oxford: Oxford University Press.

Pfeffer, J. (1998) *Competitive Advantage Through People*. Cambridge, MA: Harvard University Press.

Sewell, G. (2005) 'Nice Work? Rethinking Managerial Control in an Era of Knowledge Work', *Organization* 12(5): 685–704.

Thompson, P. (2003) 'Disconnected Capitalism: Or, Why Employers Can't Keep Their Side of the Bargain', *Work, Employment and Society* 17(2): 359–78.

Townley, B. (1994) *Reframing Human Resource Management*. London: Sage.

Critical International Management

Eduardo Ibarra-Colado

Definition: Critical International Management (CIM) is an emerging transdisciplinary field of study devoted to analysing management practices and their consequences on an international level.

---

key concepts in
critical management studies

78

INTRODUCTION

CIM proposes alternative frameworks of analysis to go beyond the narrowness of mainstream approaches in International Management in order to embrace the complex political-economic, historical and geographical configuration of the world as the diverse arena in which international management relations are produced. The recognition of diversity and the consideration of the many discourses and practices used to organise and manage local relations in global contexts reintroduces power as key to understanding the asymmetrical relations between countries and regions and the central role played by multinational corporations in producing and reproducing the world order. Instead of improving management performance and multinational companies' success, which is usually considered to be a technical issue, CIM tries to understand the consequences of such practices for the host countries and local states, in particular the impacts on the quality of life of individuals at the local community level. Moreover, a critical understanding of international management relations is a precursor to imagining alternative ways of organising and managing a world made by many worlds. It is also concerned with re(dis)covering local knowledges and practices based on different cultural rationalities that contrast with the unique market-oriented project of modern Anglo-euro-centric civilisation.

BEYOND CURRENT INTERNATIONAL MANAGEMENT

Critical international management is a new transdisciplinary space of knowledge and its emergence has been stimulated by the urgent need to understand the processes of mundialisation beyond the rhetoric of 'modernisation' and 'globalisation' as a generalisable model (Ibarra-Colado, 2006). In doing so it confronts international management approaches mainly developed in the US which analyse, from functionalist and positivistic perspectives, international aspects of management, management practices in different cultures, activities of multinational corporations, globalisation of business, management of firms in a multinational context, foreign direct investment, and cooperation through joint ventures and strategic alliances. Within these approaches, the international dimension is generally limited to the consideration of the conditions facing transnational corporations in host countries. Central is the consideration given to intercultural relations and to the variations in the forms of organisation, regulation and institutionalisation of the economic and political activities in each country. The main intention is to provide useful knowledge on international relations to improve decision-making capabilities of corporations in order to facilitate their competitiveness and economic success.

Current international management knowledge serves largely to protect the geostrategic interests of the United States and its economic allies on the world stage. This dominant discourse of international management draws from the objectivity of science for its rationale promoting a technical and systematic approach to management. Within such a discourse cultural traits are seen to explain variations in economic success and the unequal distribution of wealth is understood to be a function of national economic performance. Cross-cultural and cross-national studies are undertaken largely to distil principles of international management that specify the best way to operate within, but perhaps more significantly *over*, other countries and cultures.

CRITICAL INTERNATIONAL MANAGEMENT CHALLENGES

Faced with this dominant position heavily focused on the best interests of the corporation, and given its instrumental vocation and managerial point of view, critical international management researchers are concerned to reveal the politics underpinning this position. Established power relationships between corporations, international financial agencies, governments and a range of other interest groups linked to the company or, more broadly, to society become the focus of concern (Cairns and Śliwa, 2008). Instead of worrying about the economic performance of transnational corporations, critical researchers try to understand the implications of corporate decisions on society and the effects of their productive and commercial activities at grassroots level.

A key challenge for CIM research lies in appreciating how the international activities of corporations provoke tension and conflict as they impose dominant forms of organising and managing without taking heed of social and cultural specificity in the countries and communities in which they operate. In promoting the 'modern' values of economic competitiveness and progress the corporation, at least partly, views its actions as benefiting the host country. From the corporation's point of view, they are giving it the opportunity to modernise and learn how to progress economically. The process is typically represented as one of learning and cultural adaptation guided by expert knowledge, instead of a brand of neocolonialism resulting in subjugation (Escobar, 2007).

In order to better appreciate the variations in management and organisational forms from one place, community or country to another CIM scholars argue that we first need to consider the material conditions that historically and geographically produced each social configuration. They are concerned to reintegrate space, time and power as key dimensions to understand the relationships and processes operating in the international arena. This then allows us to appreciate the diversity and hybridity of forms in the context of their *own* modes of rationality (Özkazanç-Pan, 2008). This recognition of otherness affords an understanding of the complex asymmetries and the power–knowledge relations that govern international activities. At the same time, it reveals possible ways to transform those structures and institutions that protect and reproduce economic dependence and political subordination.

CIM researchers are also concerned with the consequences produced by the policies, strategies, structural designs and actions of transnational corporations in their competition for markets and accumulation. Research focuses on appreciating and documenting the negative consequences produced by corporations in the countries that receive them. These variously include: the conditions under which the people work, the consequences produced by the consumption of their products or services; and the so-called 'externalities' that dramatically modify the quality of life for local people and communities. Some of the main problems stem from management practices that favour international subcontracting, offshoring production (runaway shops, footloose industry and fly-by-night enterprises) and the negotiation of special tax benefits and subventions for corporations. This last point is particularly controversial in countries where the government cannot properly attend to the social security and basic needs of their own population. In addition corporations have been known to engage in practices which are illegal in their country of origin to increase profit: sweatshop labour conditions and the repression of trade unions; the hiring of children; the production of goods that have adverse health effects; engaging in unsustainable production activities that irreversibly damage the environment; and bribery, corruption and illegal activities that produce local political instability.

A truly critical approach to international management has radical transformation as its guiding principle, thus requiring the examination, not only of management practices in the international arena, but also a consideration of the organisation of the whole political and economic international order. One solution to the problems caused by capitalist globalisation involves the acceptance of diverse ways of organising and managing tightly linked to local communities. This involves the construction of a new social capacity, or set of institutions, to produce transnational dialogues and conversations to agree the basic principles of co-operation, without damaging or eliminating 'the other'. The essential contribution of this new transdisciplinary space of reflection lies in the knowledges it can provide to produce this urgent transformation.

FURTHER READING

Good discussions can be found in the Special Topic Forum on 'Critique and International Management: An Uneasy Relationship?' recently published in the *Academy of Management Review* (Jack et al., 2008) and in the edited collections by Tickner and Waever (2009) and Guedes and Faria (2010). See also the brief provocative book by Cairns and Śliwa (2008).

See also: *Alternative Organisation, Capitalism and Anticapitalism, Colonialism and Postcolonialism, Corporation, Globalisation, Neoliberalism, Political Economy, Power*

REFERENCES

Cairns, G. and Śliwa, M. (2008) *A Very Short, Fairly Interesting and Reasonably Cheap Book about International Business*. London: Sage.
Escobar, A. (2007) 'Worlds and Knowledges Otherwise: The Latin American Modernity/Coloniality Research Program', *Cultural Studies* 21(2–3): 179–210.
Guedes, A. and Faria, A. (eds) (2010) *International Management and International Relations: A Critical Perspective from Latin America*. London: Routledge.
Ibarra-Colado, E. (2006) 'The Ethics of Globalization', in S. Clegg and C. Rhodes (eds) *Management Ethics: Contemporary Contexts*, pp. 32–54. London: Routledge.
Jack, G.A., Calás, M.B., Nkomo, S.M. and Peltonen, T. (2008) 'Critique and International Management: An Uneasy Relationship?', *Academy of Management Review* 33(4): 870–84.
Özkazanç-Pan, B. (2008) 'International Management Research meets "The Rest of the World"', *Academy of Management Review* 33(4): 964–74.
Tickner, A.B. and Waever, O. (eds) (2009) *International Relations Scholarship Around the World*. London: Routledge.

key concepts in critical management studies

Critical Marketing Studies

Mark Tadajewski

Definition: Critical marketing studies is concerned with challenging marketing concepts, ideas and ways of reflection that present themselves as ideologically neutral or that otherwise have assumed a taken-for-granted status.

INTRODUCTION

It is probably fair to say that marketing is generally considered the least self-critical of all the disciplines in the business school. For many students, marketing is equated with selling people more goods. This is a reasonable assumption. Marketers, however, maintain that they do not just sell people goods and services that they do not want or for which there is not some innate or latent demand. Such assertions have not been convincing to those of a more critical persuasion over the last hundred years. Many social critics from Veblen, Rorty, Fromm, Adorno, Horkheimer, Marcuse, Lowenthal to Baudrillard, Lasch, Bauman, Kellner and so on, have, in varying ways, highlighted the negative impact of marketing and consumption on society.

Even so, the accusation that marketing is uncritical is not totally accurate. Some of the earliest marketing thinkers associated with the German historicist school were deeply concerned with distributive justice and wanted to make the marketing system work in the interests of all (Ellis et al., 2010). Furthermore, from around the time that the first debates on critical management studies were beginning to emerge in the 1970s, observers in marketing were expressing their unease about the fact that marketing was firmly bound up with the expanding military industrial establishment. For example, academics in the US affiliated with the Association for Consumer Research, most notably, wanted to distance themselves from the managerialist orientation of the marketing discipline.

Similar views motivated a critical turn in Europe during the late 1960s and early 1970s. There were calls for marketing theorists to question the then current – and still dominant – logical empiricist paradigm which invokes the ideals of objectivity and value-neutrality, and frames much of its published output using the symbolism of advanced mathematics. Against this US style of intellectual labour, European marketing academics, as well as a number of US critical and radically minded thinkers who studied the structures of American consumption from a Marxist perspective, wanted to question the role of marketing as a 'controlling science' (Heede, 1985), turning it into a 'liberating science' instead (see also Murray and Ozanne, 1991).

What Heede meant by a controlling science was basically that marketing activities and the theoretical edifice that universities constructed and disseminated was simply buttressing the existing structure of society; a structure that was predicated on ever-increasing levels of consumption. Increasing consumption, in this case, was used as a proxy for social development. Yet, the problem with this is that material wealth and houses full of consumer durables, was not and does not make people any happier. As a consequence, the existing structure of society was not necessarily benefiting the mass of people on this planet. In view of this, marketing theory and practice needed to be critically examined.

The first publication that uses the term 'Critical Marketing' appeared in the *Journal of Marketing* and aligned itself with a pluralistic range of critical social theory that continues to be an important attribute of critical marketing scholarship (i.e. Marxism, Critical Theory, Feminist thought, postcolonial perspectives, poststructuralism, etc.). If one ignores the points of divergence between these perspectives, a variety of questions provided the focus for early critical marketers. Broadly speaking, they wanted to explore the range of interests marketing was serving. To do this they drew attention to the discrepancy between the rhetoric found in marketing textbooks and the reality that confronted many people in their day-to-day lives when trying to negotiate the marketplace, with all its attendant asymmetries of power. Marketing academics and practitioners, it was argued, signalled their interest in the customer and played upon their role as the 'voice of the consumer' as a means of hiding their real interests with respect to satisfying corporate objectives and controlling the marketplace.

MACROMARKETING, SOCIAL MARKETING AND CRITICAL MARKETING

More recently attempts have been made to explore the linkages between a number of intellectual domains in marketing, specifically between macromarketing, social marketing and critical marketing. Macromarketing is probably the most consistent in outlook with critical marketing given the focus of the former on the relationship between marketing and society and concomitantly society on marketing. The major difference is that critical marketing questions the associations between neoliberalism and marketing practice that macromarketing advocates sometimes bypass. Macromarketers, put simply, view neoliberal policies as helping raise living standards across the globe, without much critical scrutiny being devoted to neoliberal doctrine and its more negative effects in the world. This said, there is a link between what is called 'critical macromarketing' and critical marketing that should be recognised in terms of the way both critique the assumptions underwriting the 'dominant social paradigm' that underpins the marketing system (Kilbourne, 2004). As Firat and Tadajewski remark, these assumptions include: an '"ideology of consumerism"… a faith in technology to avert environmental destruction, support for liberal democracy, defence of private property ownership, free markets and limited state intervention in marketplace activities' (Firat and Tadajewski, 2010: 132).

The relationship between critical marketing and social marketing is more complex. Social marketers view themselves as offering an important counterpoint to mainstream marketing activities that have some harmful or problematic effects on people. As such, they are interested in behavioural change that benefits society, e.g. encouraging people to consume less alcohol and fatty foods, or increase donations to worthy social groups. This all appears laudable. The problem is that the rhetoric of social marketing outruns its positive efficacy and reflexive self-awareness. Social marketing, some argue, has experienced a growth in interest as governments cut back spending on important social services (Tadajewski and Maclaran, 2009). Whereas the state generally has a longer time horizon upon which to evaluate such behavioural change programmes, professional social marketers are sometimes rewarded on the basis that they get a certain number of people to undergo vasectomies or other forms of fertility control (for example). By basing judgements about the 'success' of social marketing strategies on such quantitative indicators we neglect to factor in the wider consequences of these programmes (e.g. controlling fertility means that there are fewer family members available to work on farms; fewer people working on farms means less income for those living on the land and more problems in terms of achieving basic nutritional requirements).

Beyond the debates inside marketing, critical marketing can also be differentiated from critical management studies. This is in terms of the perception of 'positivist' or logical empiricist perspectives. Within critical management, for instance, scholars have been very dismissive of the way that much 'positivist' research eschews making value judgements, presents itself as politically neutral and is overly reliant on quantitative methods. Clearly, by asserting that it is value-neutral, 'positivist' research essentially makes a statement about its underlying political position, in that it demonstrates its support for the status quo. Likewise, positivistically oriented researchers are making decisions about what to study based on their own interests or those of funding organisations and thus cannot claim to be totally 'objective'.

Unlike their contemporaries in critical management studies, by contrast, critical marketers see no reason why logical empiricist perspectives should not inform critical marketing. Going further than this, historically oriented studies dealing with logical empiricism have illustrated the profoundly political orientation of this paradigm (Tadajewski, 2010). The problem has not been the uncriticality of logical empiricist (or positivist) perspectives *per se*, but the way this paradigm has been borrowed, developed and used in marketing. As a function of the political climate of the 1950s and 1960s, logical empiricism was read into marketing in a way that chimed with the desire by individual scholars, universities and funding bodies to distance themselves from intellectual orientations that appeared to be political in a non-US fashion (read: Socialist). The outcome of this was that an ostensibly objective, managerialist vision of marketing theory and practice became preeminent. Nevertheless, this does not mean that logical empiricist perspectives need to be deployed in this manner. They can play a role in the consciousness raising that forms the basis of critical marketing studies.

FURTHER READING

The three-volume collection *Critical Marketing Studies* (Tadajewski and Maclaran, 2009) reprints key articles associated with this perspective. For an introductory text that takes a critical perspective, Ellis et al. (forthcoming, 2010) is worth consulting. (See also Hackley, 2009.)

See also: *Commodity Fetishism, Consumer Culture, Critical Theory, Neoliberalism, Postmodernism, Poststructuralism, Power*

REFERENCES

Ellis, N., Fitchett, J., Higgins, M., Jack, G., Lim, M., Saren, M. and Tadajewski, M. (2010, forthcoming) *Marketing: A Critical Textbook.* London: Sage.

Firat, A.F. and Tadajewski, M. (2010) 'Critical Marketing – Marketing in Critical Condition', in P. Maclaran, B. Stern, M. Saren and M. Tadajewski (eds) *The Sage Handbook of Marketing Theory,* pp. 127–50. London: Sage.

Hackley, C. (2009) *Marketing: A Critical Introduction.* London: Sage.

Heede, S. (1985) 'The Conflict Between Ideology and Science', in N. Dholakia and J. Arndt (eds) *Changing the Course of Marketing,* pp. 147–58. Greenwich: JAI Press.

Kilbourne, W.E. (2004) 'Globalization and Development: An Expanded Macromarketing View', *Journal of Macromarketing* 24(2): 122–35.

Murray, J.B. and Ozanne, J.L. (1991) 'The Critical Imagination: Emancipatory Interests in Consumer Research', *Journal of Consumer Research* 18(2): 129–44.

Tadajewski, M. (2010) 'Critical Marketing Studies: Logical Empiricism, Critical Performativity and Marketing Practice', *Marketing Theory* 10(2): 210–22.

Tadajewski, M. and Maclaran, P. (eds) (2009) *Critical Marketing Studies,* 3 vols. London: Sage.

Critical Realism

Geoff Easton

Definition: Critical realism is a philosophical position which combines a realist ontology with an interpretivist epistemology.

INTRODUCTION

Ontology is what we believe exists in the world that we inhabit. Epistemology is our theory of knowledge of that world. Critical realists believe that there is a real world and that epistemologically it is possible to know it, but only with difficulty and in part. A philosophical position is basically a set of beliefs about the world. In practice we all take such positions since we have to act in our everyday lives according to those beliefs although, as non-philosophers, our philosophical position may be somewhat inconsistent and inchoate.

Philosophers spend a great deal of their time thinking and writing about beliefs and particular combinations or systems of beliefs which they label 'isms'. However isms can really only continue to exist if there is a group or school of scholars who accept the tenets of the ism. Realists, for example, believe that there is a real world within which we exist and act out our lives. For non-philosophers this may seem like a ludicrous statement. It would appear obvious from our sense data that there is a world out there. However, there is a school of thought, inter-pretivism or phenomenology, which argues that we cannot know the real world since we only have access to it via our senses and that our interpretations are influenced by our beliefs and past experiences. Interpretivism came into being, as is the case quite often in philosophy, largely as a reaction to positivism. Positivists implicitly believe that there is a real world but also that it is governed by laws, not just physical but also psychological and social. Much of current quantitative statistical research basically involves taking a positivist position.

The three schools of thought described above are very broad indeed and each of them can be divided into a number of subschools by adding additional belief labels to the fundamental defining belief. Critical realism is one such subschool. The philosophical literature is replete with battles between isms, the fiercest of which are often between those which seem the most similar. One such battle, by a critical realist, is described in the marketing literature by Hunt (2003), and this provides a very useful introduction to the intricacies of the various competing positions.

GENESIS

Critical realism is a relatively recent philosophical movement but one which has flourished, especially in Europe, particularly among organisation and management scholars. It now has its own journal for example. Roy Bhaskar was the progenitor of critical realism and his first efforts were set out in his book *A Realist View of Science* (Bhaskar, 1975). In its original form it was called 'transcendental realism' because it sought to conceptualise the link between the researcher and what was being researched. Normatively it was close to Marxism and mainly dealt within the philosophy of the natural sciences. However it was further developed, to include social as opposed to material worlds, by integrating elements of the critical naturalism school and hence critical realism was born. There have been many developments in the philosophical and theoretical aspects of the movement since, but it is perhaps Sayer (1984, 2000) who offers the most coherent and accessible account.

CRITICAL REALISM AND ITS ASSUMPTIONS

Ontologically, critical realism accepts that there is a real world and does not simply allow, but requires, that causal language is used. The elements of testing a theory or, in a more limited sense, a model, begin with events which can be recorded or experienced. The critical realist researcher wishes to explain these events, for example a disagreement about the outcome of a staff evaluation. In this situation there are objects or entities which form the constituents of our theory. There are human entities such as, in this case, a manager and a subordinate, and material objects such as a completed evaluation form, a desk and chairs. These all have causal powers and liabilities which may or may not be exercised in a particular situation to cause particular events to occur. For example the manager has the power to evaluate the subordinate but has the liability that she has another urgent task to complete. The subordinate has the power to disagree, actually or tacitly, about the evaluation, but is liable in terms of her inability to express herself clearly. The evaluation form and the desk have the power to help or hinder the process. Each entity may have an internal structure involving other entities; for the manager knowledge of the subordinate and a headache, for example.

Entities may have necessary relationships with other entities in terms of the way they are defined. For example a manager and a subordinate have a necessary relationship by virtue of the titles they have, the employment relationship, contracts and the organisational culture. The terms manager and subordinate necessarily stipulate the relationship between them for the purposes of theory creation. However entities can also have contingent relationships such that there may be relationships between the actors, but these will depend on the conditions. For example the manager and the subordinate may be members of the same ethnic group. This could affect the powers involved and exercised but there is no necessity that it will.

A critical realist explanation therefore comprises an account of how a particular mechanism, couched in terms of the above concepts, results in and necessarily causes a particular set of empirical observations to be generated. Thus, formally and according to Sayer, an object (X) having a structure S necessarily possessing causal powers (p) and liabilities (l) under specific conditions (c) will either result in no event (e0) or a variety of events (e1 – ex) depending on the nature of any of the specified actants.

However, critical realists accept fallibilism but argue for a position of stratification. Events are construed in the empirical world (which can be detected by researchers) but occur in the actual world (which we can only surmise) and the real world which we cannot know but can speculate about, given knowledge of the empirical. Put another way, the world is socially constructed but not entirely so. It follows that critical realists should always be searching for alternative explanations based on different interpretations of their findings.

In summary, the development of general critical realist theories in a particular field involves distinguishing the key entities, discovering their range of powers and liabilities, and determining what mechanisms cause particular kinds of events to occur.

METHODS AND POLITICS

Critical realism is generally neutral with respect to research method. However it is particularly sympathetic to case research and provides a philosophical justification for its use. It has the virtue that it can be used to investigate a set of quite complex alternative mechanisms culled from a variety of sources, e.g. metaphors and symbols. It can also study a phenomenon in great depth using a variety of research instruments and methods (Easton, 2010).

Critical realism is generally emancipatory in the sense that it presumes that discovering explanations for events provides a basis for the actors involved to make judgements about what is unacceptable and what can be done to rectify the situation. Some theorists would even see it as related to labour process Marxist approaches (Fleetwood and Ackroyd, 2000). An obvious criticism of such an approach is that research objectives and designs are implicitly value laden so the outcomes will always be biased. However the alternative approach, which would be to try to confirm by research that a situation exists where emancipation is assumed to exist can also obviously be criticised. Such research will tend to find what it expects to find.

FURTHER READING

Archer et al.'s (1998) *Critical Realism: Essential Readings*, provides a good foundational reader and Fleetwood and Ackroyd's (2004) *Critical Realist Applications in Organisation and Management Studies*, provides a excellent overview of applications.

See also: *Actor–Network Theory, Labour Process Theory, Marxism and Post-Marxism, Paradigm, Poststructuralism, Reflexivity, Subjectivity and Subjectivation*

REFERENCES

Archer, M., Bhaskar, R., Collier, A., Lawson, T. and Norrie, A. (eds) (1998) *Critical Realism: Essential Readings*. London: Routledge.

Bhaskar, R. (1975) *A Realist View of Science*. Leeds: Leeds Books.

Easton, G. (2010) 'Critical Realism in Case Study Research', *Industrial Marketing Management* 39: 118–28.

Fleetwood, S. and Ackroyd, S. (eds) (2004) *Critical Realist Applications in Organisation and Management Studies*. London: Routledge.

Hunt, S.D. (2003) *Controversy in Marketing Theory: For Reason, Realism, Truth, and Objectivity*. Armonk, NY: M.E. Sharpe.

Journal of Critical Realism, Equinox. http://www.equinoxjournals.com/ojs/index.php/ JCR/.

Sayer, A. (1984) *Method in Social Science: A Realist Approach*. London: Routledge.

Sayer, A. (2000) *Realism and Social Science*. London: Sage.

critical realism

Critical Theory

Robert Cluley

Definition: Critical theory is a social theory that examines the costraints of society and culture, assuming that by explaining and understanding them we promote rationality, freedom, individuality and community.

WHAT IS CRITICAL THEORY?

Critical theory is the parent that gives critical management studies its name. Like the relationship between any parent and child, the resemblance between them has changed over time. In this case, the child has grown increasingly independent. But this is not so much an act of rebellion on the part of critical management studies as the result of critical theory itself.

Critical theory is an interdisciplinary academic tradition that combines the humanities and social sciences – most notably political economy, psychology and philosophy – in order to ask how the world around us got to be as it is. In the process critical theory forces us to consider whether the world has to be as it is. It is, in this sense, not a theory that seeks to establish truths about the world but, rather, to investigate what makes our explanations about the world seem true in the first place. Critical theory switches the question of truth into a question of power. It tries to unmask the power relationships that lie behind our ideas of what is true.

In doing this, critical theory draws on a number of theoretical foundations (Tallack, 1995). There are two that are particularly worth bearing in mind. First, critical theory is *antifoundational* and *anti-essentialist*. It is uninterested in establishing eternal truths, facts which we must accept without question. Instead it is dialectical, in the sense that it seeks to locate truth as produced by context (Jay, 1973). Second, critical theory is *deconstructive* and *self-reflective*. Not only is it uninterested in establishing truths, it seeks to pull apart truths. This also involves pulling apart, or critiquing, its own truths.

Critical theory texts can be frustratingly difficult to read. They can be dense and appear wilfully intellectual (although they are also fascinating and incredibly interesting too). Critical theory texts are engaged in three levels of analysis. First, they work with longstanding conversations within a range of theoretical traditions. Second, they analyse historically specific events and phenomena ranging in scope from the Enlightenment project to horoscopes printed in the *Los Angeles Times*. Third, they reflect on their own validity. Whenever we read critical theory we need to recognise these three levels of analysis.

WHO ARE CRITICAL THEORISTS?

There are some notable figures whose works form the foundations of critical theory (Simons, 2002). The works of Frederick Hegel, Immanuel Kant, Karl Marx, Friedrich Nietzsche, Sigmund Freud, Ferdinand de Saussure and Max Weber are particularly important here. There are also a range of feminist theorists, postcolonial theorists, poststructuralist theorists, literary theorists and philosophers who we could include too.

Yet, critical theory, in the context of critical management studies, is most closely associated with the work of a particular group of German scholars who belonged to the Institute of Social Research at the University of Frankfurt during the middle of the twentieth century (Alvesson and Willmott, 1996). For the Frankfurt School of critical theory, or just Frankfurt School as this group of scholars became known, critical theory has a particular meaning (Jay, 1973). For theorists including Theodor W. Adorno, Max Horkheimer, Erich Fromm and Herbert Marcuse, all of whom worked for the Institute of Social Research, critical theory helped them make sense of their unique historical situation.

As Jews in Nazi Germany, Frankfurt School theorists saw firsthand how potent economic and political power could be and how easy it was for people to be controlled. Fortunately, they were able to escape from Germany and relocate the Institute in America. Never quite at home in their adopted land, they became increasingly concerned at the similarities between the fascist totalitarianism they had left back in Germany and the mass consumerism that surrounded them in America. Both systems, they believed, had gone wrong somewhere. In both societies industrial and technological progress had been matched, bizarrely, with the crushing of individuality and the rise of the mass.

With this in mind, while in America they began to analyse how capitalist ideology had come to infuse not just our relations at work but also our relationships to culture as art had become a mass-produced commodity; our relationships to each other as sex and romance were probed and prodded by an army of psychologists; and our relationship to knowledge as education had become training for life as a worker and consumer. They came to see that capitalism, like Nazism, produced an administered society of dependent masses.

This administration stretched everywhere from the design of roads to celebrity film stars. For instance, Adorno and Horkheimer (1944/1997) worried about the industrialisation of culture. Adorno was a classically trained pianist schooled in avant-garde music. He believed that the films, music and literature produced for profit by culture industries in Hollywood and Tin Pan Alley lacked real aesthetics or beauty. Instead, he thought that they offered nothing but childish stories that are, ultimately, always the same. They always have a happy ending. Of course, real life does not always have a happy ending so cultural products seem more attractive to us. Because we want the world to be like it is in the movies and in pop songs, we start to live our lives in accordance with them. We become characters in our own films, songs and novels. As such, our lives become like the mass-produced industrial products on which they are based. They become mass produced, standardised and predictable. We become products too. Cultural products distract us from the real exploitation that surrounds us every day and, in the process, stop us from confronting this exploitation.

For critical theorists, therefore, perfected administration is not a sign of our advancing social and organisational skills. Administration is never just about efficiency. Just as the Nazi party had developed a highly efficient yet repressive and brutal regime in Germany, they saw barbarism and destruction lurking behind industrialisation, consumerism and bureaucracy in capitalist societies. They wondered whether the freedom to choose between standardised industrial products was freedom at all.

As a result of these analyses, critical theorists are often unfairly portrayed as pessimists who see nothing but problems and offer few solutions. When people make such arguments against critical theory it is worth keeping in mind that critical theory offers us both concrete analyses of the world around us and it generates concepts, ideas and tools that we can use to analyse the world around us ourselves – including critical theory. Critical theorists are happy to be wrong as long as we come to our conclusions after thinking critically rather than accepting someone else's facts at face value.

In this sense, critical theory was an initial inspiration for ground-breaking work in management studies with contributors to Alvesson and Willmott's (1992) *Critical Management Studies* drawing heavily and, at times, quite directly on critical theory as a way to prise open management as something we can think about, study and change. Later critical management researchers have developed a unique engagement with critical theory that is quite distinct from the use of critical theory in areas such as cultural studies, literary studies and politics. They have used critical theory as a springboard to explore how management practices, workplace relations, human resource management and accounting systems work as political activities and allowed critical management studies to develop its own sense of what being 'critical' means.

FURTHER READING

Jay (1973) and Wiggershaus (1995) offer authoritative histories of the Frankfurt School with thorough reviews of the key writers, research and ideas.

See also: Bureaucracy, Capitalism and Anticapitalism, Class, Commodity Fetishism, Dialectics, Hegemony, Ideology, Marxism and Post-Marxism, Political Economy, Power

REFERENCES

Adorno, T.W. and Horkheimer, M. (1944/1997) *Dialectic of Enlightenment*. London: Verso Classics.

Alvesson, M. and Willmott, H. (eds) (1992) *Critical Management Studies*. London: Sage.

Alvesson, M. and Willmott, H. (1996) *Making Sense of Management: A Critical Introduction*. London: Sage.

Jay, M. (1973) *The Dialectical Imagination: A History of the Frankfurt School and the Institute of Social Research, 1923–1950*. California: University of California Press.

Simons, J. (ed.) (2002) *From Kant to Lévi-Strauss: The Background to Contemporary Critical Theory*. Edinburgh: Edinburgh University Press.

Tallack, D. (ed.) (1995) *Critical Theory: A Reader*. London: Pearson Education.

Wiggershaus, R. (1995) *The Frankfurt School: Its History, Theory and Political Significance*. London: Polity Press.

critical theory

Deconstruction

Campbell Jones

> **Definition:** Deconstruction is a definite sense that things are not yet finished.

When we hear people talking about deconstruction, there is often the sense that they are taking something apart. Usually the kind of thing that is being taken apart is some use of language. Maybe one is deconstructing a newspaper article, or a film, or a management textbook. When we say this we are talking about a strategy of critical reading that seeks to dismantle a text in order to find something that is not entirely obvious on the first reading.

On the surface of things, this might be what deconstruction is – a kind of method that could be applied here and there. And deconstruction is this, and has been used in this kind of way. The idea that deconstruction could be used to dismantle or to undo management – or at least the ways that management is usually understood – has definitely been an important part of the development of what is known as critical management studies.

Even if deconstruction is this, it is more than this. Indeed, deconstruction can be thought of more generally as a contestation of any form of containment. It involves a boiling up or a 'dissemination' that interrogates the limits that are put on things. As you might be able to see already, this applies also to the limits that are put on deconstruction. So deconstruction is a strategy of critical reading, but it is not limited to that. It is a thinking of and at the limit, that patiently and persistently asks why any such limit stands in front of us.

When we introduce deconstruction we often introduce it with examples. The classic examples of deconstruction are those that are found in the work of Jacques Derrida, one of the most important philosophers of the twentieth century. Through a painstakingly careful reading of numerous texts, Derrida asked profound questions about the limits of the Western philosophical tradition. He asked questions to which there did not seem to be any answers, such as why Plato described writing as a kind of poison and also a cure, why Aristotle thought that friends must be limited in number, and why Marx didn't like ghosts (see Derrida, 1981, 1994, 1997).

These are of course only ever examples, and some have thought that Derrida used these examples in order to show us something more general. In a certain sense there are only ever *examples* of deconstruction, and these all differ from one another. They each contain a uniqueness or singularity, which means that even if they share something, they are only ever singular instances. This is also another way of saying that deconstruction is always applied, that it is something that only ever happens to something. This is the reason for which Derrida would say, and there is clearly a reason for saying this, that 'All sentences of the type "deconstruction is X" or "deconstruction is not X" *a priori* miss the point, which is to say that they are at least false' (Derrida, 1985: 4).

It is going to be very hard, then, to find a general method called deconstruction. But at the same time, Derrida is a very serious thinker, and had no time for those who thought that any old way of thinking is as good as any other. Derrida had a profound respect for learning and thinking, for trying to understand things even when they are extremely complicated. The problem is that when we are trying to understand – when we are *really* trying to understand what something means – we sometimes realise that sense draws us in more than one direction at the same time.

This matter of being drawn in more than one direction at once is what Derrida called an encounter with an *aporia*, a Greek word that refers to an impasse or a blockage that we cannot get past. Derrida was keen to show us that we often have a tendency to proceed in such a way that we sweep aside big difficulties by boring straight through them. If we tell ourselves with enough confidence that we know where we need to go, and that nothing will be allowed to get in the way, then we will not encounter the aporia. We will drive straight through it.

This is a problem, Derrida argued. In the denial of contradictions and problems we do a lot of smoothing out, and this can lead us to be very efficient indeed. But in doing so we lose sight of what is suppressed or closed down in the process. That which is excluded or denied in this is what Derrida and other thinkers refer to as 'the Other'.

So when asking why Aristotle says that friends must be restricted in number, Derrida asks against Aristotle if it makes any sense to speak of friendship only with those that we have tested, know we can trust, and know will love us in return. This is, he shows, not friendship but indeed a *limit* to friendship, a limit based on a dangerous enclosure.

When Derrida deconstructs something like friendship, his point is not to show that friendship can be deconstructed, or that a method of deconstruction can be applied to something like friendship. To think this would be to think of deconstruction as something that is applied from the outside. Derrida rather shows the way that things like friendship are already deconstructing themselves. Think of the way that this works when we meet someone new who charms us or impresses us. In such experiences we are drawn out of ourselves and put in a relation with an other that takes us beyond what we previously knew or thought. We might do all that we can to insulate ourselves from such experiences, which is what we do when we lock ourselves up and close ourselves off from the Other.

When it comes to management studies, then, what can one do with deconstruction and with the ideas of Derrida? A number of authors have sought to 'deconstruct' the foundational texts of management and to show the problems that they involve (see Kilduff, 1993; Jones, 2007b). Others have taken domains in management studies, such as Total Quality Management, and sought to deconstruct them (Steingard and Fitzgibbons, 1993), and others have found speech or texts in organisational life and have sought to deconstruct them (Calás and Smircich, 1991).

These have made important contributions to the critical study of management. There is, however, much more that can be done with the ideas of Derrida than in the idea of deconstructing particular texts. It is perhaps possible to say today that this work of deconstruction was one definite but finite set of examples. And today, beyond these examples, much more remains to be done.

More remains to be done because Derrida invites us into a terrain that is not the one that is usually the staple fare of students of management. He invites us to ask again and again about the limits of our education and about the limits of what is seen to be management. In doing so, if we take deconstruction seriously then it is not a particular technique for reading texts, but a general expansion of the limits of what can be thought. It is a social practice and indeed an ethos that calls us to persistently look beyond what is taken as the limits of our universe. This is why Derrida insisted that 'deconstruction is justice' (Derrida, 1992: 15).

There is in deconstruction then something that is relentlessly optimistic. Nothing could be further from the flippant cynical laughter that is often mistaken for critique of management. Yes, the world in which we live is funny, and we must laugh at it. But seeing through its pretences is only the first step. Beyond that, with one foot in the past remembering what is best in our democratic traditions and our traditions of critical thinking, we can see that our other is stretched out into both the unfinished dreams and the unimaginable horrors of a radically different future.

FURTHER READING

Jones, C. (2004) 'Jacques Derrida', in S. Linstead (ed.) *Organization Theory and Postmodern Thought*, pp. 34–63. London: Sage.
Jones, C. (2007a) 'Deconstruction', in Stewart Clegg and James Bailey (eds) *International Encyclopedia of Organization Studies*, pp. 366–70. London: Sage.

See also: Alternative Organisation, Capitalism and Anticapitalism, Discourse, Poststructuralism, Utopia and Utopianism

REFERENCES

Calás, M. and Smircich, L. (1991) 'Voicing Seduction to Silence Leadership', *Organization Studies* 12(4): 567–602.
Derrida, J. (1981) 'Plato's Pharmacy', in *Dissemination*, trans B. Johnson. London: Athlone.
Derrida, J. (1985) 'Letter to a Japanese Friend', in D. Wood and R. Bernasconi (eds) *Derrida and Différance*. Warwick: Parousia Press.
Derrida, J. (1992) 'Force of Law: The "Mystical Foundation of Authority"', in D. Cornell, M. Rosenfeld and D.G. Carlson (eds) *Deconstruction and the Possibility of Justice*. New York: Routledge.
Derrida, J. (1994) *Specters of Marx: The State of the Debt, the Work of Mourning and the New International*, trans. P. Kamuf. New York: Routledge.
Derrida, J. (1997) *Politics of Friendship*, trans. G. Collins. London: Verso.
Jones, C. (2007b) 'Friedman with Derrida', *Business and Society Review* 112(4): 511–32.
Kilduff, M. (1993) 'Deconstructing Organizations', *Academy of Management Review* 18(1): 13–31.
Steingard, D. and Fitzgibbons, D. (1993) 'A Postmodern Deconstruction of Total Quality Management (TQM)', *Journal of Organizational Change Management* 6(5): 27–42.

deconstruction

Dialectics

Philip Hancock

> **Definition:** Dialectics emphasises the production of ideas and social formations through the conflict between, and the possible unification of, contradictions.

The origins of the dialectic as a means of acquiring knowledge and understanding of the world can be traced back to the Socratic philosophy of ancient Greece. Here it emerged as a technique of reasoning and debate by which a proposition is confronted by its own contradictory qualities or outcomes in order to raise the original proposition to a higher level of truth or self-understanding. This strategy of arriving at knowledge through disputation is perhaps most aptly illustrated in the Socratic dialogues that comprise Plato's consideration of the ideal political state, *Republic*.

By the eighteenth century, dialectics had evolved in the work of German idealist philosopher G.W.F. Hegel (1770–1831) from a predominantly epistemological system into one that also encompassed an ontology of human history. For Hegel, both the subject (humanity) and object (society) of history are dialectically interrelated, with each progressively raising the other to a higher condition of truth and self-knowledge, driven by the overcoming of the contradictions inherent within the dominant ideas of any given age. From this perspective, therefore, dialectics was the only means by which humanity could acquire a genuine understanding of itself and its relationship to the world it creates. This was by virtue of the fact that only dialectical thinking reflects the dialectical manner in which human consciousness brings the social world into being and is then itself shaped by the objectified ideas and practices of that world.

It was, however, Hegel's most notable disciple Karl Marx (1818–83) who recognised dialectics to be the key to a truly critical approach to understanding human societies. Marx is commonly credited for inverting Hegel's idealistic dialectic – by which it is the contradictions between our ideas and experiences of the world that drive human history forward – into a materialist one concerned with the dynamics of economic systems. In particular, Marx identified the contradictions thrown up by the demands engendered by the dominant economic system prevalent at any point in time, and the class structure that it brought into existence, as the driving force of history. What continued to unite Hegel and Marx, however, was the presence of a progressive, teleological basis to their work. So whereas Hegel considered the end of history to be an inevitable outcome of a dialectical process that would ultimately reveal the role humanity's own ideas and beliefs play in shaping the character of the social world, for Marx it was the final overcoming of the socio-economic contradictions of capitalism through the revolutionary emergence of socialism, and finally classless communism, that would witness the global culmination of the materialist dialectic and the end of history.

As a body of political thought, Marxism fragmented during the twentieth century with many of its largely supportive critics pointing to the continuation of such an unwarranted teleological strand as one of the dialectics' primary weaknesses. Theodor Adorno (1903–69), for instance – a leading figure of the Frankfurt School – while sympathetic to the centrality of a form of dialectics as a means of grasping the contradictory qualities of capitalist social relations, considered this to be the root of a vulgar determinism that viewed the overthrow of capitalism to be inevitable, despite the failures of the international communist movement. Indeed for Adorno (1973: 320), the very idea of historical progress was a questionable pretence, albeit one that was itself profoundly dialectical in that, as he put it, 'No universal history leads from savagery to humanitarianism, but there is one leading from the slingshot to the atom bomb'. Instead Adorno practised what he termed a *negative dialectic:* one that he claimed recognised the descent of reason into a tool not of liberation but domination and, rather than searching for the seeds of progress within the contradictions of economy and society, sought to explore the fetters that existing modes of social and cultural organisation placed upon them.

DIALECTICS IN CRITICAL MANAGEMENT

It is probably fair to say that any approach to management and organisation studies that claims a Marxist heritage of one form or another could identify its underlying method to be dialectical. The labour process tradition that derives from the pioneering work of Harry Braverman (1974) has, for instance, strong claims to represent the continuation of a tradition of analysis that focuses on industrial change as it is brought about through the contradictions inherent within the capitalist mode of production and the struggles these engender between the social forces of capital and labour. Nonetheless, the work that perhaps marks the self-conscious arrival of dialectics as a theory of organisation and, in turn, helped to establish the foundations of critical management studies, is Benson's (1977) article in *Administrative Science Quarterly*, 'Organizations: A Dialectical View'.

Drawing selectively on elements of the dialectical method characteristic of Marx's work, Benson highlights what he considers to be the essentially processual character of organisations. Combining this understanding with the complementary categories of totality, contradiction and praxis, he argues that one should not assume that organisational life is an essentially rational and determinate condition. Rather, he points to the need for a critical focus on the processes and actions that seek to produce and reproduce this idealised condition, and the contradictions and instabilities that these in turn generate. Furthermore, Benson presents dialectics as an engaged approach in that it is 'concerned with the active reconstruction of organizations' (Benson, 1977: 18). By this he is concerned not simply with a critique of existing workplace relations, but with establishing the possibilities open for active participation by those who work in organisations to 'freely and collectively control the direction of [organisational] change on the basis of a rational understanding of social process' (Benson, 1977: 18).

In a further approach that owes much to the work of Adorno and fellow members of the Frankfurt School, Philips and Brown (1993) argue for a dialectical approach to the study of organisations that they term *critical hermeneutics*. This is grounded in the proposition that all critical organisational analysis should contain both a hermeneutic (i.e. interpretative), and a structural dimension, in order to grasp the ways in which human subjectivity is invested in, reproduces and reacts to, the apparent objectivity of organisational relations. Thus, by acknowledging the fact that organisational life possesses both an experiential 'solidity', yet exists solely as an outcome of human ideas and practices, critical hermeneutics promotes a dialectical understanding of the mutually productive, and yet at one and the same time, mutually contradictory relationship between subjective structures of meaning and those socio-cultural relations that constrain and enable them.

It would be wrong to suggest, however, that dialectics as a means of exploring managerial and organisational activity has been adopted solely by those who might identify with a critical approach to their subject matter. Indeed one might even say that it has almost become fashionable to profess a dialectical method in order to establish conditions by which, for instance, higher forms of organisational efficiency or cooperation might be achieved through collaboration and synthesis. Nevertheless, dialectics continues to underpin a range of critical explorations of organisational life, ranging from Hegelian interpretations of the production of employee subjectivity (Hancock and Tyler, 2001) to the dialectics of managerial control and resistance (Mumby, 2005). As such, while neither a prediction of how organisational life will be, nor a methodological straitjacket, dialectics reminds students of critical management studies to question and explore the processes and contradictions that reside at the heart of contemporary organisations and management practice.

FURTHER READING

There are few works available that provide a clear and simple introduction to dialectics, not only due to the complexity of the concept, but also because of its multifaceted and contested nature. One general Marxist text that does manage this, however, is Ollman's (1993) *Dialectical Investigations*, which provides a useful starting point. In addition to Benson's (1977) aforementioned article, another useful source in relation to organisation and management studies is Burrell and Morgan's (1979/1992) text, particularly chapters 8 to 11.

See also: *Commodity Fetishism, Critical Theory, Ideology, Labour Process Theory, Marxism and Post-Marxism*

REFERENCES

Adorno, T.W. (1973) *Negative Dialectics*. New York: Continuum Publishers.
Benson, J.K. (1977) 'Organizations: A Dialectical View', *Administrative Science Quarterly* 22(1): 1–21.
Braverman, H. (1974) *Labor and Monopoly Capital*. New York and London: Monthly Review Press.
Burrell, G. and Morgan, G. (1979/1992) *Sociological Paradigms and Organisational Analysis*. Aldershot: Ashgate.

Hancock, P. and Tyler, M. (2001) 'Managing Subjectivity and the Dialectic of Self-consciousness: Hegel and Organization Theory', *Organization* 8(4): 565–85.

Mumby, D. (2005) 'Theorizing Resistance in Organization Studies', *Management Communication Quarterly* 19(1): 19–44.

Ollman, B. (1993) *Dialectical Investigations*. London: Routledge.

Phillips, N. and Brown, J.L. (1993) 'Analyzing Communication in and Around Organizations: A Critical Hermeneutic Approach', *Academy of Management Journal* 36(6): 1547–76.

Discourse

Cliff Oswick

Cliff Oswick

Definition: Discourse is a process of meaning-making through talk and text.

INTRODUCTION

The study of discourse has emerged out of two different disciplinary traditions. On the one hand, discourse can be traced back to the field of socio-linguistics and its concern with the fine-grain analysis of language use. On the other hand, discourse has origins in philosophy and social theory with a focus on broader perspectives and interpretations. An overriding feature of discourse is that it has a constructivist orientation in which reality is seen to be subjective in nature and mediated by processes of social negotiation. In effect, discourse is 'language use relative to social, political and cultural formations – it is language reflecting social order but also language shaping social order, and shaping individuals' interaction with society' (Jaworski and Coupland, 1999: 3).

Following the linguistic turn in the social sciences, the discursive analysis of management phenomena has grown considerably over the past two decades. Management scholars have subjected a wide range of issues to discursive scrutiny (e.g. strategy, organisational change, corporate culture, leadership styles, and sense-making). Within the field of critical management studies, the most popular foci of inquiry have been aspects of identity, power and ideology.

The analysis of discursive phenomena can be undertaken through a variety of methodological approaches, including: conversation analysis, ethnomethodology, narrative analysis, and critical discourse analysis (Boje et al., 2004). Discourse can be examined from several different perspectives and there are different levels of analysis. These issues will be discussed in the two subsequent sections.

MODES OF DISCURSIVE ENGAGEMENT

Discursive approaches have been used for contrasting epistemological and ontological ends. The three dominant modes of discursive engagement can be described as 'positivist uni-vocalism', 'critical bi-vocalism', and 'postmodern pluri-vocalism' (Oswick and Richards, 2004). A positivist approach positions discourse as a means of establishing the definitive or unequivocal reading of a particular text or social situation. In this regard, the discursive outcome is a singular and coherent interpretation. This approach has not been widely used within management for two reasons. First, mainstream management scholars (i.e. who adopt a positivist stance) are predisposed to employ methods which are easier to defend because they are likely to offer more extensive, generalisable and aggregated results (e.g. case studies, interviews, and survey-based techniques). Second, while discourse-based methods are extensively employed by critical management scholars, the antithetical nature of a positivist epistemology means that they do not embrace this perspective on discourse.

The critical perspective on discourse draws attention to the contested nature of meaning and discursive exercise of power. More specifically, this mode of inquiry explores the existence of a hegemonic struggle between a privileged discourse and a marginalised discourse (Mumby and Stohl, 1991). This approach highlights the way in which certain views and accounts dominate while others are suppressed or silenced. Rather than reinforcing the uni-vocal coherence associated with a positivist approach, this mode of discursive engagement reveals bi-vocal contestation arising from opposing discourses. This approach to discourse has been widely used in critical management studies to challenge dominant interests. In particular, it has been applied in relation to issues of race and gender, governance, corporate social responsibility, business ethics, workers' rights, and to challenge corporate capitalism.

A postmodern approach to discourse engages with multiple interpretations of reality and the indeterminacy of meaning. Unlike a positivist approach which centres on a single discourse (i.e. uni-vocal coherence) or a critical approach which reveals opposing discourses (i.e. bi-vocal competition), a postmodern approach is far more relativistic and plurivocal in orientation and it highlights multiple discourses (Boje et al., 2004). This approach has been used by management scholars to deconstruct and undermine traditional modernist assumptions, but it falls short of championing alternative discourses in the manner advocated by more critically oriented scholars. That said, the philosophical foundations of postmodern discursive approaches have, at least to a certain extent, provided the foundations for the more politically motivated agenda of critical discursive approaches.

LEVELS OF DISCURSIVE ENGAGEMENT

Alvesson and Karreman (2000) have asked the question: 'Is discourse best understood as a highly local, context-dependent phenomenon to be studied in detail or does it mean an interest in understanding broader, more generalized vocabularies/ways of structuring the social world?' (Alvesson and Karreman, 2000: 1129). Arguably, the answer is to view discourse as operating at different, but non-competing, levels ranging from the microconversational (e.g. one-to-one interaction) to the macrodiscursive (i.e. grand narratives and metadiscourses such as feminism and neoliberalism). Alvesson and Karreman draw a distinction between 'Discourse' (with a capital 'D') and 'discourse' (with a lower-case 'd'). For them, discourse is characterised as being 'myopic' (i.e. a close-range interest in a local-situated context) while Discourse is described as 'grandiose' (i.e. a long-range interest in a macrosystemic context). An interest in discourse has developed out of the socio-linguistic tradition and it utilises micro-oriented methods such as conversation analysis and ethnomethodology. Inquiry based upon Discourse can be linked to philosophy and social theory, and more specifically 'Foucault-inspired work' (Alvesson and Karreman, 2000: 1134). It is less focused on local arrangements and is concerned with identifying general patterns and overarching themes. In addition to the extremes of micro and macro levels of discourse, there are intermediate or meso-levels of discourse. The analysis of meso level discourse involves the consideration of situated talk or written text, but not at the level of the actual words or language used. Instead, the focus of concern is emergent themes which have a narrative structure and that can be interrogated through narrative analysis. In effect, meso-level approaches hold a middle position in so far as they are removed from the immediacy of the text, but do not go as far as forming distanced macrosystemic perspectives.

The delineation of macro, meso and micro levels of discursive engagement has been challenged by Fairclough (1992, 1995). He proposes an approach referred to as 'critical discourse analysis' (CDA) in which a discursive event is 'simultaneously a piece of text, an instance of discursive practice, and an instance of social practice' (1992: 4). As a result, the analysis of discourse requires: (i) examination of the language in use (*the text dimension*); (ii) identification of processes of textual production and consumption (*the discursive practice dimension*); (iii) consideration of the institutional factors surrounding the event and how they shape the discourse (*the social practice dimension*). In effect, CDA seeks to address how local texts are influenced by wider contextual factors and vice versa.

DISCOURSE: CHALLENGES AND THE FUTURE

There are two major concerns about discourse in relation to critical management studies. First, it has been suggested that discourse has been too narrowly focused on talk and text at the expense of considering other semiotic phenomena (such as logo, pictures, body language, video footage, etc.). Second, it has been argued that discourse unduly privileges the socially constructed nature of reality and systematically fails to address issues of materiality and the structural conditions which constrain discourse. Hence, there are two major challenges for critical management studies: (i) to broaden and enrich the scope of discursive inquiry by incorporating the investigation of other non-traditional visual media and artefacts in management (i.e. to move beyond the study of talk and text); and (ii) to meaningfully engage with critical realist concerns by considering the interplay between, and interconnectedness of, the social world and the material world.

FURTHER READING

An excellent overview of the variety of interdisciplinary approaches that can be applied to discourse is provided in *The Discourse Reader* edited by Jaworski and Coupland (1999). For a collection of readings that engage with discourse from an organisational viewpoint see Grant, Hardy, Oswick and Putnam (2004). Finally, an accessible treatment of the study of discourse from a critical perspective is offered by Fairclough (1995).

See also: Deconstruction, Hermeneutics, Identity, Ideology, Postmodernism, Power

REFERENCES

Alvesson, M. and Karreman, D. (2000) 'Varieties of Discourse: On the Study of Organizations through Discourse Analysis', *Human Relations* 53(9): 1125–49.
Boje, D.M., Oswick, C. and Ford, J.D. (2004) 'Language and Organization: The Doing of Discourse', *Academy of Management Review* 29(4): 571–7.
Fairclough, N. (1992) *Discourse and Social Change.* Cambridge: Polity.
Fairclough, N. (1995) *Critical Discourse Analysis: The Critical Study of Language.* London: Longman.
Grant, D., Hardy, C., Oswick, C. and Putnam, L. (eds) (2004) *The Sage Handbook of Organizational Discourse.* London: Sage.
Jaworski, A. and Coupland, N. (eds) (1999) *The Discourse Reader.* London: Routledge.
Mumby, D. and Stohl, C. (1991) 'Power and Discourse in Organization Studies: Absence and the Dialectics of Control', *Discourse and Society* 2(3): 313–32.
Oswick, C. and Richards, D. (2004) 'Talk in Organizations: Local Conversations, Wider Perspectives', *Culture and Organization* 10(2): 107–23.

Environmentalism

David L. Levy

Definition: Environmentalism refers to a social movement and associated body of thought that expresses concern for the state of the natural environment and seeks to limit the impact of human activities on the environment.

INTRODUCTION

Environmentalism has grown out of concerns that the natural environment and human health are adversely affected by the rapid growth of urbanisation, industrialisation, population and consumption in the modern era. These processes are associated with loss of natural habitats and endangerment of species, land degradation, natural resource depletion, and pollution of air, land and water due to waste products. Environmental concerns have shifted over time and vary by location (Guha, 2000). Urbanisation and industrialisation have created expressions of environmentalism directed toward urban effluent and hazardous factory wastes. Wilderness conservation and species protection have played a key role in the United States, through the national parks system and private land trusts. North American environmentalism has traditionally highlighted the intrinsic, experiential and recreational value of nature for humans. In Europe, where high population density and industrialisation largely preceded the rise of environmentalism, efforts have focused more on managing industrial pollution and waste, protecting human health from toxics and nuclear risks, and energy efficiency. More recently, attention has shifted to regional and global issues such as acid rain, ozone depletion and climate change. In developing countries, priority has been given to desertification, water resources, soil erosion and degradation.

Economists regard environmental pollution and resource depletion as negative externalities, costs that are imposed on society and not taken into account by private firms in their decision-making. The ability of firms to externalise environmental costs while appropriating profits from production generates incentives for firms to overproduce goods with harmful environmental impacts and to underinvest in measures to reduce these impacts (Stavins, 1989). The standard economic solution is to force firms to internalise the environmental costs by taxing environmentally harmful products or processes, enabling legal processes for damages, or direct regulation (Portney and Stavins, 2000). It is therefore not surprising that business has traditionally viewed environmental concerns as a threat to profitability and managerial autonomy. Business has generally opposed new environmental regulations and the establishment of regulatory authorities, frequently contesting the scientific basis for understanding harmful impacts and pointing to high compliance costs.

The wave of environmental activism in the 1960s and 1970s, originating with the publication of Rachel Carson's book *Silent Spring* in 1962, led to the establishment of the US Environmental Protection Agency in 1970 and similar agencies in other countries. Business acquiesced partly to assuage key stakeholders, including consumers, non-governmental organisations (NGOs), and government agencies, and partly because federal regulation would pre-empt an expensive patchwork of varied and sometimes stricter state laws. Business opposition to environmental regulation grew during subsequent decades as standards became more extensive and stringent. Business perceived that environmental risks were not balanced against compliance costs, and that direct regulation was an inefficient and blunt tool to address environmental concerns. During the 1990s, regulatory authorities began to experiment with market-based measures, such as the trading system for SO_2 and industries launched self-regulation initiatives such as the US chemical industry's 'Responsible Care' programme. Business, NGOs and governmental agencies experimented with partnerships and voluntary agreements as part of the increasingly complex field of societal environmental governance (Prakash and Potoski, 2006). The decade also saw the rise of a 'win–win' discourse of corporate environmentalism that framed environmental and economic goals as potentially complementary, and the emergence of environmental management as an academic field (Hoffman and Ventresca, 2002).

PARADIGMS OF ENVIRONMENTALISM

Egri and Pinfield (1996), in a review of the literature on organisation theory and the environment, identify three paradigms for understanding the relationship between environment, society and economy. The dominant social paradigm is anthropocentric and neoliberal, encompassing assumptions that human welfare is aligned with the maximisation of economic growth, personal consumption, and corporate pursuit of profits. Unlimited economic growth is assumed to flow from exploiting infinite natural resources, technological innovation, the primacy of markets, and a minimal role for government. The environment, in this paradigm, is regarded as an instrumental economic input, perhaps a constraint, but its sole purpose is the generation of economic value for humans.

Radical environmentalism, by contrast, is biocentric, emphasising the intrinsic value of nature and the dependence of human economic and social life within larger dynamic ecosystems. In this paradigm, environmentalism derives less from concerns about resource depletion or harmful toxics, but more from respect for other species and appreciation of the interconnected complexity and fragility of ecosystems. Various schools of radical environmentalism have different points of departure (Merchant, 1992). Neo-Marxist variants emphasise production for profit under capitalism and the political power of corporate elites (Pepper, 1993). Deep ecologists also critique modern industrialism but focus on cultural and normative anthropocentrism, in which humankind is distinct from and superior to nature, entitled to control and subdue it (Naess, 1989).

These 'red–green' debates raise significant theoretical issues. Neo-Marxists accuse deep ecologists of lacking an analysis of class and power, and view the cultural infatuation with consumption and technology as part of the ideological superstructure of capitalism. Deep ecologists accuse neo-Marxists of harbouring modernist anthropocentric ambitions to harness nature for human benefit. Neo-Marxists reply that ecocentrism is both undesirable in its potential for misanthropism and misguided in its efforts to assign intrinsic value and moral consideration to nature. Ecofeminists share this critique of anthropocentrism but point to patriarchy as the ideological underpinning of the construction of nature as feminine and its subjugation by industry, technology and the military (Salleh, 1992).

Reform environmentalism, a third paradigm, is a more pragmatic approach that recognises the limits of natural systems and attempts to address them within the parameters of the existing order. Reform environmentalism has roots in various theoretical traditions, including systems theory, which emphasises the interdependence of the economy and the environment, and the stakeholder perspective, which points to corporate obligations towards, and dependence on, groups other than shareholders, including consumers, the community, and government. Axiomatic for reform environmentalism is the reconciliation of environmental and economic goals, expressed in the concept of 'sustainable development', defined by the Brundtland Commission of the United Nations as development that 'meets the needs of the present without compromising the ability of future generations to meet their own needs'. Ecological modernisation, or eco-modernism (Hajer, 1995) is an optimistic expression of reform environmentalism that places considerable faith in technology, entrepreneurship and markets in the pursuit of efficient use of environmental resources and sustainable development. Rather than view economic growth as the source of negative environmental externalities, it posits that growth enables investment to address environmental issues, giving a bell-curve relationship between pollution and national income. Simultaneously, growth and modernisation lower population pressures on the environment.

ENVIRONMENTAL MANAGEMENT

Ecological modernisation theory has provided fertile ground for the rapid growth since the mid-1990s of environmental management as an academic field and as managerial practice. Gladwin, Kennelly and Krause (1995), for example, proposed a 'sustaincentric' synthesis of traditional and ecocentric paradigms, which would privilege humans as intelligent stewards of the environment, embraces innovation, and offers a managerialist approach to prevent business activity from exceeding ecosystem constraints. Environmental management proponents argue that successful firms proactively seek profitable 'win–win' opportunities to reduce pollution or develop new green product markets. Environmental management is held to offer the prospect of lower costs for energy, materials, waste disposal and litigation, and the potential for higher sales stemming from green product differentiation.

Implicit in the field of environmental management are a number of ideological assumptions that are rarely articulated (Levy, 1997). One is that the environment can and should be managed at industrial scale, a second is that win–win opportunities give corporate managers the financial motivation to do so, a third is that corporations are the best-equipped societal organisations, in their possession of financial and technical resources, to accomplish this task, and a fourth is that existing forms of management are readily adaptable to the cause. A larger question is whether environmental management efforts at the level of individual firms addresses sustainability efforts at the macro level of the economy–ecosystem interface.

Hajer (1995: 34) asks whether ecological modernisation is 'the first step on a bridge that leads towards a new sort of sustainable modern society' or whether it is a 'rhetorical ploy that tries to reconcile the irreconcilable only to take the wind out of the sails of "real" environmentalists'. Perhaps ecological modernisation and environmental management can best be understood as an accommodation between business and environmental concerns, in which environmentalist pressures are assimilated with modest adjustments to economic systems. It is not empty rhetoric, or 'greenwash', as it demands a degree of compromise and practical steps to address environmental harms, especially those that threaten the resource base and political legitimacy of capitalist production. In mobilising the language and practices of environmentalism, leading business sectors can sustain their hegemonic position, construct alliances with key environmental groups in civil society, and marginalise radical environmentalists calling for deeper structural and cultural transformation in the social and economic order.

FURTHER READING

Levy's (1997) paper provides a useful insight into some of the complexity surrounding the issue of environmentalism as it has been mobilised in the management and other literatures. This could be followed by Hajer's (1995) critical contribution to the debate.

See also: Alternative Organisation, Feminism

REFERENCES

Egri, C.P. and Pinfield, L. (1996) 'Organizations and the Biosphere: Ecologies and Environments', in S.R. Clegg, C. Hardy and W. Nord (eds) *Handbook of Organization Studies*. Newbury Park, CA: Sage.

Gladwin, T.N., Kennelly, J.J. and Krause, T.-S. (1995) 'Shifting Paradigms for Sustainable Development: Implications for Management Theory and Research', *Academy of Management Review* 20(4): 874–907.

Guha, R. (2000) *Environmentalism: A Global History*. New York: Longman.

Hajer, M.A. (1995) *The Politics of Environmental Discourse: Ecological Modernization and the Policy Process*. Oxford: Clarendon Press.

Hoffman, A.J. and Ventresca, M.J. (2002) *Organizations, Policy and the Natural Environment: Institutional and Strategic Perspectives*. Stanford: Stanford University Press.

Levy, D.L. (1997) 'Environmental Management as Political Sustainability', *Organization and Environment* 10(2): 126–47.

Merchant, C. (1992) *Radical Ecology*. New York: Routledge.

Naess, A. (1989) *Ecology, Community, and Lifestyle*. Cambridge: Cambridge University Press.

Pepper, D. (1993) *Eco-socialism*. London: Routledge.

Portney, P., and Stavins, R. (2000) *Public Policies for Environmental Protection*. Washington, DC: RFF Press.

Prakash, A. and Potoski, M. (2006) *The Voluntary Environmentalists: Green Clubs, ISO 14001, and Voluntary Environmental Regulations*. Cambridge: Cambridge University Press.

Salleh, A. (1992) 'The Ecofeminism/Deep Ecology Debate: A Reply to Patriarchal Reason', *Environmental Ethics* 14: 195–216.

Stavins, R.N. (1989) 'Harnessing Market Forces to Protect the Environment', *Environment* 31(1): 5–7, 28–35.

environmentalism

Feminism

Jo Brewis and Michèle Bowring

> **Definition:** Feminism refers to a type of social theory or philosophy which asks why women are socially disadvantaged relative to men, and provides political solutions to correct this disadvantage.

INTRODUCTION

The term 'feminism' is in fact a misnomer because there are so many variants of feminist theory. It is therefore more accurate to speak of 'feminisms'. It is also not easy to trace feminist thinking back to its roots; although a common if arbitrary place to start is with Mary Astell, writing more than three centuries ago. As *liberal political philosophy* took hold in the west during the *Enlightenment*, arguing that all men are born with the capacity for reason and thus the capacity to be equal given the appropriate education, Astell famously riposted '*If all Men are born free, how is it that all Women are born slaves?*' (1700: Preface). She claimed that the ignorance, self-indulgence and general unreliability attributed to women at the time were all products of deficiencies in their education. If educated in the same way as men, Astell asserted, women would be just as socially useful and productive.

FEMINISM/S AND MANAGEMENT STUDIES

The *liberal feminist* philosophy, which arguments like Astell's inaugurated, starts from the premise that in all significant respects men and women are equal, and should be treated as such. It is *essentialist* because it argues for innate human qualities or essences, and is based on *sameness* and the importance of *equality*. It is liberal feminist arguments which underpin antidiscrimination laws prohibiting unequal treatment on the basis of sex in employment, education and the provision of goods and

114

services. Liberal feminism is also the most influential feminism in management studies. Its central concept is the idea of unfair organisational *segregation* predicated on sex. Segregation can be *horizontal*, where stereotypes about men and women mean they are channelled into, or even actively select, particular occupations (e.g., paediatric medicine for women and emergency medicine for men). It can also be *vertical*, meaning women are under-represented in the most senior organisational positions, again because of stereotypical constructions of their capabilities. Vertical segregation is often explained by reference to the *glass ceiling* (Davidson and Cooper, 1992). This is an invisible but hard to penetrate attitudinal barrier which makes it much harder for women to access the ranks of power. As the former UK Equal Opportunities Commission (2007: 1) puts it, there are 'nearly 6,000 women "missing" from more than 33,000 top positions of power in Britain today'.

Another important strand of feminist thinking which has influenced management studies proceeds more or less from psychoanalytical theory concerning sex-based socialisation. *Psychoanalytic feminism* contends, broadly speaking, that psychic development from infancy onwards rests on the child's relationship with his or her mother in particular. It argues that how we navigate this relationship – in most cases – depends on whether we are male or female. Like liberal feminism, psychoanalytic feminism is Western in origin, and its conceptualisations of the 'typical' family and the sex-specific socialisation which this family produces are therefore *ethnocentric*. But, unlike liberal feminism, it is a philosophy of *difference* and therefore *parity* or *equity*. In other words, psychoanalytic feminism argues that women and men tend to come to adulthood having developed different characteristics. Women are thus understood as more caring, relationship-oriented and intuitive than men, who are more individualistic, combative and assertive. When translated into management studies, psychoanalytic feminism (sometimes called the *women's ways* approach) suggests not only that men and women are different, but also that women's unique contribution to organisations should be valued as adding something that men usually cannot. For example, Rosener (1990, 1997) claims that women's more *transformational* style of workplace leadership – a participatory, inclusive and supportive approach – should be encouraged in today's unstable and unpredictable global economy, especially given increasing levels of workers' education and professionalisation.

While it is impossible to do justice to the range of feminisms in an entry like this, the third feminism which has impacted on management studies, and critical management studies in particular, over the last two decades or

feminism

115

so is the equally broad church of *postmodernist feminism*. Both liberal and psychoanalytic feminism contend that sexist stereotyping of what women 'really' have to offer explains phenomena such as the glass ceiling and segregation. Postmodernist feminism on the other hand regards the linguistic or *discursive* categories of 'woman' and 'man' as unstable – not as reflecting anything materially, biologically or psychologically real or enduring. Instead it suggests that the commonplace and longstanding labelling of certain bodies as 'male' or 'female', and certain behaviours, attitudes and values as 'masculine' or 'feminine', produces certain *power effects*. This means most of us come to understand ourselves as either male or female, and to act and interact accordingly. Equally, this means we will not act and interact in other ways because they are not 'sex-appropriate'. Moreover, the *discourse* of sex – or gender – alters across time and space. As such what it 'means' to be a man or a woman in different socio-historical locations is likewise highly variable. The rallying call of this feminist perspective is 'every way of seeing is also a way of not seeing'. It asks us to reflect on how we 'sex' or 'gender' ourselves and each other, and what sorts of entirely contingent limitations on ourselves and others we (re)produce as a result.

This is a complex set of ideas, which has necessarily been diluted here, but in management studies postmodernist feminism has been used by Thomas and Davies (2002), for example, to examine how female academics have reacted to far-reaching public sector reforms in Britain. In universities, these include the creation of the 'new' universities in the early 1990s, the advent of mass higher education and intensified public scrutiny of university performance. Thomas and Davies suggest that the discourse of the 'New Public Management' encourages the construction of a new scholarly identity. In basic terms, it encourages academics to become competitive, single-minded, individualistic, self-sacrificing publishing machines. Equally, Thomas and Davies argue, this identity is highly *masculine*. Thus, while universities have always promoted masculine behaviours, attitudes and values, NPM alters the terms of reference, requiring new kinds of masculine identity performances from academics in exchange for career success. Some female academics reacted by constructing themselves as 'honorary men' – but suffered by being defined as *non*-feminine and so somehow 'unnatural' by colleagues. Others resisted the NPM discourse by refusing to identify with its norms – but were therefore labelled as 'solid troupers' as opposed to high performers or, even worse, as 'work shy' (Thomas and Davies, 2002: 388, 391).

In the context of management studies, we might also consider *Marxist* and *socialist feminisms* which add an analysis of women's subordination to a class-based analysis to suggest that *patriarchy* (the social structures which maintain men's domination over women) combines with *capitalism* to produce specific forms of women's subjugation. *Postcolonial feminism* is a more recent entrant to the analysis of management and organisations. It argues that the legacy of *empire* in former European and North American colonies produces specific experiences for women in these parts of the world which Western feminism has failed to acknowledge. Thus postcolonial feminism focuses on the intersections between gender, *ethnicity* and the aftermath of *imperialism* to argue that much existing feminist analysis – and *activism* – has been highly ethnocentric.

FURTHER READING

Calás and Smircich (1996) provide a helpful review of how feminist theory has been used to unpick management and organisations. Alvesson and Billing (2009) offer an equally insightful analysis of the various intersections between feminism and management studies. The journal *Gender, Work and Organization* also publishes a variety of feminist analyses in the area.

See also: *Colonialism and Postcolonialism, Discourse, Gender, Identity, Marxism and Post-Marxism, Postmodernism, Poststructuralism, Subjectivity and Subjectivation*

REFERENCES

Alvesson, M. and Billing, Y.D. (2009) *Understanding Gender and Organizations*, 2nd edn. London: Sage.
Astell, M. (1700) *Some Reflections Upon Marriage*. London: John Nutt.
Calás, M.B. and Smircich, L. (1996) 'From the "Woman's Point of View": Feminist Approaches to Organization Studies', in S.R. Clegg, C. Hardy and W.R. Nord (eds) *Handbook of Organization Studies*, pp. 218–57. London: Sage.
Davidson, M.J. and Cooper, C.L. (1992) *Shattering the Glass Ceiling: The Woman Manager*. London: Paul Chapman.
Equal Opportunities Commission (UK) (2007) *Sex and Power: Who Runs Britain?* Manchester: Equal Opportunities Commission.
Rosener, J.B. (1990) 'Ways Women Lead', *Harvard Business Review* (Nov.–Dec.): 119–25.
Rosener, J.B. (1997) *America's Competitive Secret: Women Managers*. Oxford: Oxford University Press.
Thomas, R. and Davies, A. (2002) 'Gender and New Public Management: Reconstituting Academic Subjectivities', *Gender, Work and Organization* 9(4): 372–97.

feminism

Gender

Elizabeth Parsons

> **Definition:** Gender is the range of characteristics that are said to differentiate between female and male subjects. These characteristics variously include biological sex, social roles and social identities.

PERSPECTIVES ON GENDER

There are two general means by which perspectives on gender studies might be classified: in terms of their political project (i.e. the way they view society and how they might make changes to society) or in terms of their ontological and epistemological positions (i.e. their views on the nature of knowledge and knowledge production or methodology). There are significant overlaps between gender studies and feminist studies and in many cases the terms are used synonymously. However, a political project is always fundamental to feminist studies, and this is not always the case in gender studies. As this entry is about 'gender' rather than 'feminism' the methodological as opposed to political approach is discussed here. In this approach three key perspectives might be identified: 'gender as a variable', 'feminist standpoint' and 'poststructuralist feminism' (Alvesson and Billing, 2009).

The *gender as variable* perspective is concerned with looking at differences between men and women in their attainment in the labour market, with a particular focus on the conditions under which women work. This work is carried out with a view to understanding the bases of discrimination, often so that policy solutions might be developed to address them. Here gender is viewed as a unitary variable with a specific focus on women as an undifferentiated and unambiguous category. Studies in this vein use both quantitative and qualitative methods but are generally underpinned by a (neo)positivist view, where gender is conflated with sex. Here, the categories of male and female are viewed as relatively fixed entities, as realities 'out there', to be uncovered through rigorous, objective research.

The *feminist standpoint* perspective deals with gender in a very different way. Here gender is viewed as 'a fundamental organizing principle of patriarchal society' (Alvesson and Billing, 2009: 28). In this perspective the experiences of women are seen as differing fundamentally from those of men and the commonality of women's experience is emphasised. Proponents argue that women's location as a subordinated and oppressed group means that their understanding of the world not only differs from that of men, but allows them to challenge the traditional male-biased wisdom on which patriarchal societies are founded. In research terms this perspective proposes to make women's experiences, instead of men's, the point of departure. Research focuses on making women's experiences visible through exposing their points of view, and by giving them an active role and a voice in the research process.

A third perspective on gender might be termed *poststructuralist feminism*; here understandings of gender are significantly different in kind from the previous two perspectives. Gender is viewed as unstable and ambiguous and the emphasis lies on fragmentation as opposed to commonality. Poststructural feminists view earlier studies as attributing false unity to gender by conceptualising it as a 'category'. Instead they argue that the concepts of men and women are socially constructed through language and that these constructions are entirely contextually contingent. As Alvesson and Billing observe: '"men" and "women" – like other signifiers – have only a precarious, temporal meaning tied to the context in which these words (signifiers) are used' (2009: 37). Thus research explores the ways in which reality is rhetorically constructed through language as opposed to a pre-existing entity waiting to be uncovered. Researchers attempt alternative ways of representing the researched, and in using arbitrary descriptions, try to leave open the possibility of a range of interpretations.

GENDER IN ORGANISATIONAL AND MANAGEMENT STUDIES

The relationship between gender and organisations, and gender and management, is a complex one, riddled with tensions. Researchers have typically employed a mixture of the above approaches to try and capture some of this complexity. In many cases these approaches are not entirely distinct from one another, but it is still possible to identify a broad historical development within the field. Early work in the 1960s focused largely on the gender-as-a-variable and feminist-standpoint perspectives. The development from the 1990s onwards of a poststructuralist feminist perspective was linked to the wider move towards poststructuralism in critical management studies. This work has responded to criticisms of organisational theory, and indeed organisational theorists themselves, as 'Blind and Deaf to Gender' (Wilson, 1996). Concerned to reinsert gender into organisational theory and theorising (Calás and Smircich, 1992) researchers have variously explored the ways that gender is practised, reproduced and maintained within the cultures and management of organisations. In its focus on performativity this work has also brought embodiment to the forefront of debates (Tyler and Taylor, 2001).

An early example of this more recent approach to gender is Gherardi's (1995) seminal book *Gender, Symbolism and Organizational Cultures*. In the book she highlights the ambiguous and elusive nature of gender in organisational life. She demonstrates how organisational cultures are pervasively gendered, arguing that organisations, 'despite their claim to be neuter and neutral, are structured according to the symbolism of gender' (1995: 3). Linstead and Thomas (2002) place a similar focus on gender as fluid and inconsistent in their study of managers. They use the concept of the gender mask to explore the ways in which middle managers (re)create their sense of self in the uncertain context of organisational restructuring. Drawing from the narratives of four middle managers they observe the ways in which they 'draw, implicitly and explicitly on gendered masks to construct and legitimize their generic roles and identities as managers, regardless of being male or female' (2002: 15). The masks they identify include 'the hired gun', 'the old soldier', 'the male breadwinner' and 'a better man than the men'. They observe that these masks themselves are 'masks of masculinities' and as such 'serve to reinforce the masculine signifiers of organization' (2002: 16). They also explore the ways in which this masking serves to bridge the public and private in the identity work of these managers, as the discourses of management and organisation encroach on their domestic, as well as working, lives.

While emphasising a fractured and fragmented view of masculinity, Kerfoot and Knights (1998) also recognise a predominant mode of masculinity amongst managers. They surmise that 'This form of masculinity offers many men a secure and "comfortable" identity in generating and sustaining feminine dependence and a sexuality of men that displaces intimacy' (1998: 7). They argue that this mode of masculinity is also used as a yardstick against which both men and women are judged and thus its operation serves to privilege men over women in the workplace.

Recent focus on gender has been informed by a wide range of theoretical perspectives including psychoanalysis, critical race theory, masculinities and queer theory. This work acknowledges not only the fluidity of gender but also that the gender construct is cross cut with the constructs of sexuality, class and race.

FURTHER READING

For up-to-date discussions of the relations between gender, work and organisation see the journal of the same name (*Gender, Work and Organization*). Alvesson and Billing's (2009) book also provides an excellent entry point into current debates.

See also: *Feminism, Queer Theory, Sexuality*

REFERENCES

Alvesson, M. and Billing, Y.D. (2009) *Understanding Gender and Organizations*, 2nd edn. London: Sage.

Calás, M.B. and Smircich, L. (1992) 'Re-writing Gender into Organizational Theorizing: Directions from Feminist Perspectives', in M. Reed and M. Hughes (eds) *Rethinking Organization*, pp. 227–53. London: Sage.

Gherardi, S. (1995) *Gender Symbolism and Organizational Culture*. London: Sage.

Kerfoot, D. and Knights, D. (1998) 'Managing Masculinity in Contemporary Organizational Life: A "Man"agerial Project', *Organization* 5(1): 7–26.

Linstead, A. and Thomas, R. (2002) 'What Do You Want From Me? A Poststructuralist Feminist Reading of Middle Managers' Identities', *Culture and Organization* 8(1): 1–20.

Tyler, M. and Taylor, S. (2001) 'Flight Attendants and the Management of Gendered "Organizational Bodies"', in K. Backett-Milburn and L. McKie (eds) *Constructing Gendered Bodies*, pp. 25–38. London: Palgrave.

Wilson, F. (1996) 'Organizational Theory: Blind and Deaf to Gender?', *Organization Studies* 17(5): 825–42.

gender

Globalisation

Subhabrata Bobby Banerjee

> **Definition:** Globalisation refers to the processes behind the spread of markets and a consumer culture across the globe.

The definition of globalisation depends on the context in which it is being used. Economic globalisation refers to the emergence of a global political economy that is characterised by increasing interdependence of national economies and the reduction of trade barriers to facilitate the flow of capital across national boundaries. Cultural aspects of globalisation reflect both the emergence of a global consumer culture as well as the production and transmission of cultural products across the globe. Political aspects of globalisation describe the global organisation of the political economy.

The global integration of financial markets has both temporal and spatial effects. New financial instruments in the form of securities and hedge funds coupled with advances in communication technologies have led to instantaneous financial transactions that can affect stock markets and currency markets all over the world. Policies of deregulation and privatisation and the internationalisation of economies and financial markets also create a new spatial competitive environment (Banerjee, Clegg and Carter, 2009). Some popular readings of globalisation (Thomas Friedman's *The World is Flat*, 2005, is a case in point) celebrate the emergence of the global era as marking the end of the dominance of nation-states and multinational corporations as the world converges to a global political economy where geographical boundaries have become meaningless. Such simplistic approaches to globalisation are problematic because they construct a false opposition between globalisation and the territorial state.

Sassen (1998) argues that the national/global binary opposition does not capture the complexities of globalisation processes. The dualism tends to focus attention on industrial outputs while eliding issues relating to processes and relations of production. It privileges capacity for information transmission but does not take into account the infrastructure required to build this capacity. National/global categories are not mutually exclusive but their elements are intertwined and embedded in national and international institutions. Even the most global industries – finance, media, information technology – operate through a global network located in national sites where strategic decisions on the deployment of capital and location of resources serve to strengthen the international division of labour and strategic concentration of infrastructure.

The global economy is predicated on a system of nation-states. Globalisation in such a reading is characterised not by the vanishing nation-state but, on the contrary, by the central implication of the territorial state in the production of a globalised world. The state provides a 'structured permanence' that enables the organisation of space and the control of its networks (Banerjee, Chio and Mir, 2009). The nation-state, then, is a fundamental building block of globalisation, in the working of multinational corporations, in the creation and maintenance of a global financial system, in the institution of policies that determine the mobility of labour, and in the creation of the multistate institutions such as the United Nations (UN), the International Monetary Fund (IMF), World Bank and World Trade Organisation (WTO) (Banerjee and Linstead, 2001).

There is also a political aspect of globalisation in the sense that processes of globalisation also reflect relationships of power, domination and subordination. Market expansion was very much a part of the colonial and imperial project. Thus, globalisation has its historical roots in the modern era where military strength secured the global control of raw materials, which, through industrialisation in turn, enabled the creation and control of world markets sustaining the competitive and economic advantage of the industrialised countries. Today, international institutions and transnational corporations are writing the rules of globalisation. Global political exchanges often involve coercion (the various trade embargoes orchestrated by Western powers), surveillance (as evidenced by several World Bank and IMF policies), legitimacy (as offered by the WTO) and authority (granting of 'most favoured nation' status by the United States).

Advances in information technology have also seen the emergence of global media that have facilitated the transformation of citizens into global consumers. While some scholars claim that globalisation has created cultural homogenisation resulting in the emergence of a 'global culture', others argue homogenisation is always accompanied by some form of indigenisation of global cultural flows at the local level (Appadurai, 1990). The global cultural economy can be understood as a series of disjunctures between economy, culture and polity leading to multiple cultural flows through a series of what Appadurai (1990: 296) calls 'scapes': *Ethnoscapes* refer to the diversity of people in transition: tourists, immigrants, refugees, exiles and other mobile groups. *Technoscapes* refer to the global configuration of technology; *finanscapes* to the globalisation of capital; *mediascapes* to the production and dissemination of information; and *ideoscapes* to the nation-state development ideologies and the counter-ideologies of social movements. These scapes are neither truly global nor purely local but reflect instead the simultaneity of the global and the local, of the particular and the universal.

Globalisation is also a contested process as evidenced by the many protest movements across the world organised by diverse groups such as labour unions, human rights activists, environmentalists, women's rights groups, indigenous rights groups and others. There are winners and losers in the global economy – what Bauman (1998) calls the first world of the globally mobile and the second world of the locally tied. The emergence of a new global underclass is different from earlier geographical distinctions of First, Second and Third Worlds. Instead we increasingly find First World segments within the Third World and Third World segments within the First World, a division which is opening up between the mobile and the immobile within *all* societies as a further consequence of the increasing flexibility of investment and those who are paid to follow it, and the increasing restriction of choice for those who are subject to its fluctuations.

FURTHER READING

For a good review of key debates see David Held and Anthony McGrew's (2007) *Globalization/Anti-Globalization: Beyond the Great Divide.*

See also: Capitalism and Anticapitalism, Consumer Culture, Colonialism and Postcolonialism, Ideology, Neoliberalism, Power

REFERENCES

Appadurai, A. (1990) 'Disjuncture and Difference in the Global Cultural Economy', *Public Culture* 2(2): 1–24.

Banerjee, S.B., Chio, V. and Mir, R. (2009) 'The Imperial Formations of Globalization', in Banerjee, Chio and Mir (eds) *Organizations, Markets and Imperial Formations: Towards An Anthropology of Globalization*, pp. 3–14. Cheltenham: Edward Elgar.

Banerjee, S.B., Clegg, S. and Carter, C. (2009) 'Managing Globalization', in M. Alvesson, H. Willmott and T. Bridgman (eds) *Handbook of Critical Management Studies*, pp. 186–212. Oxford: Oxford University Press.

Banerjee, S.B. and Linstead, S. (2001) 'Globalization, Multiculturalism and Other Fictions: Colonialism for the New Millennium?' *Organization* 8(4): 683–722.

Bauman, Z. (1998) *Globalization: The Human Consequence*. Cambridge: Polity.

Friedman, T. (2005) *The World Is Flat: A Brief History of the Twenty-first Century*. New York: Farrar, Strauss and Giroux.

Held, D. and McGrew, A. (2007) *Globalization/Anti-Globalization: Beyond the Great Divide*. Cambridge: Polity.

Sassen, S. (1998) *Globalization and its Discontents: Essays on the New Mobility of People and Money*. New York: The New Press.

Governmentality

Kaspar Villadsen

Definition: this term designates a particular rationality for governing the population which has become ubiquitous in modern societies.

Governmentality is closely associated with Michel Foucault, who adopted the term from Roland Barthes. The latter used it to describe a 'naturalized myth' that represented the state as an omnipotent and benevolent instigator of all social relations (Barthes, 1972: 129). Foucault was similarly interested in opposing overestimations of the state as the centre of society and a source of power. Yet, he does not employ the term as a concept in the traditional sense – that is, as a descriptor which represents a particular phenomena or a delimited part of reality. Rather, governmentality serves as a category which guides empirical descriptions and is calibrated differently depending on the type of intellectual provocation it invokes in each instance. The term serves at least three functions:

First, governmentality constitutes an *analytical perspective* which offers guidelines for studies of modern forms of power. A key principle is to avoid reducing political (and other kinds) of power to the state or the formal state apparatus. Rather than accepting the state as an already given substance, Foucault sought to mark out all those different strategies of regulation which historically made possible the modern state and still permeate it. In order to denaturalise the concept of state, he suggested an analytical 'decentring' as opposed to an institutional-centric approach (Foucault, 2007: 116), a move similar to his prison study, in which Foucault moved 'outside' the institution in order to locate it in relation to more general strategies of power. To describe governmentality thus implied examining a range of strategies for dealing with practical problems and establishing new objects of knowledge, which gradually made possible our modern ways of conceptualising the state and political power. Whereas discipline corrects and controls the behaviour of individual bodies, modern government seeks to influence the self-regulation and self-reflection of free persons. Governmentality directs analytical attention to the connections between practices of government and practices of the self – governmental technologies and self-technologies (Foucault, 1988: 19).

Second, governmentality designates a *specific political reasoning* which gradually emerged from the seventeenth century onwards through a series of transformations. In 1978 Foucault defines governmentality as the ensemble formed by different institutions, analyses and strategies permitting an exercise of power that has the population as its target, political economy as its major form of knowledge, and apparatuses of security as its technical instrument (2007: 108). This complex statement indicates a historical process comprising at least three major phases. The first phase is characterised by *raison d'état* originating in the seventeenth century, a time marked by mercantilist economy that aimed to protect the wealth of the state by disciplining national production and export. This reason of state revolved around the goal of maximising its own power. A strategy that involved a military-diplomatic technology of foreign politics combined with an internal technology of 'police science' comprising administrative techniques and statistical knowledges concerned with maximising the volume, productivity and health of the population.

• This rationality is transfigured in the second phase in the process of governmentalisation, where state reason is confronted by criticisms that

key concepts in critical management studies

it governs too much at the expense of the economical order, which should be governed according to principles of laissez-faire. It is at this point that the population comes into view not as something to regulate and control in every detail but rather as a self-regulating reality, a 'naturalness of society' (2007: 349), which governmental intervention should not violate. In the second phase thus arises a new problem of governing while allowing those governed particular forms of freedom – freedom not justified in inviolable rights, but as an indispensable element for this new governmentality itself (Gudmand-Høyer and Hjorth, 2009).

The scepticism against excessive government continues in the third phase, where Foucault traces the governmental interconnection of security, economy and population within two versions of twentieth-century neoliberalism. First, a new governmentality appears within German Ordo-liberalism of the 1930–40s, contrary to the tradition advocating that society should be governed for the market and not vice versa. Second, this neoliberal governmentality is further developed by the American neoliberalism of the 1960–70s, which promoted an expansion of economic analysis and programming to vast areas of social life. Following the presupposition common to liberal and neoliberal governmentality that the primary field of intervention for government is neither state nor market, but a civil society inhabited by a self-regulating population, Foucault alternatively defines governmentality as 'the way in which one conducts the conduct of men' (2007: 186).

Third, the term governmentality is *diagnostic* in as far as it describes our present as an era in which this modern rationality of government has become ubiquitous, self-evident, and (partly for this reason) something precarious. In this use, governmentality serves to indicate a general threshold, a transformation which still bears upon us, at which power relations begin to assume an increasingly governmental character. As far as individuals' self-relations became crucial for the workings of political power, it is impossible to separate each individual's self-practice (ethics) from the governing of the state (politics) and vice versa. The same point goes for the increasingly intricate intertwinements of the management of organisations and organisational members' self-management.

Critical organisation studies (COS) has witnessed an explosion of work inspired by Foucault, particularly from the early 1990s onwards. While a great part of these studies treat problems pertaining to the governmentality theme, the term itself appears surprisingly rarely in COS. In a related area, however, Miller and Rose (1990) argued that authorities in advanced liberal societies seek to 'govern at a distance' by employing technologies that can align personal conduct with political and managerial objectives. Key consideration was given to technologies that transform the calculative procedures of economic agents, including enterprises, managers and the producing subjects. Miller and Rose's work thus reflects Foucault's injunction to study the connection between forms of government of the state and government of the self.

Foucault's concepts pertaining to governmentality have proved particularly useful for studying new forms of antibureaucratic, flexible and entrepreneurial management. Du Gay et al. (1996) studied recent attempts to reconstitute managers – their conduct and self-conduct – along entrepreneurial lines. The vision of good managerial competence is demonstrated to increasingly rest on individualised types of business functions and the establishment of market-like relations within organisations. In this way, Du Gay et al. applied Foucault's insight that the market has become the emblematic site at which to find the formative principles of social regulation. That antibureaucratic government often involves sensibilising, making professionals and managers more sensitive towards those that they attempt to govern, is demonstrated by Karlsen and Villadsen (2008). Their study focuses on the proliferation of internal organisational dialogues which are used as a popular governmental technology emerging across a range of institutional settings as a result of the critique of authoritarian management and expertise. While dialogue technologies demand that leaders and professionals should speak less and allow the subordinate to speak, they nevertheless subtly regulate organisational domains of speech. Dialogue technologies thus display the paradox of governing freedom: they aim to dig out free, 'authentic' statements, but pre-shape the conversational space through regulatory procedures.

Recently some COS academics have argued that Foucault's concepts are inadequate for analysing current managerial power. Some scholars have found inspiration in Deleuze's call for a move from 'disciplinary societies' to 'societies of control' (1997). On this basis they point at the emergence of new forms of managerial power which dissolve institutional boundaries and depart from the rigidity of disciplinary segregation of time, bodies and space. This development is seen to be spurred by new information technology and biotechnologies. However, the recent publication of Foucault's lectures on governmentality from 1978–9 makes evident that those characteristics of 'non-disciplinary power', allegedly instantiated by this emerging society of control, were already vividly indicated by Foucault in these lectures. Many interesting perspectives on current organisational life still wait to be explored using this work.

FURTHER READING

Michel Foucault's work is an essential starting point (e.g. 2007), especially lecture 4. For clarification of analytical concepts, see Miller and Rose (1990).

See also: Neoliberalism, Poststructuralism, Power, Surveillance

REFERENCES

Barthes, R. (1972 [1957]) *Mythologies*. New York: The Noonday Press.
Deleuze, G. (1997) 'Postscript on the Societies of Control', in Deleuze (ed.) *Negotiations 1972–1990*. New York: Columbia University Press.
Du Gay, P., Salaman, G. and Rees, B. (1996) 'The Conduct of Management and the Management of Conduct', *Journal of Management Studies* 33(3): 263–82.
Foucault, M. (1988) *Technologies of the Self*. Amherst: University of Massachussetts Press.
Foucault, M. (2007) *Security, Territory, Population*. New York: Palgrave Macmillan.
Gudmand-Høyer, M. and Hjorth, T. (2009) 'Liberal Biopolitics Reborn. Review Essay: Michel Foucault, The Birth of Biopolitics: Lectures at Collège de France, 1978–1979', *Foucault Studies* 7: 99–130.
Karlsen, M.P. and Villadsen, K. (2008) 'Who Should Do the Talking: The Proliferation of Dialogue as Governmental Technology', *Culture & Organization* 14(4): 345–63.
Miller, P. and Rose, N. (1990) 'Governing Economic Life', *Economy and Society* 19(1): 1–31.

governmentality

Hegemony

Robin Klimecki and Hugh Willmott

Definition: Greek hēgemoniā from hēgemōn, leader, ruler – a specific form of political relation and achievement wherein a particular group, or an entity such as an organisation, represents its particular demands as universal and thereby exercises 'intellectual and moral leadership'. Hegemony may rely upon the use of force but, more importantly, it operates through creating consent and 'common sense' via legitimising certain ideological norms and values.

THEORETICAL BACKGROUND

In political theory, hegemony refers to the power of one state over others, such as the French Hegemony over Europe under Napoleon or Sparta as the *Hegemon* of the Peloponnesian League in the sixth century. The term hegemony first emerged in a Marxist context in the writings of Georgi Plekhanov (1857–1918) and other Russian Marxists (e.g. Lenin) to designate the necessity of the working class, as an emergent political group, to forge political alliances rather than limiting their resistance to economic struggles to overthrow the tsarist regime.

The key figure in contemporary theorising of hegemony is the Italian Marxist Antonio Gramsci (1891–1937) who developed Lenin's strategic use of the term into a theoretical concept. For Gramsci, hegemony characterises the process by which a group transcends its particular 'economic corporatist' interests to provide 'intellectual and moral leadership' (Gramsci, 1971: 182, 269) to diverse groups within society. The Gramscian understanding of hegemony can be defined as a socio-political situation in which a certain idea of reality becomes widely disseminated. Institutions and private life are informed by a spirit which shapes taste, morality, customs, religion, politics, and the intellectual and moral content of social relations.

Hegemonic projects comprise intricate, contradictory, and contingent alliances of forces within the spheres of the state and the economy as well as civil society, with the latter field comprising the church, trade unions, schools, the family, etc. Gramsci calls the dominant configuration of these heterogeneous elements in a given period of time a 'historical bloc', and tends to identify civil society as the primary vehicle, or ideological ground, to cement hegemony.

The centrality of struggle is retained as a defining feature of Marxist thought where hegemonic struggles take the form of a 'war of positions', a 'cultural war' where persuasion predominates, across social institutions rather than being limited to the 'frontal attack' of direct political confrontation. Resistance is always present within this framework because, due to the contradictory and contingent nature of the alliance of forces, historical blocs are unstable. Leadership is always fragile and threatened by shifting alliances and resistance arising from competing hegemonic projects. The precariousness of hegemonic regimes makes it possible for counter-hegemonic forces to emerge that articulate a critical conception of established ideas and eventually seize power.

As an example, 'Thatcherism' has been analysed as a hegemonic project as it had wide popular appeal and attracted fervent political support beyond traditional Conservative voters. In effect, Margaret Thatcher, together with her circle of financial and political backers and intellectuals, supplied the leadership to fill a vacuum that had opened up as the postwar corporatist settlement became discredited. 'Thatcherism' garnered support by, for example, appealing to voters' petty-bourgeois interest in becoming members of a 'property owning democracy' through the selling off of council houses and the privatisation of public utilities (Hall, 1988). But Thatcherism also fermented both resistance and expectations that it failed to fulfil, its attack upon corporatist commonsense was itself challenged by praxis (Mumby, 1977) that questioned its potent combination of individualism and nationalism.

Gramsci's concept of hegemony is notoriously open to interpretation. Among those scholars recognised in the wider social sciences, and also in critical management studies, are Ernesto Laclau and Chantal Mouffe (2001), who develop a poststructuralist/post-Marxist analysis of hegemony. Their genealogy of the concept of hegemony in Marxism advances further the anti-economist position of Gramsci with the aim of 'reactivating' Marxist categories in an entirely non-essentialist way. For them, hegemony is a form of social relation within which 'a particular social force assumes the representation of a totality that is radically incommensurable with it' (Laclau and Mouffe, 2001: x). So, for example, 'Thatcherism' aspired to be totalising and drew strong support from all sections of society. But it also acted to stimulate opposition that refused to equate 'Thatcherism' with society or sought to distance it from true 'One Nation' Conservativism. In the end, its 'incommensurability' was exposed by generalised and violent opposition to the Poll Tax.

For Laclau and Mouffe, hegemony is understood to be politically constructed as well as contingent and inherently unstable, but the notion of fundamental classes as privileged historical agents is abandoned in favour of a more radical conception of how 'interests', and associated 'positions', are discursively constituted rather than structurally allocated. The universalisation of particular interests or demands is therefore, and contrary to Gramsci, not ultimately tied to an essential class like the proletariat or the bourgeoisie. Instead, 'politico-hegemonic articulations' are conceived to 'retroactively create the interests they claim to represent' (Laclau and Mouffe, 2001: xi). Given that every universal incarnation is always 'contaminated' by its status as a particularity, universality, in the sense of a 'universal truth', can never fully be achieved and is thus always reversible. Additionally the concept of hegemony has also found its way into other traditions such as critical realism (Joseph, 2002; Delbridge, 2007).

HEGEMONY AND CRITICAL MANAGEMENT STUDIES

The concept of hegemony in the field of critical management studies (CMS) is still underexplored since the application of Gramscian ideas to manufacturing in Michael Burawoy's *Manufacturing Consent* (1979). A revival of Gramscian ideas, so called neo-Gramscianism, has predominantly occurred in the academic disciplines of cultural and communication studies, international relations (IR) and international political economy (IPE). These approaches broaden the theoretical framework of hegemony and apply it beyond the struggles of conflicting class configurations envisaged by Gramsci to other social actors and constellations of forces – such as the importance and power of capital markets within a global US-centred hegemonic world order. In CMS, the work of David Levy focuses on how international business shapes and sustains certain taken-for-granted power relations. Levy (2008) situates global production networks (GPN) within a hegemonic framework that involves collaboration as well as resistance among a variety of diverse actors such as companies, non-governmental organisations (NGOs), state bodies, trade associations, etc.

GPNs are not understood to be mere outcomes of rational economic processes such as the 'laws' of competition but politically and socially created and legitimised. GPNs such as those of the coffee sector are both results of, and contributors to, a neoliberal hegemonic regime that promotes 'competitiveness' and 'free trade' by means of organisations such as the World Bank. Such a discourse is often built on severe power imbalances as exemplified in the exploitation of coffee producers or sweatshop workers. Since hegemonic orders are always an unstable and fragile alliance of forces, as is illustrated by the plurality of positions and interests of the social actors involved in a GPN, they are vulnerable to contestation. An example in the coffee sector would be successful fair-trade campaigns. Here, Gramsci's theoretical concepts such as 'historical bloc' or 'war of position' provide relevant conceptual resources to illuminate ongoing struggles and changes. 'War of position' becomes a central hegemonic strategy as sheer economic strength or political contacts are usually not sufficient to preserve or challenge the power of social actors such as international firms. As Levy and Egan (2003: 810) state: 'Actors seek to build coalitions of firms, governmental agencies, NGOs, and intellectuals who can establish policies, norms and institutions that structure the field in particular and inherently precarious ways.'

In addition to neo-Gramscian approaches, a growing literature in CMS has taken up the ideas of Laclau and Mouffe. For example, Spicer and Böhm (2007) deploy the concepts of Laclau and Mouffe to illustrate how diverse social movements challenge the hegemony of management in the form of a collective but heterogeneous counter-hegemonic struggle. The expansion of managers and managerial ideology throughout the business world, and penetrating deep into everyday life, is conceived as the result of a particular social force aspiring to universal status. Managerial hegemony aims at providing solutions for the entire ensemble of social relations. This, however, can never be fully achieved as it cannot escape its particularity and associated limits. Managerialism provokes multiple forms of protest and contestation in the workplace and civil society alike. The resistance of social agents – unions, pressure groups, NGOs, activists, employees and so forth – is theorised as elements of a more or less associated counter-hegemonic struggle that is propelled not by underlying economic or structural forces but, rather, by common, antagonistic opposition to the hegemony of management.

Other applications of the concept of hegemony to CMS include analyses of corporate culture, organisational storytelling, management education, manufacturing, marketing and development, resistance including infrapolitical forms of resistance, intra-organisational power struggles, and institutional entrepreneurship.

FURTHER READING

A seminal study worthy of further exploration is Burawoy's (1979) *Manufacturing Consent*, which could be read alongside more recent contributions such as Levy (2008), Collinson (1992) and Spicer and Böhm (2007).

See also: *Critical Realism, Discourse, Ideology, Marxism and Post-Marxism, Political Economy, Poststructuralism, Power*

REFERENCES

Burawoy, M. (1979) *Manufacturing Consent: Changes in Labour Process and Capitalism*. Chicago: University of Chicago Press.

Collinson, D. (1992) *Managing the Shop Floor: Subjectivity, Masculinity and Workplace Culture*. Berlin: de Gruyter.

Delbridge, R. (2007) 'Explaining Conflicted Collaboration: A Critical Realist Approach to Hegemony', *Organization Studies* 28(9): 1347–57.

Gramsci, A. (1971) *Selections from the Prison Notebooks*. London: Lawrence & Wishart.

Hall, S. (1988) *The Hard Road to Renewal: Thatcherism and the Crisis of the Left*. London: verso.

Joseph, J. (2002) *Hegemony: A Realist Analysis*. London: Routledge.

Laclau, E. and Mouffe, C. (2001) *Hegemony and Socialist Strategy*. London: Verso.

Levy, D.L. (2008) 'Political Contestation in Global Production Networks', *Academy of Management Review* 33(4): 943–63.

Mumby, D. (1997) 'The Problem of Hegemony: Rereading Gramsci for Organizational Communication Studies. *Western Journal of Communication* 61(4): 343–375.

Spicer, A. and Böhm, S. (2007) 'Moving Management: Theorizing Struggles against the Hegemony of Management', *Organization Studies* 28(11): 1667–98.

key concepts in
critical management studies

Hermeneutics

John O'Shaughnessy

Definition: A term derived from the Greek *hermeneia* for 'interpretation', it has become an umbrella term for all interpretive approaches to social science.

Historically, the importance of hermeneutics was highlighted at the time of the European Reformation when Protestants rejected the exclusivity of using tradition for the interpretation of the scriptures. While called the 'art of interpretation' by Friedrich Schleiermacher and the 'art or technique of understanding and interpretation' by Hans-Georg Gadamer, the term has been expanded beyond studies of rhetoric and scripture to treating potentially everything as a *text* for hermeneutic study, so even science could be viewed as studying the text of nature.

A systematic interpretation of a text requires both identifying its sense-meaning as well as trying to gauge its referential-meaning, or the aspect of reality to which it refers. It was once thought that hermeneutics could, like the natural sciences, be an objective search for truth, but no longer. What distinguishes interpretation from deductive inference is that interpretation always involves some conjecture. While some interpretations are better than others, in the sense that they make most sense and account for more of the relevant 'facts' with the minimum of conjecture, there can be no one final interpretation.

As to hermeneutic methods, it was Friedrich Schleiermacher (1768–1834) who developed the concept of the *hermeneutic circle* in which the parts of the text are interpreted in reference to the whole and the whole understood by reference to the parts. On the question of where to start in the circle, Schleiermacher argued the problem is resolved intuitively, leaping into the circle, moving from the parts to the whole and the whole to the parts. Schleiermacher expanded the concept of hermeneutics by adding a psychological dimension to hermeneutic interpretation. This was his psychological claim that understanding a written text

hermeneutics

135

requires putting oneself in the mind of the author, justified on the ground that there is 'a little of everyone in all of us'. Later in the century Wilhelm Dilthey (1833–1911) viewed history as a text to be deciphered and used hermeneutics for his own study of history, claiming the social sciences cannot use the same methods as the natural sciences but need to employ understanding (in German, *verstehen*). Still later Max Weber (1864–1920), the German sociologist, was to describe hermeneutics and *verstehen* (empathy, in the sense of 'putting oneself in the other's shoes') as distinctive approaches to the social sciences.

Martin Heidegger (1889–1976), the German philosopher, moved away from any concern with psychology to grounding every text in the question of the meaning of 'being in the world' whose very strangeness cries out for interpretation. Heidegger argued that the hermeneutic circle was not something solved by any intuitive leap in the circle but as interplay between the traditions reflected in the text and the interpreter.

Heidegger's reformulation of the hermeneutic circle led Hans-Georg Gadamer (1900–2002), his former student, to argue that everyone enters the hermeneutic process with prejudices. As Gadamer says, the mind is not a *tabula rasa*, a clean slate that records all experiences without distortion. He rejects the claim that prejudices are necessarily negative. The belief that this is so has prevented us from seeing that understanding always involves pre-judgement or 'prejudice'. It could be argued then that there are legitimate 'prejudices' based on the recognition of authority, a form of which is tradition. The notion of bringing an existing standpoint to our going about a study or how we interpret findings, echoes 'perspectivism' that argues that every study is carried out through the conceptual lens provided by some perspective.

Gadamer is the major figure in twentieth-century hermeneutics, a position established by his *Truth and Method* (1960). Gadamer claims the interpreter's own slant on a tradition (perspective) is part of the interpreter's 'horizon' that is set against the different 'horizon' of the text. What was needed was a fusion of horizons. In other words, there was a need to fuse the two different perspectives, leading to a more open perspective. This process of fusing perspectives or horizons is never final, even if there is sufficient closure to proceed. But this fusing is confusing if it suggests the two horizons should become a single unity, as this is not what Gadamer has in mind. He realises tension will remain when the horizons (perspectives) are very different. For Gadamer it is not sufficient to master meanings-in-use in respect to the concepts of an alien culture. The real need is for enlightenment into the culture by fusing its concepts with one's own way of thinking. The resulting inter-play of the person's own perspective and the other perspective is what gives depth of understanding.

The notion that a legitimate prejudice could be based on tradition is disputed by Jürgen Habermas (1981) and supporters of 'critical theory'. Habermas agrees about the usefulness of Gadamer's hermeneutics for the humanities but argues that linking legitimacy and tradition together downplays the way tradition can be a source of power that distorts processes of communication. Drawing on the perspective of psychoanalysis, Habermas drew up a sketch for what he called a 'depth-hermeneutical' discipline where the focus returned to the text, without talk of belonging to a tradition.

Paul Ricoeur (1981) takes a different view of the function of hermeneutics in arguing that it should be concerned with uncovering what is *not* said rather than being focused on the recovery of meanings. This is what Ricoeur calls the 'hermeneutics of suspicion' which has roots in Nietzsche, Marx and Freud and where the goal is to 'liberate' by unmasking the hidden meanings that underpin social and legal practices. The hermeneutics of suspicion can be viewed as an attack on the belief in objective truth, since claims to objective truth can be fronts for vested interests.

Hermeneutics has had an impact on the social sciences, and for Clifford Geertz (1973), the anthropologist, it is central to ethnographic interpretation and to understanding the modes of thought of people in another culture. He talks about doing ethnography as analogous to reading a faded manuscript in the foreign language, full of ambiguities and vagueness that leads to complications. The influence of hermeneutics on studies of organisations is not direct, but it is one of the currents of thought that has shaped contemporary work in interactionist, social constructionist and interpretivist studies, in particular those that rely on ethnographic and qualitative approaches.

FURTHER READING

The interested student should begin with one of the more detailed over-views of hermeneutics and critical hermeneutics in the management literature. Prasad (2002) is a good starting point, as is Phillips and Brown (1993). For an application of critical hermeneutics, see Prasad and Mir (2002).

See also: Critical Theory, Ideology, Reflexivity, Subjectivity and Subjectivation

hermeneutics

REFERENCES

Gadamer, H.-G. (1960/1975) *Truth* and *Method*. London: Continuum.

Geertz, C. (1973) *The Interpretation of Cultures*. New York: Basic Books.

Habermas, J. (1981) *The Theory of Communicative Action*, vol. 1. Boston: Beacon Press.

Phillips, N. and Brown, J.L. (1993) 'Analyzing Communication in and Around Organizations: A Critical Hermeneutic Approach', *Academy of Management Journal* 36(6): 1547–76.

Prasad, A. (2002) 'The Contest Over Meaning: Hermeneutics as an Interpretive Methodology for Understanding Texts', *Organizational Research Methods* 5(1): 12–33.

Prasad, A. and Mir, R. (2002) 'Digging Deep for Meaning: A Critical Hermeneutic Analysis of CEO Letters to Shareholders in the Oil Industry', *Journal of Business Communication* 39(1): 92–116.

Ricoeur, P. (1981) *Hermeneutics and the Human Sciences: Essays on Language, Action and Interpretation*, ed. and trans. J.B. Thompson. Cambridge: Cambridge University Press.

Identity

Rolland Munro

> **Definition:** Meaning literally 'the same' (as in identical), the term customarily refers to characteristics that mark off a particular group as a *collective*.

Identity has moved from the lexicon of social scientists into a fashionable everyday trope. Wider use tends to 'individuate' identity, so that in everyday discourse it has also come to stand not only for our belonging to groups, but also for what makes each of us distinctive and unique. All this results in a wide range of social, political and psychological registers (see Wetherall, 2010), only some of which are covered in this discussion.

Anthropologically, the notion of identity emphasises what is at stake is the arts of living and working. Straddling political, economic and cultural mores, forms of *collective identity* thus index technologies as well as territories. Identities draw on differences in rituals and customs, as much as they pick up on exchanges of goods common to specific social groupings. In the UK, for instance, the ways of country people are held to be distinct from 'townies'.

Sociologically, identity is analysed in its collective forms of division, typically denoted by class, ethnicity, gender and age. Attempts to classify people in this manner may be overly general, but this is to miss the links that exist within collectives between identity and power. In the tradition of conflict sociology, people are granted agency as a result of their representing the *struggles* for domination and legitimation. Someone without identity has nothing to struggle for – or against; and in consequence has no place in the world.

Politically, identity is indicative of division within social orders. From civil rights movements in the US onwards, attention has focused increasingly on what is called *identity politics*. Typically this is where people forming a minority come together with a programme to insist on their rights to be treated equally with those making up the majority. Where identity politics departs significantly from earlier forms of collective identity is its demand for recognition on the very grounds on which recognition previously was denied: it is *as* women, *as* blacks, *as* pensioners that groups demand recognition. Respect and dignity are called for on the basis of difference, rather than our being the same.

In this way identity is closely tied to feelings of *belonging*. This raises issues of organisation and power. Specifically, where people share feelings of belonging, they have the potential to act in concert or unison. This may happen as much from sharing mutual interests and understandings, organic forms of solidarity, as from ingrained habit and custom, mechanical forms. After the influential Hawthorne studies, the theme of *group identity* was very prominent.

As has often been pointed out, however, identity is often more potent in giving people a sense of what they stand against, rather than what they are for. Inasmuch as what binds is having a common enemy, 'identity groups' are thus associated with notions of resistance. In particular the Chicago School studies of the 1930s and 1950s identified distinctive mores arising in different institutions, with the police or hospital doctors and nurses. Over the second half of the last century, however, many business firms shifted their attention from groups and co-opted in their

identity

place discourses of culture and identity. Differences between distinct 'groups' have likewise tended to be examined in terms of subcultures (e.g. Parker, 2000).

That identity is a hot topic today is partly a result of this organisation turn to culture. Visions of unity, however, prove elusive in practice. No doubt this is in part due to business corporations mainly seeking to exploit notions of identity in the workplace for profit. Indeed, negatively, many corporate agendas seem aimed at eroding feelings of belonging, often replacing group identities with notions of 'teams'. Where the focus is on installing forms of *corporate identity* (e.g. Kunda, 1992), attempts to 'change culture' typically undermine indigenous forms of solidarity in favour of an individuated sense of 'responsibility'.

In all this, the notion of identity has long been associated with *place*. People are accorded identity first by their place of work, or their place of origin. Then secondly by the 'place' each occupies within a status category, or other form of hierarchy. Identities thus come to matter most when someone is deemed to be 'out of place'. For example, the figure of the stranger is the subject of a community's fears and curiosity. The village fool is given their tag as someone who cannot easily conform to local mores. A 'dinosaur' is someone who resists progress as seen by the eyes of managers. And those with upward social mobility might be accused, even today, of 'moving in circles above their station'.

In a double sense of place, talk of identity also focuses on how someone can be 'placed'. For everyday purposes, identity is *individuated* largely through a marking of difference. As such, orderings of identity are every bit as tied to the 'locutions' of daily interaction as they are bounded by its locations. Whenever the 'accounts' that people give also become part of the mundane conflict, or struggle 'taking place' in everyday interactions, there are winners or losers to be found. Questions of identity should thus not be understood simply in terms of 'Who is she to me?' They can be framed, instead, if momentarily, in terms of 'Whose side is she on?'

This individuation in the 'turn' to identity should not surprise. The major trope that governs thinking on identity, I suggest, has mutated somewhat from 'place' to 'face'. Erving Goffman draws attention to what he calls *facework*; such as broadening one's smile on greeting someone, or timing a wave when passing in the street. His studies of 'front' and his distinction between 'frontstage' and 'backstage' are seminal here. Goffman's (1959) writings on 'impression management', however, are much more subtle than is usually noted and emphasise the constraints of the 'neglected situation'. The nub of *The Presentation of Self in*

Everyday Life is to show how minutely custom and ritual are open to calculation and manipulation. Indeed, it is just this emphasis on institutions that distinguishes Goffman's work from neoliberal ideologies that make identity out to be a matter of choice.

Identity is granted by others. As such, identity has to be *reflexive* to institutions – 'ways of doing' that are conceived broadly in terms of precedent and custom. Otherwise one may not 'pass' whatever forms of social surveillance are in place. For these reasons, what is at stake over identity is often transient. This work of 'situating' persons – deeming their facework to be 'in place' or 'out of place' – is also more intricate wherever interactions are swift and numerous. This said, as is often the case in the workplace and in city life, questions of identity may intensify even where the encounter is 'thin'. As much as relations and relationships may appear liquid (Bauman, 2004) when people are on the move, socially and geographically, there are no *rights* of passage.

In all this, notions of place or face are complex ideas since they commonly refer less to matters of fact and reflect more the 'interpretive' nature of interaction. And this again is why identity matters. For example, not everyone who 'loses their place' – say when talking – also 'loses face'. In what is commonly referred to as *identity work*, figuring people out becomes not so much a matter of knowledge *per se*, but more an ongoing process of our 'readings' of identity: a matter of picking up on, and running with, the cues and clues people offer as they conduct themselves at work or set about their daily tasks (cf. Knights and Willmott, 1999).

An influential take on identity relates it to the possession of goods, displays of *belongings* rather than feelings of belonging. In the process known as 'commodity fetishism' Marx identifies a fantastic reversal of reality, wherein what he takes to be the real nature of society is obscured as human beings confront each other as possessors of commodities as well as agents of economic entities. Where human beings are dominated by their products and compelled by the power commodities have over them, identity is open to what is called the 'tactics of consumption'. More recently, Mary Douglas has argued persuasively how identity is communicated through consumption, the purchase of a good acting as a display of one's belonging to this culture rather than that (Douglas and Isherwood, 1979).

Inasmuch as artefacts display identity, it seems that people's worlds are *motile* to their social construction. Taking belongings into consideration as 'prosthetic extensions', it is possible to rethink identity more radically in terms of cultural performance (Munro, 1999). Although much scholarly

identity

attention has fixed on stable identities, what is striking is the suddenness with which identities can be altered or changed from moment to moment. This is not the same as 'multiple identities'; the ruthless businessman by day becoming the loving father by night, and so on. Although the issues are complex, the idea of multiple identities implies too rigid a link between identity and role; as if, in order to change face, persons also had to change place. A moment's thought suggests this need not be so. Where identity and world move together, then what is 'taking place' can vary, even radically, at ostensibly the same place.

Identity work might be more provisional and ongoing than earlier stories of origins indicate. It is always what is 'taking place' that matters. And this is what opens up identity to interpretation. An encounter soon transcends the physical place as the site in which the social drama is happening. This fact led me to theorise identity as that which is being *punctualised* in the here and now (see Munro, 2004), rather than something permanently in place. In other words the scholarly Rolland Munro appears when responding to the Editors' call to write this piece. Concomitantly, he is not the same animal when attending a cricket match. We often talk about people wanting different things from us, but more often than not it is one very specific identity, rather than another, that we are being 'called' upon to perform and make present on time, every time.

In summary, against being left in the hands of others, readings of identity are guided by a 'tactics of consumption' as much as by the manipulation of custom and practice. What is called identity work thus moves between a concern to mark someone out as belonging to this or that grouping and the performances associated with self and a quest for personhood. Identity can thus focus either on the demographics of origin, a biographical register of where someone comes from and what she or he has done, or more dubiously on what might be called the democratics of choice, a palimpsest of that person's aspirations and interests. What must be stressed, nonetheless, is both forms of identity work 'take place' as social dramas within everyday interactions and are intricately tied to larger struggles for identity and power.

FURTHER READING

Goffman's (1959) *The Presentation of Self in Everyday Life* is a seminal text. Martin Parker's (2000) *Organizational Culture and Identity: Unity and Division at Work* provides a good overview of identity issues in relation to organisational life and is particularly useful for critical management scholars. The Sage Handbook of Identities offers a wide set of perspectives.

See also: *Accountability, Power, Subjectivity and Subjectivation*

REFERENCES

Bauman, Z. (2004) *Identity: Conversations with Benedetto Vecchi. Cambridge*: Polity Press.

Douglas, M. and Isherwood, B. (1979) *The World of Goods: Towards an Anthropology of Consumption*. New York: Basic Books.

Goffman, E. (1959) *The Presentation of Self in Everyday Life*. London: Penguin.

Knights, D. and Willmott, H. (1999) *Management Lives: Power and Identity in Work Organizations*. London: Sage.

Kunda, G. (1992) *Engineering Culture*. Philadelphia: Temple University Press.

Munro, R. (1999) 'The Cultural Performance of Control', *Organization Studies* 20(4): 619–39.

Munro, R. (2004) 'Punctualising Identity: Time and the Demanding Relation', *Sociology* 38(2): 293–311.

Parker, M. (2000) *Organizational Culture and Identity: Unity and Division at Work*. London: Sage.

Wetherall, M. (2010) 'The Field of Identity Studies', in Wetherall and C.T. Mohanty (eds) *The Sage Handbook of Identities*, pp. 3–26. London: Sage.

Ideology

Armin Beverungen

Definition: To speak of ideology is to inquire into the relation between material reality and ideas, and to consider how particular discourses, forms of consciousness or practices might serve power.

The concept of ideology has a long history, dating back to the eighteenth century and the writings of Destutt de Tracy, but its theoretical importance is based on its development in the work of Karl Marx (see Balibar, 1995). While we can find many contradictory definitions of ideology in Marx's work, the one most frequently used is that associated with a dominant ideology, that is, the notion that the ideas of the ruling classes lend intellectual support to their material dominance and perpetuate the alienated existence of the ruled classes. In this iteration, the task of ideology critique was to unmask the functions of such dominant ideas, and a Marxist science was to offer an alternative representation of society. The concept of ideology has subsequently been widely used. Central to its early history are the writings of Georg Lukács, who emphasised the importance of Marx's concept of commodity fetishism as ideology and developed a theory of the consciousness of the proletariat. Equally important is the work of Antonio Gramsci, who was preoccupied with the role of intellectuals and the production of hegemony (see Eagleton, 2007: ch. 4). Perhaps the most famous critique of the concept of ideology is that offered by Foucault, who proposed to replace a (Marxist) study of the economics of untruth with a study of the politics of truth. Foucault (1976/2000: 119) suggests that the notion of ideology 'cannot be used without circumspection', because it relies on an opposition of truth and falsity, necessarily refers to a subject as its originator, and depends on a crude base–superstructure model. Drawing loosely on Foucault, discourse analysis consequently positioned itself largely against ideology critique, and abandoned a truth/falsity distinction, avoided reference to a subject purposefully producing discourse, and refused to see discourse as an epiphenomenon of economic relations.

By the 1970s the 'end of ideology' had been declared, together with the death of Marxism, and by the 1990s history was also said to have ended. Theoretically, the concept of ideology had been widely rejected and replaced by concepts of discourse. However, the abandonment of the concept of ideology turned out to be premature, as history was far from over, and Francis Fukuyama's neoliberalism turned out to be yet another ideology prevalent in the early twenty-first century, accompanied in different quarters by a resurgence of religious extremism. Theoretically, Žižek (1994: 17) was not the only one to point out that to claim to be outside or beyond ideology is an ideological move *par excellence* – a trap many had fallen into. Still, for Žižek, it is equally dangerous to claim that everything is ideological, since this renders the concept of ideology useless. It remains vital for ideology critique to insist again and again on the possibility of a space outside ideology, an empty space whose boundaries must be continuously redrawn.

In response to this history and the critiques of the concept of ideology it underwent a variety of reformulations. Žižek (1994: 7–15) proposes to organise various notions of ideology around three axes: 'ideology as a complex of ideas', 'ideology in its externality, that is, the materiality of ideology', and 'the most elusive domain, the "spontaneous" ideology at work at the heart of social "reality" itself'. The first notion, that of ideology as mostly a phenomenon of ideality, is still the most prevalent but also the most crude conception of ideology – one that is often the target of reductive critiques which accuse anyone speaking of ideology of believing that 'the masses' are simply 'duped', or that to speak of ideology one assumes that there is 'false consciousness' opposed to a right one. Purporting to move away from such an idealist conception of ideology, Louis Althusser (1970/2001) developed the concept of 'ideological state apparatuses' to emphasise the materiality of ideology. There ideology is understood to be first and foremost a question of material practices, with Althusser referring to Pascal's statement 'Kneel down, move your lips in prayer, and you will believe' (1970/2001: 114) to indicate that we must look for ideology not merely in the mind, but rather in the body. Although Althusser's analysis bears resemblance to Foucault's work on discipline and biopower, Althusser places the question of subjection through ideology squarely within a problematic of the reproduction of capital, with the state as main actor of such subjection. Finally, the third notion of ideology, that of a spontaneous ideology, Žižek associates most clearly with Marx's and Lukács' work on commodity fetishism, where commodity fetishism is understood as the spontaneous ideology of the market, where the reality of exchange is structured by something ideal ascribed to the commodity, i.e. 'value'. Žižek's own work contributes a psychoanalytic conception to this third notion of ideology, focusing on how cynicism is a contemporary form of ideology that leaves the workings of capitalism intact.

While early work in critical management studies, by Mats Alvesson, Peter Anthony and Dennis Mumby among others, drew extensively on the concept of ideology, the turn to Foucault precipitated a rejection of it. Nonetheless, many different concepts of ideology are present in CMS. An early example is Willmott's (1993) study of culture management, where he draws on a classic concept of ideology as distortion in George Orwell's *1984* to explore how the language of culture management systematically distorts its actual practices and effects, specifically by denying the autonomy it purports to promote. Parker (2002) provides perhaps the starkest plea for an ideology critique, of what he calls market managerialism, the 'generalized ideology of management' (Parker, 2002: 10). While Parker does not specify the concept of ideology in use, he draws widely on conceptions of ideology as the ideas of the ruling classes, in this case the managerial classes, characterises market managerialism as hegemony, and suggests that this ideology functions primarily by limiting our imagination of what organisation could be. Ideology critique here becomes a hegemonic struggle over ideas of organisation. An example of work drawing on psychoanalysis and focusing specifically on the affective aspects of ideology, i.e. on the way ideology relies on emotional attachment, is Fleming and Spicer's (2003) article on working at a cynical distance. Drawing on the work of Peter Sloterdijk and Žižek, they argue that cynicism is a particular form of dis-identification from ideology that nonetheless can be understood as a predominant form of ideology today, in that this dis-identification has no effect: work is still performed to the expected standards and beyond. The biggest task for CMS is perhaps to challenge what Mark Fisher (2009), drawing on Fredric Jameson and Žižek, calls 'capitalist realism': the contemporary ideology that means we cannot imagine the end of capitalism – an ideology also visible in the business school.

FURTHER READING

Eagleton (2007) provides an excellent history of the concept of ideology. Žižek (1994) contains key contributions to this history. Parker (2002) provides a current example of ideology critique in critical management studies.

See also: Commodity Fetishism, Marxism and Post-Marxism, Subjectivity and Subjectivation

key concepts in

critical management studies

146

REFERENCES

Althusser, L. (1970/2001) 'Ideology and Ideological State Apparatuses', in *Lenin and Philosophy and Other Essays*, pp. 85–126. New York: Monthly Review Press.
Balibar, E. (1995) 'Ideology or Fetishism: Power and Subjection', in *The Philosophy of Marx*, pp. 42–79. London: Verso.
Eagleton, T. (2007) *Ideology: An Introduction*. London: Verso.

Fleming, P. and Spicer, A. (2003) 'Working at a Cynical Distance: Implications for Power, Subjectivity and Resistance', *Organization* 10(1): 157–79.

Fisher, M. (2009) *Capitalist Realism: Is There No Alternative?* London: Zero Books.

Foucault, M. (1976/2000) 'Truth and Power', in J.D. Faubion (ed.) *Michel Foucault: Power (Essential Works of Foucault 1954–1984, Volume 3)*, pp. 111–33. London: Penguin Books.

Parker, M. (2002) *Against Management*. Cambridge: Polity Press.

Willmott, H. (1993) 'Strength is Ignorance; Slavery is Freedom: Managing Culture in Modern Organizations', *Journal of Management Studies* 30(4): 515–52.

Žižek, S. (ed.) (1994) *Mapping Ideology*. London: Verso.

Immaterial Labour

Armin Beverungen

Definition: Immaterial labour is a concept developed to account for the new figures of labour emerging in contemporary capitalism.

(Post)Workerism is a variant of Marxism emerging out of Italy. One of its features is the aim of identifying historical periods not by characterising different capitalist modes of production but instead by tracing different figures of labour, since it is labour and its resistance that is seen to be prior to capital and its control. Where earlier workerists theoretically explored the figure of the 'mass worker' that emerged with Fordism (circa 1920s), postworkerists have attempted to comprehend changes in the nature of labour since. Some schools of thought, such as the Regulation School in France, call the epoch commencing in the 1970s 'post-Fordist' to describe how production is no longer predicated upon mass production and mass consumption but is instead characterised by technological innovation, flexible manufacturing and niche marketing. Where Antonio Negri first identified the new subject at work in post-Fordism as the 'socialized worker' – a worker for whom communication and knowledge are central to work – he later developed the concept of immaterial labour together with Michael Hardt, Maurizio Lazzarato, Paolo Virno and others (Virno and Hardt, 1996). While it traces developments that are usually understood in critical management studies through concepts such as 'knowledge work' and 'emotional labour', for theorists thinking about the changes in production and marketing the concept of 'immaterial labour' has become extremely important. It marks an attempt to develop a Marxist vocabulary that accounts for these phenomena.

Lazzarato defines immaterial labour as 'the labour that produces the informational and cultural content of the commodity' (1996: 133); Hardt and Negri define it as 'labour that produces an immaterial good, such as a service, a cultural product, knowledge, or communication' (2000: 290). The types of skills involved in this labour are primarily intellectual (producing culture and information), manual (combining creativity and imagination), as well as entrepreneurial and managerial (managing social relations) (Lazzarato, 1996: 137–8). There has also been an increasing focus on the affective qualities of immaterial labour (see Dowling et al., 2007), that is, on the way in which this work engages not merely cognitive but also emotional capacities. This labour of communication, knowledge and affect requires new forms of organisation, such as networks (Lazzarato, 1996: 137; Hardt and Negri, 2000: 294), and its emergence coincidences with new forms of technology, in particular information and communication technologies. Where the technologies of Fordism, such as the assembly line, were particularly restrictive for labour, often limiting its ability to socialise and to communicate, in immaterial labour they are more amenable to labour and support its sociality – the technical and social organisation of immaterial labour coincide (Hardt and Negri, 2000: 113). Overall, immaterial labour challenges our conceptions of the types of skills, technologies and forms of organisation operating in a capitalism preoccupied with the immaterial aspects of its products and services.

Immaterial labour is an expansive concept; it does not simply describe a particular sector or an occupational group, even if it is partly conceptually derived from work in the cultural industries, marketing and advertising, the service sector or the internet economy. Hardt and Negri suggest that information technologies have led to a homogenisation of labour processes and that this has reduced their heterogeneity, with all kinds of labour increasingly resembling each other, and immaterial labour becoming hegemonic (2000: 292). Hardt and Negri identify three varieties of immaterial labour: industrial production where the labour process has been transformed by information and communication technologies; analytical, symbolic, and routine symbolic tasks; and the production and manipulation of affect (Hardt and Negri, 2000: 293). Thus, immaterial labour attempts to describe the farmer trained in advanced biochemistry, and the nurse providing emotional support to patients, as much as the banker constantly staring at numbers on screens and the philosophy student working part time for an advertising agency. But immaterial labour does not just seek to describe the new realities of work, it provides an analytic of such work that emphasises 'the technical and subjective-political composition of the working class' (Lazzarato, 1996: 133).

Three particular consequences stand out. First, immaterial labour is said to be immediately collective: it is based on a social labour power independent of business (Lazzarato, 1996: 138), and social interaction and co-operation are immanent to it, not imposed from the outside (Hardt and Negri, 2000: 294). Where in Fordism capital and management were needed to organise the production line, in immaterial labour – with knowledge being shared, communication easy to achieve, and affect a personal capacity – neither capital nor management are needed to organise production. Harney (2005) claims that this explains why management is a cliché: since labour is always already organised by itself, management can only ever seek to copy these independent forms of organisation and therefore is an intellectual parasite. The consequence of this is that labour is potentially autonomous and able to valorise itself, i.e. able to produce value for itself, all by itself. For Hardt and Negri, immaterial labour even 'seems to provide the potential for a kind of spontaneous and elementary communism' (2000: 294). Another term postworkerists use to explain this state of affairs is that of 'general intellect', which captures the idea that today knowledge and information are held in common and shared, with everyone potentially able to draw on them to increase their labouring capacities.

Second, this general intellect means that a transformation has taken place in the nature of labour-power. Where previously labour-power was primarily defined through physical rather than mental capabilities, now 'it encompasses within itself, and rightfully so, the "life of the mind"', Virno (2004: 81) claims. Where previously capital might only have been interested in how well a worker can use a tool or serve a machine, today it is increasingly interested in minds – not only in what knowledge or information they contain, but also in what they desire or imagine. This

immaterial labour

149

explains the emphasis on control through the formation of particular types of subjectivity in contemporary labour processes and beyond (Lazzarato, 1996: 134–5; Virno, 2004: 84–5): labour must be disciplined but it must also be actively and positively involved in production, so capital tries to 'manage culture' and workers must become 'entrepreneurs'. Yet, and this is the third consequence, subjectivity is not simply important for control, as Michael Burawoy already taught us. Instead, subjectivity is put to work 'both in the activation of productive cooperation and in the production of the "cultural" contents of commodities' (Lazzarato, 1996: 143). It is only because labour invests its desires and fantasies in production that capital knows what it has to produce and how.

The reception of the concept of immaterial labour in critical management studies has been mixed. Thompson (2005) suggests that it has little to offer to labour process theory, since the way it understands contemporary labour is unrealistic and conceptually confused, but others were more forthcoming. In contrast, Harney (2006) suggests that we should consider the optimism that the thesis entails, allowing us to imagine different, more social forms of work and organisation, and he proposes a socialist programme for immaterial labour, one which would help in a political struggle to establish new realities of work. Elsewhere, Shukaitis (2009) starts from the immaterial labour thesis to explore the 'imaginal machines' that bring forth new forms of autonomy and self-organisation in everyday life, proposing that it is to the struggles taking place around immaterial labour that we can look to rediscover our imagination. Such affirmative engagements with the concept of immaterial labour, as well as related debates around the general intellect and cognitive capitalism, will occupy critical management studies in the future.

FURTHER READING

Key early writings from the journal *Futur Antérieur*, in which the immaterial labour thesis was developed, are available in Virno and Hardt (1996). Vital discussions are presented in a special issue of *ephemera* (Dowling et al., 2007) and a research stream on cognitive capitalism, immaterial labour and the general intellect in the journal *Historical Materialism* (see Toscano, 2007).

See also: Capitalism and Anticapitalism, Labour Process Theory, Marxism and Post-Marxism, Subjectivity and Subjectivation

REFERENCES

Dowling, E., Nunes, R. and Trott, B. (2007) 'Immaterial and Affective Labour: Explored', *ephemera: theory & politics in organization* 7(1): 1–7.

Hardt, M. and Negri, A. (2000) *Empire*. Cambridge, MA: Harvard University Press.

Harney, S. (2005) 'Why is Management a Cliché?', *Critical Perspectives on Accounting* 16(5): 579–91.

Harney, S. (2006) 'Programming Immaterial Labour', *Social Semiotics* 16(1): 75–87.

Lazzarato, M. (1996) 'Immaterial Labor', in P. Virno and M. Hardt (eds) *Radical Thought in Italy: A Potential Politics*, pp.133–49. Minneapolis: University of Minnesota Press.

Shukaitis, S. (2009) *Imaginal Machines: Autonomy & Self-Organization in the Revolutions of Everyday Life*. New York/London: Autonomedia/Minor Compositions.

Thompson, P. (2005) 'Foundation and Empire: A Critique of Hardt and Negri', *Capital & Class* 29(2): 73–98.

Toscano, A. (2007) 'From Pin Factories to Gold Farmers: Editorial Introduction to a Research Stream on Cognitive Capitalism, Immaterial Labour, and the General Intellect', *Historical Materialism* 15(1): 3–11.

Virno, P. (2004) *A Grammar of the Multitude*. New York: Semiotext(e).

Virno, P. and Hardt, M. (eds) (1996) *Radical Thought in Italy: A Potential Politics*. Minneapolis: University of Minnesota Press.

Labour Process Theory

Armin Beverungen

> **Definition:** Labour process theory is an approach to the historical and contemporary study of work under capitalism emanating from Marx.

The first book of Karl Marx's *Capital: A Critique of Political Economy* deals with the process of the production of capital. Marx discovers that commodities apparently possess a certain value. This value of commodities, however, is not produced in the sphere of circulation where commodities are endlessly exchanged. Consequently capital is also not produced in this sphere, since any increase in value is merely accidental, and no capitalist can bank on the endless exchange of commodities to increase his or her monetary wealth. The capitalist, to become more than simply a money-owner, must find ways of producing value. The capitalist discovers a peculiar commodity that is capable of producing value: labour-power.

Marx defines labour-power as 'the aggregate of those mental and physical capabilities existing in the physical form, the living personality, of a human being, capabilities which he sets in motion whenever he produces a use-value of any kind' (1976: 270). What makes this commodity special is that its consumption potentially yields value. The use-value of labour-power is labour, and in order to benefit from this use-value the capitalist must put this commodity to work – the owner of this labour-power, the worker, must be made to produce. Here we enter the 'hidden abode of production, on whose threshold hangs the notice "No admittance except on business"' (1976: 279–80). And, with leaving the sphere of circulation, we also note a change in the relations between people: in the sphere of production, relations are decidedly unequal, with the worker now following the capitalist 'like someone who has brought his own hide to market and now has nothing else to expect but – a tanning' (1976: 280).

What follows in *Capital* is Marx's conceptual and historical exploration of the labour process under capitalism. Marx first asks us to 'consider the labour process independently of any specific social formation' (1976: 283), with the human using his or her natural powers to change nature and simultaneously his or her own nature. Marx further specifies that every labour process has three simple elements: purposeful activity, the object of work, and the instruments of work (1976: 284). At this primordial stage the labour process is still 'purposeful activity aimed at the production of use-values' only (1976: 290). It is only with the formal subsumption of the labour process under capital that it also becomes a process for the production of exchange-value and surplus-value. First the capitalist is restricted to producing absolute surplus-value, where work is simply extended or intensified. Here the labour process remains largely unchanged. It is only with real subsumption that relative surplus-value is produced and 'the entire real form of production is altered and a *specifically capitalist form of production* comes into being' (1976: 1024; emphasis in original), with new technology, new forms of organisation, and new relations of production between workers and capital.

Labour process theory is nothing more or less than the attempt to theorise the consequences of this subsumption of the labour process under capital, with the production process understood as a labour process which is at the same time a process for the production of commodities and of capital itself. After Marx's study of early capitalist forms of production in *Capital*, it was only with the publication of Harry Braverman's (1974/1998) *Labor and Monopoly Capital* that such a Marxist study of capitalist production was resuscitated. Braverman was particularly concerned with tracing the effects of Taylorism on work, which he considered important because it represented the 'explicit verbalization of the capitalist mode of production' (1974/1998: 60) and rendered 'conscious and systematic, the formerly unconscious tendency of capitalist production' (1974/1998: 83). Braverman famously characterised Taylorism as the degradation of work, where labour was divided between conception and execution, craft skill was destroyed, the worker was reduced to an automaton and management became practically omnipotent through its abuse of science.

Since for Braverman this degradation of work was seen to be an irrefutable feature of capitalist work in the middle of the twentieth century, much of the 'Bravermania' that followed was intent on assessing to what extent these trends could actually be said to be true. The historical and empirical work in the late 1970s and 1980s explored capitalist work in different industries, developing various typologies of control and maps of skill. A concern that gained particular importance at that time was the issue of subjectivity. Braverman had self-consciously limited his analysis to the '"objective" content of class' (1974/1998: 19), and for many commentators it suggested the complete destruction of the subjectivity of workers to be a necessary consequence of Taylorism. Against this Michael Burawoy's influential study in *Manufacturing Consent* (1979) demonstrated how the subjectivity of workers was not destroyed by work under capital, but enrolled to ensure the manufacture of consent on the shop floor.

When towards the end of the 1980s attempts were made to formalise labour process theory, it was the issue of subjectivity that took centre stage, with Paul Thompson arguing that the 'construction of a full theory of the *missing subject* is probably the greatest task facing labour process theory' (1990: 114; emphasis in original). While there was general agreement on the need for such a theory, it was this issue that was to destroy the unified project of labour process theory. The collection edited by David Knights and Hugh Willmott (1990) simply entitled *Labour Process Theory* was one of the last books in which many of the key writers were to be found together. With Knights and Willmott and others turning towards Foucault and other theorists to reflect on subjectivity, subsequently establishing critical management studies as a rival field to labour process theory, it was left to Thompson, Paul Edwards and Chris Smith among others to attempt to articulate a core for labour process theory (see Thompson, 1990; Thompson and Smith, 2010).

While this 'core theory' still took its cue from Marx's identification of labour-power as a peculiar commodity, it distanced itself consciously from Marx, claiming no longer to be Marxist (Thompson, 1990: 102). In particular, it rejected both Marx's theory of value and the commitment to social revolution based on class struggle. Consequently, 'core' labour process theory arguably has little in common with the analyses developed in Marx, Braverman and Burawoy, and struggled with explaining empirical descriptions of labour processes with reference to changes in capitalism. Where Braverman rejected a specific sociology of work for denying the objective conditions of capitalist work (1974/1998: 20), and where Burawoy warned against an organisation theory that ignored the capitalist character of modern work organisations (1979: 7), labour process theory in the 1990s largely seemed oblivious to such concerns.

The merits of labour process theory remain fundamentally contested. On the one hand, the 1990s saw a proliferation of empirical studies of labour processes, with a focus on diverse new topics such as knowledge management, emotion work and creative labour, and the project to fortify core theory continued while it opened itself up to more diverse approaches (see Thompson and Smith, 2010). On the other hand, labour process theory is deemed to have taken on many of the features of the labour processes it sought to criticise (O'Doherty, 2009), while innovative theorisations of contemporary capital and its labour processes is often to be found outside its realms (e.g. Berardi, 2009).

FURTHER READING

Chapter 7 of *Capital Volume 1* on 'The Labour Process and the Process of Valorization' (Marx, 1976: 283–306) is the starting point for a Marxist study of the labour process. Braverman's explorations in *Labor and Monopoly Capital* (1974/1998, esp. chs 4 and 5) are essential reading.

See also: Commodity Fetishism, Dialectics, Ideology, Immaterial Labour, Marxism and Post-Marxism, Subjectivity and Subjectivation

REFERENCES

Berardi, F. (2009) *The Soul at Work: From Alienation to Autonomy*. New York: Semiotext(e).

Braverman, H. (1974/1998) *Labor and Monopoly Capital: The Degradation of Work in the Twentieth Century*. New York: Monthly Review Press.

Burawoy, M. (1979) *Manufacturing Consent: Changes in the Labour Process under Monopoly Capitalism*. Chicago: University of Chicago Press.

Knights, D. and Willmott, H. (eds) (1990) *Labour Process Theory*. London: Macmillan.

Marx, K. (1976) *Capital: A Critique of Political Economy, Volume 1*, trans. B. Fowkes. London: Penguin.

O'Doherty, D. (2009) 'Revitalizing Labour Process Theory: A Prolegomenon to Fatal Writing', *Culture and Organization* 15(1): 1–19.

Thompson, P. (1990) 'Crawling from the Wreckage: The Labour Process and the Politics of Production', in D. Knights and H. Willmott (eds) *Labour Process Theory*. London: Macmillan.

Thompson, P. and Smith, C. (eds) (2010) *Working Life: Renewing Labour Process Analysis*. Basingstoke: Palgrave Macmillan.

Managerialism

Martin Parker

> **Definition:** Managerialism is the discourse or ideology which assumes the need for one occupational group to coordinate the aims and activities of organisations, usually in return for higher pay and status than their subordinates.

One of the most unexamined pieces of common sense is one of the most common – that ordinary people need to be managed by others. Since the rise of the large corporation, the university business school and the consultant, 'management' has been the subject of a huge public relations campaign. It is now often assumed, even after the financial crises of 2008, that MBA-trained managers will be able to understand the 'needs' of the market and convert them into an efficient and (in the private sector) profitable organisation. However, whilst it would be odd to assume that complex organisations do not need coordination, there is no logical reason why this needs to be done by a permanent cadre of individuals, or why these people should attract very markedly higher pay than other individuals performing essential labour for a large organisation.

Even if there is no logical reason, there are plenty of social reasons why management will claim to be indispensable. Like many other occupational groups, it is the interests of managers (and those who train them, sell them services and so on) to claim that what they do requires particularly rare expertise or personal qualities. If this claim is successful, then their reward and status is likely to be increased. In the case of management, added to this is their function as delegates or agents of the owners of capital, or of an increasingly marketised public sector. In both cases, using managers to naturalise the decisions forced by the 'bottom line' is an effective way of displacing the politics from organising in the name of a 'no alternative' economics. This is useful, when the claims of citizens, customers, employees, trade unions and social movements might be contesting the logic of an institutional decision. Managers can then claim that they had no choice, and the interests of the state or capitalist are effectively effaced.

The idea of a class of experts is not new, and can be found in much utopian politics, from Plato's *Republic* with its philosopher kings to H.G. Wells' 'voluntary nobility' in his *Modern Utopia*. Compared to the random cruelties of hereditary monarchy, the idea of a class of experts had strong egalitarian appeal, and could easily be articulated as a revolutionary development. In the early nineteenth-century writings of Saint Simon and Comte, the rise of a class of professional industrialists was seen as a development which would lead to a progressive reduction in inequalities of production and distribution. However, the rise of a managerial class in the twentieth century appears to have failed to meet these radical aspirations, instead solidifying into patterns of inherited privilege backed by certain sorts of knowledge claims about social progress.

First, it is assumed that progress is equivalent to our ability as human beings to increasingly control the natural world around us. Management is one of the ways in which we articulate this control over things by making them manageable, subject to the control of human beings. Secondly, management is also a way for human beings to be controlled. By using the various sciences of the human, management can develop human beings towards a more productive future. Third, management is also implicated in an account of the development of control strategies themselves. According to this account, the forms of social organisation that characterise early societies were autocratic and cruel so when the autocrat evolves into the responsible manager, the greatest good of the greatest number has been achieved.

I have used the word 'management' in a very general sense here. Indeed, it might be said that management is being conflated with modernity itself. But the very generality of management reflects a claim that this is a form of knowledge that can be made widely applicable across a huge variety of domains. Once it has been learnt, management can be applied anywhere, to anything and on anyone. The etymology of the word reflects this gradual expansion of its claims. It seems to be derived from the Italian *mano*, hand, and its expansion into *maneggiarre*, the activity of handling and training a horse carried out by *maneggio*. From this form of manual control, the word gets expanded into a general activity of training and handling people. The later development of the word is also influenced by the French *mener* (to lead) and its development into *ménage* – household, or housekeeping – and the verb *ménager* – to economise. So an intimate technology of the hand or of the household grows to become a technology of the workplace, and eventually of the state too. But it doesn't stop there because the later generalisation of the word also follows from its subsequent division into three meanings – a noun, a verb and an academic discipline.

First, management is the plural noun for 'manager'. We can describe them as an occupational group who have engaged in a very successful strategy of collective social mobility over a century or so. From a disparate collection of occupational nouns – owner, supervisor, superintendent, administrator, overman, foreman, clerk – this collective term has emerged that represents anyone engaged in the coordination of people and things. Whilst the historical effects of the division of labour have usually been to subdivide tasks, and their attached labels, this word is a successful attempt to undivide, to create a general term which covers many occupations. Whilst there might be qualifiers added to the noun (marketing manager, human resource manager) and there are other occupational terms that can be subsumed within management (accountant, director), the general category is one that would be recognised across most of the world, and in every sector of the economy. Through this merging, a new class of people is created. Perhaps not a class in the classical Marxist sense, though that might be worth investigating further, but certainly a class in the sense of concepts.

Second, the noun can also be translated into a verb. This is a verb that can be applied to the processes of ordering and controlling people and things. It implies a separation between the actual doing of whatever is being managed (engineering or teaching) and the higher-level function of control of these processes. In other words, management is not *about* engineering or teaching, but the coordination of the doing of these things. In some sense, management is constituted as a higher order of brain work which requires an elevation from mundane functions in order to gain a better perspective. Though management may be etymologically linked with the hand, it is no longer a practice that is 'hands-on'. In substantive terms, management usually refers to what managers do – marketing, strategy, finance and so on – but the word is spreading beyond such restrictive definitions. Thus there is increasing talk of the management of everything – children, sex lives, careers and so on. The division performed here is between managing something, which is good, and not-managing, which is bad. The not-managing usually gets less attention but seems to include both bad management (mismanagement) and no management, in other words both doing things badly and leaving things alone altogether. Both, it seems, can be repaired by better management.

Finally, this is also the name of university departments where people are paid to read, write and talk about what the management does and what management is, and sometimes talking to managers about what they do. This is certainly not a practice that can be isolated from the other two, simply because much of the output of this 'discipline' is shaped by, and in turn shapes, contemporary practices in both of the other areas. In the simplest of terms, political-economic problems of organisation are reduced to matters of human-systems engineering. Even when the intent is avowedly 'soft' or 'humanist', the subtext stresses the imperatives of managing and the necessity of control. This is one of the largest institutional legitimation and public relations campaigns in the history of thought, though it is rarely recognised as such. In that sense, even though it is developed in such departments, CMS would tend to be critical of managerialism. This is either hypocrisy or a productive tension, depending on how you look at it.

FURTHER READING

A good early history of management can be found in Jacques (1996). Whyte (1961), Braverman (1974), MacIntyre (1981) and Bauman (1989) have put forward well-known diagnoses of the problems with the manager–technocrat. Grey (1999) and Parker (2002, 2009) develop critiques of contemporary managerialism and Hancock and Tyler (2009) extend this into the managerialisation of everyday life.

See also: Alternative Organisation, Bureaucracy, Class, Corporation

REFERENCES

Bauman, Z. (1989) *Modernity and the Holocaust*. Oxford: Polity.

Braverman, H. (1974) *Labor and Monopoly Capital*. New York: Monthly Review Press.

Grey, C. (1999) '"We are All Managers Now"; "We Always Were": On the Development and Demise of Management', *Journal of Management Studies* 36(5): 561–85.

Hancock, P. and Tyler, M. (eds) (2009) *The Management of Everyday Life*. London: Palgrave Macmillan.

Jacques, R. (1996) *Manufacturing the Employee: Management Knowledge from the 19th to the 21st Centuries*. London: Sage.

MacIntyre, A. (1981) *After Virtue*. London: Duckworth.

Parker, M. (2002) *Against Management*. Oxford: Polity.

Parker, M. (2009) 'Managerialism and its Discontents', in S. Clegg and C. Cooper (eds) *The Sage Handbook of Organisational Behaviour: Volume II. Macro Approaches*, pp. 85–98. London: Sage.

Whyte, W.H. (1961) *The Organization Man*. Harmondsworth: Penguin.

managerialism

Marxism and Post-Marxism

Stefano Harney

> **Definition:** Marxism is the inseparable theory and practice inaugurated by Marx and Engels of seeking a communist society in the face of the exploitation, expropriation, and subsumption by capitalism of the social relations of global societies.

Critiques of private wealth, of property, and of exploitation existed long before either capitalism or Marxism came into existence. Cedric Robinson (2001) demonstrates how Marxist debates drew on late-classical and medieval European movements of liberation. Marxism continued to benefit from encounters with such critiques as they emerged globally, embracing antislavery struggles in the nineteenth century, anticolonial struggles of the early twentieth century, struggles against racism and patriarchy in the mid-century, and emerging anti-globalisation struggles at the end of that century. At the same time Marxism brought something important to such struggles, even as it was changed by them. At the level of theory, Marxism saw in capitalism a very specific kind of social relations, prefigured in chattel slavery, in which private property emerges through the advancing dispossession and enclosure of all alternative forms of life, and ways of staying alive. The dynamic of this advancing expropriation is a new kind of exploitation where the labour of the many comes to generate wealth for the few through the social invention of wage labour. With all other means of survival increasingly cut off by the privatisation of property, and by aggressive state and vigilante action against all those who try to invent new means of survival, the wage comes to be the dominant social relation in nation-states making the transition to capitalism.

The origins of this transition to capitalism are complex and much debated. One reason for this social invention was the growing resistance to feudal forms of exploitation and need to quell this resistance. Another reason was the growing surplus of money, first from trade with the Near and Far East, and then from the plundering of the New World and the enslavement of Africans in the resulting colonies. More commonly, clashes between an urban merchant and banking class, and the aristocracy and Christian church are said to have given rise to a new revolutionary class in Europe, the bourgeoisie. First through the French Revolution and then via the Industrial Revolution, this class is said to have made the modern world, and is the protagonist of Marx and Engels' founding text, the *Communist Manifesto*, in which the bourgeoisie chases capital all around the globe, battering down 'all Chinese walls', attempting to resist these new social arrangements.

For Marx and Engels this bourgeois revolution brought into being a new and total kind of class struggle. With nothing to lose but their chains, the industrial proletariat was understood to be capable of seeing the need for an entirely new world. In the second and third decades of the twentieth century this proletariat in northern Italy, Germany and then Spain did indeed imagine that another world was possible, before being cruelly defeated by the forces of this world. Instead, it was in other kinds of class societies in Russia, China, Cuba, Algeria, Angola and Vietnam that communist revolutions, inspired by Marxism, saw victories. From then on, the practice of Marxism would come to dominate its theorisation. This was not only the case with revolutionaries like Lenin, Mao, Fanon, and Che Guevara, but with those primarily engaged in theory (even if mixed with practice) such as W.E.B. Du Bois, C.L.R. James, and even a figure such as Louis Althusser who was heavily influenced by Mao's writings.

Marxism is also a theory of its own coming into being. Marx believed his writings were only possible because of a certain stage of social development generally, and were equally limited by this development. In this sense Marxism's real subject – socialisation – is also its biography. The three great books of Marx's *Capital* are the tale of how capital throws together humans and the natural world into new intimacies and extended relationships. At first, the protagonist seems again to be the bourgeoisie, but gradually we see that this is the story thus far of what Marx calls the society of producers, the associated world brought about by the way capitalism forces people together but without any clear idea of what to do with them beyond expropriating their labour. That European Marxists sometimes confused this story with the story of Europe should not blind us to the fact that Marxism was global long before business named itself so.

Critical management studies has availed itself of very little of this world revolutionary tradition. This may have something to do with the problem of imagining itself as an academic subject, perhaps uniquely among disciplines, in a future society without capitalism. Nonetheless, we can identify its initial interest in labour process theory, its dalliance with post-Marxism, and its ongoing commitment to the problem of alienation, as emanating from the theoretical side of Marxism. Alienation specifically refers to a separation that occurs between man and nature, man and himself, man and other men, and man and society, all brought about because capitalism forces people to sell their labour to make commodities they cannot immediately use, in order to survive. The founding text of labour process theory is Harry Braverman's *Labour and Monopoly Capitalism* (1998) and although the book is about much besides industrial deskilling, it provided a way to theorise the degradation, alienation, and estrangement that characterised both industrial and service work. As sociology departments came under attack and were defunded by, for example, the Thatcherites in the 1980s, industrial sociologists found new employment and opportunity in the expanding business schools in the UK. They came to form the nucleus of an international critical management studies, and brought with them this kernel of Marxism from Braverman.

These scholars soon began to question approaches to alienation based on deskilling, in part influenced by the social development Marx originally identified. Some thus turned away from Marxism as part of the tenor of the times, seeking 'postideological' positions. Others began to question the humanist premise of alienation, which implied that people began whole and were fractured by capitalism, rather than seeing the human as a yet to be completed project. Drawing on philosophers like Michel Foucault, they found new ways to account for what the working life both thwarted and brought into being (e.g. Garsten and Grey, 1997). A theoretically tentative but politically committed feminism also emerged at this time to assert itself. The influence of the Frankfurt School, and particularly its critique of the culture industry as another form of alienation and domination, allowed critical management scholars to think about work beyond the world of work, in its modes of representations, symbols, and consumption (e.g. Hancock and Tyler, 2004). Still others flirted with post-Marxism, a chastised and even chaste politics that acknowledged exploitation and domination in the world but feared equally the anticommunist caricature of the revolutionary option. This

key concepts in
critical management studies

period also saw the flourishing of a specifically Marxist critique of accounting (Harney, 2006).

By the turn of the new century, critical management studies was established as an academic subdiscipline inside of which specific positions could be identified, no longer centred for the most part around Marxism's initial kernel. But once again events in the world unsettled this academic arrangement. Anticapitalist and alter-globalisation movements, which had their origins in anti-IMF riots in the Global South, burst onto the Northern scene with the Battle of Seattle in 1999. The anticapitalist spirit of these movements caught the imagination of many. These movements were not specifically Marxist in the main and some saw this as confirmation of a post-Marxist zeitgeist. But then in 2000, Hardt and Negri published *Empire*. Based in the revolutionary Marxist tradition of Italian workerism and postworkerism, this book slowly began to burn its way through the consciousness of activists, and of a younger generation of scholar-activists. Introducing concepts like immaterial labour to a wider audience, Hardt and Negri provided a way to think about many of the terms current in orthodox business and management, like knowledge management and the symbolic analyst, without losing the politics of struggle that underpinned them. Moreover, for the first time since the 1970s, Marxism seemed ready to align its theory and practice, and to do so anywhere on the globe. This new turn offers the possibility of an engagement with more global forms of Marxism that never made it to critical management studies. It remains to be seen, however, if critical management studies will take up its own globalisation.

FURTHER READING

The Marx and Engels reader listed in the references below will provide the interested student with an introduction to some of the issues discussed above. Hardt and Negri's important book should also be consulted.

See also: *Commodity Fetishism, Consumer Culture, Critical Theory, Feminism, Immaterial Labour, Labour Process Theory*

REFERENCES

Braverman, H. (1998) *Labor and Monopoly Capitalism*. New York: Monthly Review Press.

Garsten, C. and Grey, C. (1997) 'One to Become Oneself: Discourses of Subjectivity in Postbureaucratic Organizations', *Organization* 4(2): 211–28.

Hancock, P. and Tyler, M. (2004) '"MOT Your Life": Critical Management Studies and the Management of Everyday Life', *Human Relations* 57(5): 619–45.

Hardt, M. and Negri, A. (2000) *Empire*. Cambridge, MA: Harvard University Press.

Marx, K. and Engels, F. (1978) *Marx and Engels Reader*, 2nd edn, ed. R.C. Tucker. New York: W.W. Norton.

Harney, S. (2006) 'Management and Self-Activity: Accounting for the Crisis in Profit-Taking', *Critical Perspectives on Accounting* 17(7): 935–46.

Robinson, C. (2001) *An Anthropology of Marxism*. Aldershot: Ashgate.

 Materiality

Janet L. Borgerson

Definition: Materiality concerns the relationships, the interactions, and the co-creation of subjects and objects and their contexts. This understanding includes notions of human subjects' relations with other human subjects; but also interactions with non-human subjects, with material objects, and with human beings, perceived as objects.

From a CMS perspective, materiality studies might provoke investigation into co-creation of organised selves in contexts constituted through management practices or consumer cultures (e.g., Hancock and Tyler, 2001). In this way, studies in materiality explore the variations through which self and society form, particularly in relation to experiencing otherness, or that which is perceived to be different from the subject, or self. Materiality invokes exploration into the constitution, or organisation, of subjects and objects. Indeed, particular ontological assumptions – varying notions of being and non-being – lead to diverse understandings of processes, such as subject formation, co-creation and intersubjectivity that guide studies of materiality (Borgerson, 2005). For example, can we always distinguish between subject and object, or the self and the other, and determine boundaries and borders without distorting that which we hope to understand? Materiality as explored here emphasises how relationships and interactions form and function; attempts to avoid pre-emptively designating particular versions of 'entities,' such as subject and object; and resists defining material qualities said to belong to independent entities or autonomous things.

Recognising processes of materiality can shed light on activities basic to CMS, and studies of the aesthetics of an organised world (Gagliardi, 1990). Consider, for example, claims within marketing that consumer experiences, consumer products and material objects generally express and create, emancipate and transform the consumer self and, moreover, communicate self-concept and status to others. Studies in materiality might interrogate the relationships and co-creative processes that are being proposed, or assumed, when consumers are seen as seeking out brands, and other aspects of material culture (including those aspects perceived as immaterial), in pursuing various identity projects.

Furthermore, a fundamental assumption of current brand research suggests that brands provide resources for construction of self and community. Companies encourage consumers not only in consumption activities, but production activities as well; for example, in the sense that consumers are called upon to create and produce their own identities, and co-create brand meaning and value as well. Indeed, participatory activities basic to social networking sites, brand communities, and 'happenings' such as T-Mobile's brand-led crowd performances allow companies and their brands to appropriate consumer creativity, spontaneous innovation, and consumer embodiment of brand values. Moreover, related processes allow employers to engage employees in activities of embodying the brand as an integral part of everyday work.

Anthropologist Daniel Miller's work (1995, 2008) has offered a theory of materiality based in ethnographically generated understandings of material culture and subject/object hybridity. Miller's theory of materiality engages philosopher G.W.F. Hegel's dialectic, evoking notions of co-creation and co-production. This approach suggests that values and social relations take cultural forms, but 'are created in the act by which cultural forms come into being' (Miller, 1995: 275). In other words, values and relations do not exist prior to their emergence in interaction and activity. Miller highlights the materiality of artefacts, from which a rethinking of the subject follows. He argues that acknowledging the subject allows one to recognise effects of objects in the subject and thus infer the existence of related objects.

materiality

Miller points out that anthropologist Marilyn Strathern (2000) focuses on people's conceptualisation of each other, including the materiality of artefacts. Thus, both researchers attempt to transcend the simple dualism of persons and objects, and as such, persons may constitute the 'objects' that have effects. According to Miller, social theorist Bruno Latour investigates the material nature of social worlds, countering the general disregard for non-humans and their effects. On the question of materiality, Latour (1987) proposes an actor–network theory of constraints and effects, with objects as actors that possess agency, as effects, inseparable from social and material aspects in the social world. However, from Miller's perspective, Latour ignores the study of material culture and the importance of social perception, leaving aside people's conception of objects and agency.

In exploring materiality, an explicit connection emerges between various understandings of subject and object agency. In other words, materiality raises fundamental questions of agency, often understood simply as the ability to act. A human subject or self may be said to have agency, including the capacity to undertake action, purposively initiate effects, or cause things to happen in the world, often in interaction with objects and other agents. Actions become expressive of a particular agent, ultimately in so far as the agent uses uncoerced decision-making powers to choose between alternatives based upon an understanding of circumstances and available options. The contexts of such circumstances and options; the variable nature of what is meant by 'understanding'; and, furthermore, the range of human abilities to distinguish relevant pieces of information all figure into notions of agency, especially as this relates to 'ethical' agency, or cases in which one is said to be responsible for one's actions.

Miller's theory of materiality calls the agency of both subjects and objects into question, as agency appears to emerge in relation, not as a quality of either subjects or objects. In this way, Miller has criticised the way in which Latour adopts a metaphor of subject-based agency to serve as object agency's interpretative model. For example, the term 'agent' may designate sites of interaction, or effects, in the sense that it is at such sites that an agent emerges or appears as a marker. Such understandings call into question the effect-causing identified 'agent', disrupting the basic notion that we can designate a cause of a particular effect.

Philosopher Harry Frankfurt has argued that assumptions regarding causal antecedents are unsatisfactory, yet he supports the importance of social perception, arguing that a theory of action must allow the agent to account for what is happening in the present. He writes, 'the problem of action is to explicate the contrast between what an agent does and what merely happens to him, or between bodily movements that he makes and those that occur without his making them' (1988: 69). For example, some conceptualisations of materiality might suggest that co-creation and intersubjectivity exhaust the possibility for a subject to act on his or her own accord or make autonomous, purposive or intentional choices. Having, and acting upon, an intention, which is often the root of any notion of agency, becomes for Frankfurt a matter of more or less effective agent intervention. In other words, agency becomes a kind of participatory intervention in an attempt to accomplish purposes that might otherwise be dissipated in the wake of intervening forces.

Despite the pressure that notions of materiality place upon questions of agency, unexpected insights emerge through materiality's lens. Recently, the United States Park Service re-evaluated a category of objects that had come into their possession. Collected from along the base of Maya Lin's Vietnam Veterans Memorial in Washington, DC, objects left by visitors – in memory of relationships severed by death in war – were transported to 'lost and found'. Initially categorised as things forgotten, as if by mistake, that later might be claimed by their owners, this myriad miscellany now forms a museum collection dedicated to meaningful memorial objects. In this example, human subjects – both present and absent, living and dead – and objects come together in a complex dance of interaction, form and change each other over time.

A focus on materiality draws attention to questions fundamental to management studies. For example, differing versions of materiality invoke varying conceptions of identity constitution, co-creation, and intersubjectivity. Moreover, exploring assumptions basic to management studies, such as relationships and interactions between employees and corporate values, or consumers and brands, opens new understandings at the core of materiality.

FURTHER READING

Miller's (2008) *The Comfort of Things* offers a theory of materiality based on a micro-ethnography of material culture. See Borgerson's (2009) interview with Miller for an examination of some of the emergent themes. For an application of materiality to organisational theory see Gagliardi (1990).

See also: Aesthetics, Actor–Network Theory, Consumer Culture, Identity, Subjectivity and Subjectivation

REFERENCES

Borgerson, J. (2005) 'Materiality, Agency, and the Constitution of Consuming Subjects', *Advances in Consumer Research* 32: 439–43.

Borgerson, J. (2009) 'Materiality and the Comfort of Things: Drinks, Dining and Discussion with Daniel Miller', *Consumption, Markets and Culture* 12(2): 155–70.

Frankfurt, H. (1988) *The Importance of What We Care About*. Cambridge: Cambridge University Press.

Gagliardi, P. (1990) 'Artifacts as Pathways and Remains of Organizational Life', in P. Gagliardi (ed.) *Symbols and Artifacts: Views of the Corporate Landscape*, pp. 3–38. Berlin: de Gruyter.

Hancock, P. and Tyler, M. (2001) 'Managing Subjectivity and the Dialectic of Self-consciousness: Hegel and Organization Theory', *Organization* 8(4): 565–85.

Latour, B. (1987) *Science in Action: How to Follow Scientists and Engineers Through Society*. Milton Keynes: Open University Press.

Miller, D. (ed.) (1995) *Acknowledging Consumption*. London and New York: Routledge.

Miller, D. (2008) *The Comfort of Things*. Cambridge: Polity.

Strathern, M. (2000) 'Accountability and Ethnography', in M. Strathern (ed.) *Audit Cultures*. London: Routledge.

McDonaldisation

Alan Bryman

Definition: McDonaldisation refers to the diffusion throughout the economy and society of the principles exemplified by McDonald's restaurants.

INTRODUCTION

According to George Ritzer, McDonaldisation is 'the process by which the principles of the fast-food restaurant are coming to dominate more and more sectors of American society as well as the rest of the world'

(Ritzer, 2008: 1). As such McDonaldisation does not refer to the spread of McDonald's restaurants or to the fact that more and more areas of life are copying McDonald's but to the diffusion of their underlying principles of doing business.

McDonaldisation is an aspect of the continuing rationalisation of more and more areas of social life. The concept draws on a number of developments that precede the emergence of fast-food restaurants, especially scientific management, Fordism and bureaucracy. These three trends, all of which are features of creeping rationalisation, are seminal influences on the process of McDonaldisation.

Ritzer outlines four dimensions of McDonaldisation:

- *Efficiency*. This refers to the implementation of the optimum means for a given end. A McDonald's restaurant is efficient in a number of ways, but particularly in the sense that it is geared to allowing a large number of people to be supplied with food. It is efficient from the point of view of both the restaurant and the consumer.
- *Calculability*. This means an emphasis on things that can be counted. In the specific case of McDonald's restaurants, this is revealed in a number ways. Restaurants used to proclaim the number of millions and later billions of burgers that McDonald's had sold. But more significantly for Ritzer, they convey the impression that the consumer is getting a *large* amount of food for a *small* expenditure of money (e.g. Big Mac).
- *Predictability*. When you go into a McDonald's restaurant, anywhere in the world, you will not encounter any great surprises. Minor national variations are sometimes introduced, but by and large the menu will be recognisable to anyone familiar with McDonald's fare. Also, if you do order a Big Mac it will be the same in terms of size, contents, taste, appearance, wrapping, and even how it was cooked and put together, as one bought anywhere else.
- *Control through non-human technology*. Both customers and workers are controlled through non-human technologies. Customers in a McDonald's restaurant are controlled through the queuing system, whilst workers are controlled through production technologies that measure the precise amount of ketchup or the cooking time.

McDonaldisation is evident in its diffusion in many spheres of modern life. Thus, Ritzer and various other writers have considered its flow into areas such as theme parks, sport, healthcare, shopping, tourism and even birth and death (Ritzer, 2008, 2010). Of particular interest to readers of this book is the suggestion that higher education itself is becoming McDonaldised. For example, Ritzer (1998) suggested that American sociology, a discipline that has been a major influence on critical management studies, has been mechanised. It exhibits predictability by virtue of the standardised format of journal articles, which are further rationalised by the peer review process, while the computer and software control (in the form of a non-human technology) the writing process. Bryman and Beardsworth (2006) have suggested that McDonaldisation is in evidence in much quantitative research in sociology and that qualitative research, which has been a significant methodological approach for critical management researchers, is also showing signs of McDonaldisation. They argue that the growing use of quality criteria, more structured forms of qualitative data analysis, and data analysis software are pushing it in a McDonaldising direction.

Ritzer writes very much as a critic of McDonaldisation, though he also displays a grudging admiration for it. The critical hue is apparent in his identification of what he terms *the irrationality of rationality* in relation to McDonaldisation. The irrationality of rationality seems to serve as a further dimension of McDonaldisation in some of Ritzer's writings. The point about it is that frequently McDonaldisation leads to the *opposites* of the four features mentioned above. In the case of the rationalised jobs that are so central to McDonaldisation, the irrationality of rationality is revealed in the fact that McDonaldised work is invariably dehumanising leading to high labour turnover and frequently to difficulty in finding replacements.

McDonaldisation has been criticised on several counts. It is sometimes accused of not taking the perspective of the user into account and of instead placing the emphasis on Ritzer's own views about others' experiences. He has been accused of providing a simplistic view of the globalisation process that takes little notice of local adaptations to the global spread of McDonaldisation's principles. It is also sometimes suggested that Ritzer minimises the role and significance of countervailing trends, such as post-Fordism with its implications of variety and customisation in place of standardisation and the mass market. However, in more recent writings on McDonaldisation he has focused on additional trends such as Starbuckisation.

McDONALDISATION AND DISNEYISATION

One trend that was influenced by the concept of McDonaldisation but which seeks to draw attention to additional features of modern society is Disneyisation which refers to 'the process by which *the principles* of the Disney theme parks are coming to dominate more and more sectors of American society as well as the rest of the world' (Bryman, 2004: 1).

In outlining the nature of Disneyisation, Bryman identifies four components of the process, which are:

- *Theming*. This term refers to the application of a narrative that is largely external to the object to which it is applied but which infuses that object with an exotic aura. Thus, the Disney theme parks are themed in the sense that the different regions of the parks are portrayed using motifs such as foreign adventure and via associations with cinema releases.
- *Hybrid consumption*. This feature is concerned with the hybridised nature of many areas of social and economic life that previously have been separate. In the Disney theme parks this component is revealed in the way in which it is difficult to disentangle its nature as an amusement park from the fact that it also seems to be the context of shopping and eating opportunities.
- *Merchandising*. This refers to the promotion of goods that are based upon copyrighted images and logos. Its most obvious manifestation in the Disney theme park is in terms of the large amount of merchandise that is for sale, replete with park logos and Disney images.
- *Performative labour*. This refers to the growing tendency for work to be regarded as a performance, especially in service industries. One of the main ways in which this is revealed is in emotional labour which refers to the way in which employees in service occupations frequently are constrained to exhibit emotions of a particular kind. Increasingly, employees are enjoined to exhibit positive emotions in order to create a more uplifting experience for visitors.

Weaver, who has proposed that cruise ship tourism has become McDonaldised (2006a), has also proposed that it has become Disneyised (2006b): cruise ships are sometimes themed or comprise themed areas; they exhibit hybrid consumption through the sale of a host of products and services on board; there is growing evidence of merchandising, for example, through branded credit cards; and finally, performative labour in the form of emotional control among front-line service staff is very much in evidence.

Whereas McDonaldisation is rooted in traditional associations with modernity and rationalisation, Disneyisation relates much more closely to the consumerist ethic. Disneyisation is part and parcel of a process of injecting the consumption process with new experiences for the consumer, in particular through the creation of entertaining encounters. As such, Disneyisation serves as a mechanism for differentiating companies' products and services that might otherwise not be distinguishable from each other. In this way, it is closer to the post-Fordist economy, with its emphasis on differentiation and customisation, than to Fordism, with which McDonaldisation is more closely aligned.

Ritzer's writings on McDonaldisation have provided a provocative concept that encapsulates several trends in modern society but in a manner that is accessible beyond the academy.

FURTHER READING

Ritzer's (2008) latest edition of *The McDonaldization of Society* is the natural starting point and his edition text (2010) is a useful collection of assessments of the concept and of the diffusion of McDonaldisation. A useful discussion of both McDonaldisation and Disneyisation in an interview with Ritzer can be found at http://uk.youtube.com/watch?v=WM8LU8TaGFs (accessed on 16 April 2010) and is referred to as 'Disneyization, Super Size Me, and Fast Food Nation'.

See also: Consumer Culture, Critical Theory, Governmentality

NOTE

Parts of this entry are based on the author's entries on McDonaldisation and Disneyisation in G. Ritzer (ed.) *Sage Encyclopaedia of Social Theory*, Thousand Oaks, CA: Sage, 2005.

REFERENCES

Bryman, A. (2004) *The Disneyization of Society*. London: Sage.
Bryman, A. and Beardsworth, A. (2006) 'Is Qualitative Research Becoming McDonaldized?', *Methodological Innovations Online* [Online], 1(1). Available at: http://sirius.soc.plymouth.ac.uk/~andyp/viewarticle.php?id=20.
Ritzer, G. (1998) *The McDonaldization Thesis*. London: Sage.
Ritzer, G. (2008) *The McDonaldization of Society 5*. Thousand Oaks, CA: Pine Forge Press.
Ritzer, G. (2010) *McDonaldization: The Reader*, 3rd edn. Thousand Oaks, CA: Pine Forge Press.

key concepts in
critical management studies

Weaver, A. (2006a) 'The McDonaldization Thesis and Cruise Tourism', *Annals of Tourism Research* 32(2): 346–66.
Weaver, A. (2006b) 'The Disneyization of Cruise Travel', in R.K. Dowling (ed.) *Cruise Ship Tourism*, pp. 389–96. Wallingford: CABI.

Neoliberalism

Jo Grady and David Harvie

Definition: Neoliberalism is both an ideological and a practical or political project. It holds that human welfare and the social good will be maximised by extending market and property relations into every sphere of human interaction.

September 11, 1973. Santiago, Chile. Fighter jets strafe the presidential palace, whilst the democratically elected government hunkers down inside. Faced with limited choices President Salvador Allende takes his own life. Allende's cabinet is arrested at gunpoint. Thousands of communists, socialists, trade unionists and other 'subversives' are rounded up in Santiago's football stadiums. Many are tortured and/or executed. Over the next few years at least 3,200 Chileans are executed or 'disappeared', more than 80,000 are imprisoned and 200,000 are exiled (Klein, 2007: 77).

To help undo Chile's three-year experiment with socialism, General Augusto Pinochet, leader of the *coup d'état*, calls on the 'Chicago Boys', a group of Latin American economists trained at the University of Chicago by such figures as Milton Friedman and George Shultz – under scholarships funded by the Ford Foundation. Nationalisations are reversed and other public assets privatised. Markets are deregulated and opened up to foreign investors, as are natural resources – with the interests of indigenous groups frequently trampled upon. Social spending is slashed, social security is privatised and taxes are cut. Friedman approvingly describes the reforms as 'shock treatment'.

neoliberalism

173

Over the next three decades, similar neoliberal policies are implemented across the planet: Deng Xiaoping's liberalisation of China's economy; 'structural adjustment' in Africa and other Latin American countries in the wake of the international debt crisis; Ronald Reagan's supply-side reforms of the United States' economy; 'shock therapy' (prescribed by Jeffery Sachs) in Bolivia, Poland and Russia; the 'free market fundamentalism' ordered in Iraq by Paul Bremer, head of the US-appointed Coalition Provisional Authority.

Britons get their first taste of neoliberalism in 1976, when the Labour government is forced to implement austerity measures – public spending cuts and wage constraints – in exchange for an emergency loan from the IMF. As in the US and elsewhere, the eschewing of Keynesian economics and the shift to neoliberal policies is occasioned by the global capitalist crisis of the 1970s. In fact it can be understood as a counter-attack against the growing power of workers, peasants and 'new social subjects', whose struggles have caused the crisis. As the ruling class rethinks the management of capitalism, the ideas of Friedman and the Austrian economist Friedrich von Hayek find favour. Both men advocate free markets and a minor economic role for the state – which must concentrate on enforcing private property rights.

Margaret Thatcher, like her friend Reagan, is an ardent free-marketeer and a devotee of the writings of Friedman and Hayek. In 1979, as leader of the Conservative party, she is elected prime minister, with a strong mandate to implement neoliberal reforms to the British economy. Describing Thatcherites as the 'crack assault troops of insurgent neoliberalism', Daniels and McIlroy (2009: 32) highlight that under Thatcher the Conservative government aggressively introduced a new social, political and economic ideology into the governance to Britain. The Thatcher government's onslaught of neoliberal legislation struck at the heart of what was identified as 'welfare/dependency culture' and reliance on the 'nanny state'. The neoliberal solution was multifaceted but included policies to:

- reduce direct taxation;
- allow 'inefficient' or unprofitable enterprises to go bankrupt;
- privatise nationalised industries;
- introduce market mechanisms into public services not immediately suitable for privatisation;
- substantially reduce welfare payments and other social provision; and
- remove distortion from the operation of markets, including financial and labour markets, the latter involving anti-trade union legislation.

This set of policies was controversial, of course, and led to both the most significant industrial dispute in Britain's post-Second World War history and its worst riot in a century. In 1984, her popularity buoyed by victory over Argentina in the Falklands/Malvinas war, Thatcher takes on Britain's coal miners' union, the country's most militant, politicised and powerful, which she describes as 'the enemy within'. A strike is provoked by the announcement of a wave of redundancies and the closure of 'uneconomic' collieries. After a year-long dispute, bitter and often violent, with the police deployed in a paramilitary fashion, Thatcher again emerges victorious leaving Britain's union movement weak and divided and its industrial heartlands obliterated with little regard to the human cost.

Thatcher is eventually forced to resign in 1990, after attempting to replace a local property tax with a flat-rate per capita tax – a poll tax – on every adult. The tax's introduction provoked a mass non-payment campaign – with up to one in three refusing to pay – and a series of riots around the country, including the so-called Battle of Trafalgar in March 1990, a national demonstration-turned-10-hour-riot, which saw more than 500 police officers and thousands of protestors injured and 491 arrests (Burns, 1992). But Thatcher's successors have continued in the same vein and her (in)famous statement that *'there is no alternative'* was echoed, a decade and a half later, by Tony Blair: 'These forces of change driving the future don't stop at national boundaries. Don't respect tradition. They wait for no one and no nation. They are universal' (cited by McMurtry, 2002: 13).

Neoliberalism is 'in the first instance a theory of political economic practices that propose that human well being can be best advanced by liberating individual entrepreneurial freedoms and skills within an institutional framework characterised by strong private property rights, free markets, and free trade' (Harvey, 2005: 2). This fundamental underpinning of neoliberalism – that the market is the best means to best advance human wellbeing – encouraged the rise of the entrepreneurial self pursuing personal freedoms. As a result there has been increased political concentration on the individual, their rights and responsibilities, their freedom to succeed or fail based on their own skills and hard work.

Neoliberalism has always had two sides. On the one hand, we can understand it as a counter-attack by elites against social gains won by workers' and other movements from the 1930s onwards – their response to the crisis of the 1970s and an attempt to shift wealth back up the social ladder. This understanding makes sense of the frequently violent nature of its implementation and strong role of the state. But we can also

neoliberalism

understand neoliberalism as an ideological project claiming to rid 'the markets' of unwarranted intervention by governments and their ilk. It is the American dream gone global: get rich or die trying. As part of this ideology, social inequality is accepted as part of the wide disparities that human competition creates. In 2010 the gap between richest and poorest Britons was at a record high, with the richest 10 per cent owning a hundred times the wealth of the poorest 10 per cent.

With the financial and economic crisis of 2007 onwards, the ideological element of neoliberalism has lost a lot of its purchase: astronomical sums (£850 billion in the UK alone) have been paid to bail out banks – a clear case of money flowing uphill – and there is now widespread acceptance that markets do not always work. The neoliberal 'deal' of cheap credit and the possibility of self-advancement in exchange for deregulated labour markets and stagnant wages is clearly null and void. But here we encounter a third side of neoliberalism, the way it has trained people – through a forced engagement with markets in every aspect of their lives – to view themselves as rational benefit-maximisers, as *Homo economicus*. Thus, although neoliberalism no longer 'makes sense' in policy terms, its logic keeps stumbling on.

FURTHER READING

David Harvey's *A Brief History of Neoliberalism* (2005) and Naomi Klein's *The Shock Doctrine* (2007) are both excellent reads. On the neoliberal 'deal' and zombie-liberalism, see Turbulence Collective (2009).

See also: *Capitalism and Anticapitalism, Managerialism, Political Economy*

REFERENCES

Burns, D. (1992) *Poll Tax Rebellion*. Edinburgh: AK Press and London: Attack International.

Daniels, G. and McIlroy, J. (eds) (2009) *Trade Unions in a Neoliberal World*. New York: Routledge.

Harvey, D. (2005) *A Brief History of Neoliberalism*. Oxford: Oxford University Press.

Klein, N. (2007) *The Shock Doctrine: The Rise of Disaster Capitalism*. New York: Metropolitan Books.

McMurtry, J. (2002) *Value Wars: The Global Market Versus the Life Economy*. London: Pluto Press.

Turbulence Collective (2009) 'Life in Limbo?', *Turbulence: Ideas for Movement* 5: 3–7. Available at http://turbulence.org.uk/turbulence-5/life-in-limbo/.

key concepts in critical management studies

Paradigm

Mark Tadajewski

> **Definition:** A paradigm provides a way of thinking about, researching and understanding the social world.

The paradigm concept is one of the most contested terms in social theory. The key literature that uses the term can be traced back to the historian and philosopher of science Thomas Kuhn. Although Kuhn has been widely criticised for his ambiguous use of the paradigm concept, we can best understand it in the following way: very broadly speaking, scientists are guided by a set of shared rules of scientific interpretation that allow participants in one branch of science to test and assess various claims to knowledge according to particular agreed upon conventions.

The paradigm concept, by providing scientists with a way of seeing, structures the way we look at the world, highlighting certain facets while redirecting our attention away from others. This could have the implication that scientists remain only within the consensually defined limits of the paradigm, looking at the world in a similar way because they are trained to do so. This makes it unlikely that they will chance upon some revolutionary new way of thinking about any given topic. For Kuhn, this argument was misplaced. Like other occupations, the practice of science requires a division of labour, so that many scientists focus on one 'small aspect of nature in great empirical detail' (Kuhn, 1970: 42). He goes further and claims that this specialisation is of great value with respect to scientific understanding, letting scientists work on refining research areas that require further development. It was perfectly possible that scientists working in this way could trigger scientific revolutions that redefine the way we think about and understand the world.

Within management studies, the major work that uses the paradigm concept – albeit in a slightly different way to Kuhn – is the book by Burrell and Morgan, *Sociological Paradigms and Organisational Analysis*. In this text they aim to map the key paradigms in organisation studies.

paradigm

For Burrell and Morgan, the term paradigm 'is intended to emphasise the commonality of perspective which binds the work of a group of theorists together in such a way that they can usefully be regarded as approaching social theory within the bounds of the same problematic' (Burrell and Morgan, 1979/1992: 23).

For instance, research associated with the functionalist paradigm usually adopts a realist ontology, seeing society or an organisation as having a real existence, not dependent on the idiosyncratic perception of any individual. Research in this tradition is associated with the 'sociology of regulation', seeing society as tending towards order and regularity. Scientific research is believed to be objective and draws on the hypothetico-deductive method, with the researcher producing a variety of hypotheses and then subjecting these to refutation and revision. The knowledge produced by scholars working through this paradigm is 'pragmatic, useful knowledge' and usually produced in the interest of solving some managerial problem (Hassard, 1991: 277).

PARADIGMS AND POLITICS

Burrell and Morgan claim that their use of Kuhn's terminology was a political move: they wanted to use theoretical language that many readers would be familiar with (Burrell, 1997); and by broadening Kuhn's use of the term, they were able to subsume the majority of scholarship produced in organisation studies under the banner of one paradigm, namely functionalism. This had the added bonus of allowing them to position the remaining three paradigms, radical humanism, radical structuralism and the interpretive paradigm, as reflecting 'virgin territory' that required further exploration.

Each of the four Burrell and Morgan paradigms has its own set of metatheoretical assumptions, that is, assumptions that are the basis for thinking about social research and the structuring of society. These are derived from philosophy in the first instance, taking into account ontological and epistemological precepts, as well as particular views of human nature and methodology (Burrell and Morgan, 1979/1992: 1). The other assumptions are taken from sociology and relate to how we understand society (i.e. as tending towards regulation or radical change).

As Burrell and Morgan are at pains to point out throughout their work, many of the assumptions they use to contrast the different paradigms are often extreme positions that few people completely endorse and, as such, even those who are affiliated with the same paradigm may contest some of the statements their colleagues articulate. So, subscription to one paradigm does not mean that each scholar thinks about their research in an identical fashion. There is room for both convergent and divergent thought. Nevertheless, 'The paradigm, does ... have an underlying unity in terms of its basic and often "taken for granted" assumptions, which separate a group of theorists in a very fundamental way from theorists located in other paradigms' (Burrell and Morgan, 1979/1992: 23).

What is most interesting about Burrell and Morgan's scholarship and all of the later discussions about 'incommensurability,'[1] is that they emphasise that researchers, should they wish to, can move between paradigms. In doing so, the intellectual horizons of the scholar concerned are widened; they see their subject in new and interesting ways, thereby avoiding paradigmatic myopia.

Burrell and Morgan, then, essentially stress a role for paradigmatic anthropology (Booth, 2002). Each paradigm is treated as if it provides only a partial view of whatever phenomena concern us, which can then either be used as a supplement or to deliberately contrast existing ways of thinking. As Arndt appreciates, when a discipline is characterised by multiple paradigms rather than just one, there is the potential for 'interparadigmatic criticism' which encourages 'scientists to refine and improve their formulations' (1985: 20). Yet, in equal measure, some would argue that a proliferation of paradigms, theories and metaphors can also contribute to intellectual fragmentation and a decline in the scientific credibility of the discipline.

Nevertheless, although scholars often claim to be interested in interparadigmatic dialogue, it remains unclear how far such statements are translated into reality. Furthermore, there are still relatively few researchers who shift from one paradigm to another in their work. This said, there have been calls for the greater use of multiple rather than mono-paradigm analysis. However, before we rush into embracing multiple paradigm research, it is worth bearing in mind that simply producing a study based on multiple paradigms is not guaranteed to result in 'more comprehensive explanations of the organizational world. If the various paradigmatic positions adopted in a research investigation each have theoretical or empirical deficiencies, then research based on a combination of these may actually lead to sub-optimal analysis' (Hassard et al., 2008: 8).

To conclude, notwithstanding the various attempts to rethink the paradigm concept and the Burrell and Morgan typology, their two-by-two matrix remains one of the most important readings of social theory into organisation studies. This is not to say that it is unproblematic. The question remains how we could reduce the complexities of postmodern, feminist theorising or postcolonial approaches to a single paradigm. But let us remember that Burrell and Morgan only intended to offer a sketch of the paradigms available, they never meant for their typology to remain unaltered. Just as they were concerned with destabilising existing functionalist orthodoxy, they would probably be worried if their exploratory sketch delimited our attention rather than encouraged us to expand our intellectual horizons.

FURTHER READING

Both Kuhn's (1970) and Burrell and Morgan's (1979/1992) work should be the starting point for students interested in this concept. In terms of recent developments in the paradigm debate, the overview provided by Lewis and Kelemen (2002) is excellent.

See also: *Critical Marketing Studies, Critical Theory, Marxism and Post-Marxism, Postmodernism, Poststructuralism*

NOTE

1 We can think of this mainly in terms of people who self-associate with different paradigms weighing the contribution to knowledge of research produced using other paradigms in a way that is skewed in favour of their own paradigm.

REFERENCES

Arndt, J. (1985) 'On Making Marketing Science More Scientific: Role of Orientations, Paradigms, Metaphors, and Puzzle Solving', *Journal of Marketing* 49(3): 11–23.

Booth, C. (2002) '"Maps and Chaps": Metaphors of Travelling, Mapping and Surveying in Burrell & Morgan's (1979) Sociological Paradigms and Organisational Analysis'. Working Paper Proposal. Available at: http://group.aomonline.org/cms/Meetings/Denver/booth.htm.

Burrell, G. (1997) 'Organization Paradigms', in A. Sorge and M. Warner (eds) *The IEBM Handbook of Organizational Behavior*, pp. 33–47. London: International Thompson Business Press.

Burrell, G. and Morgan, G. (1979/1992) *Sociological Paradigms and Organisational Analysis*. Aldershot: Ashgate.

Hassard, J. (1991) 'Multiple Paradigms and Organization Analysis – A Case Study', *Organization Studies* 12(2): 275–99.

Hassard, J., Kelemen, M. and Wolfram Cox, J. (2008) *Disorganization Theory: Explorations in Alternative Organizational Analysis.* London: Routledge.

Kuhn, T.S. (1970) *The Structure of Scientific Revolutions,* 2nd edn. Chicago: University of Chicago Press.

Lewis, M.W. and Kelemen, M.L. (2002) 'Multiparadigm Inquiry: Exploring Organizational Pluralism and Paradox', *Human Relations* 55(Feb.): 251–75.

Political Economy

Paul Adler

Definition: 'Political economy' refers to the combined and interacting effects of economic and political structures or processes, and by extension, to the scholarly study of this domain.

The term originated in the seventeenth and eighteenth centuries to refer to the economic policies of the nation-states of the time. The writings of that period (such as by the Physiocrats and Mercantalists) focused on taxes and trade policy. The meaning of the term was broadened in the nineteenth century to refer to the manifold ways in which economic structures and market processes influenced, and were influenced by, political power at local, national and international levels. The great theorists of that period were Adam Smith, David Ricardo, Richard Malthus, John Stuart Mill and Karl Marx.

Starting in the late nineteenth century, political economy as a scholarly field was increasingly displaced by economics. This shift reflected the celebration of the market as an autonomous mechanism for spontaneous coordination that ostensibly neither required nor induced any political structuring. The displacement was facilitated by the development of increasingly elegant mathematical models, whilst the study of political economy is by nature more context dependent, more institutionally specific, and requires a more heterogeneous mix of concepts and approaches.

Notwithstanding the great analytic successes of economic orthodoxy, and despite its hegemony in universities across the non-communist world, the stark facts of the interdependence of economic and political phenomena – the variable role of governments in monetary, fiscal, trade and industrial affairs, and business's role in shaping government policy and socio-economic inequality – have stimulated continued research in political economy.

A FRAGMENTED FIELD

Political economy today is a fragmented field. It is fragmented, first, by the heterogeneity of theoretical traditions, of which the main ones are:

(a) *Class-based*, in the form of (i) a Marxist or Marxist-inspired tradition, building on scholars such as Ernest Mandel, Michel Aglietta, Giovanni Arrighi, Robert Brenner, Paul Baran, Paul Sweezy, David Gordon, Richard Edwards and Michael Reich; and (ii) a 'post-Keynesian' tradition, in the work of scholars such as Hyman Minsky and James Crotty.

(b) *Institutionalist*, which differs from the first mainly by its less economic and more sociological roots, building on Marx but also on Thorstein Veblen, John R. Commons and Karl Polanyi; some key contemporary scholars in this tradition are Paul Evans, Fred Block, Geoffrey Hodgson and William Lazonick. This tradition has been particularly strong in international political economy and in a growing body of feminist political economy.

(c) *Rational choice*, where the 'mainstream' economic tradition addresses political economy by using its standard tools and concepts, via (i) 'public economics' – the study of how government tax and expenditure policies affects individuals and firms, and how a 'social-welfare maximising' policy-maker should design these policies; and (ii) 'public choice' theory, which extends the *homo economicus* model to politics by assuming that politicians behave in ways that maximise their individual self-interest. The more adventurous edges of this orthodox research have rejoined heterodox political economy's interest in exploring the origins of institutions and cultures.

THE VARIOUS USES OF POLITICAL ECONOMY IN CMS

As a resource for critical management studies, political economy can be contrasted with several other popular approaches to CMS, most notably those focused on culture and those grounded in phenomenology and symbolic interactionism that give priority to the social construction of shared meanings. Political economy research also differs from some other strands of CMS in its reliance on an epistemology that is more typically critical realist if not simply positivist.

Political economy figures in CMS in two main ways: (a) as an argument about the importance of the broader, 'macro' structures of political economy to the activity within and the behaviour of organisations (mainly business organisations), and (b) as the study of the 'micro' political-economic structuring of relations within and between organisations themselves.

Concerning the former, macro approach, CMS has argued against a long tradition within management studies that has sought to assert its independence from the broader fields of sociology, economics or political economy. CMS researchers have argued that such a conceptual strategy risks naturalising features of contemporary organisations, making their historically contingent features – and most notably their specifically capitalist features – appear inevitable and universal. The CMS critique is exemplified in labour process theory, which I take to be part of the broader CMS field, notwithstanding its opposition to the poststructuralist stands of theory that have been popular within CMS. Labour process theorists have long argued that we miss something essential if we fail to note the pervasive effect on organisational structure and process of the class antagonism between workers and managers (as representatives of capital within the firm). Marxist political economy has been particularly strongly represented in this line of work (reviewed in Adler, 2009; Adler, forthcoming). Studies of the mutations in the macro structures of political economy been linked to changing subjective identities via a number of paths discussed by theorists such as Karl Marx, Norbert Elias and Jürgen Habermas. We should note too some writing on the political-economic analysis of the emergence of CMS itself (Hassard et al., 2001).

Macro political economy has also informed critically oriented research on the strategic conduct of firms. Hymer's Marxist analysis of multinational corporations was a very influential precursor. Marens (2009) discusses a range of Marxist-inspired political economy scholarship and its significance for corporate strategy and structure. Political economy has also informed CMS critiques of corporate claims to social responsibility (e.g. Banerjee, 2009). CMS has to date had little to say about strategic action by organisations (business or advocacy groups) oriented towards the polity and its policies: Jacobs (1999) and Levy (e.g. Levy and Egan, 2003) are exceptions.

As concerns the micro perspective on the political economy of organisations themselves, Mayer Zald and J. Kenneth Benson were important precursors for CMS work that aimed to reveal the political stakes of apparently neutral technical/administrative exigencies. Michael Burawoy (1979) argued that the firm should be understood as a political-economic structure with its own internal 'state apparatus'. Pfeffer and Salancik's 'resource dependency' theory provides a political-economic theory of interfirm behaviour, integrating economic profit and political power considerations in the analysis of corporate board interlocks and other strategic ties. Mark Mizruchi (Mizruchi and Yoo, 2002) and Donald Palmer (Palmer and Barber, 2001) continue a long tradition of Marxist research that studies the ways these political and economic ties reflect and enact macro-level class structures.

FURTHER READING

For overviews of the competing perspectives in political economy, see Caporaso and Levine (1992) and Miller (2008). Ackroyd et al. (2005) provide an overview of various strands of research on work and organisations that are strongly grounded in political economy.

See also: *Capitalism and Anticapitalism, Class, Corporation, Marxism and Post-Marxism, Neoliberalism*

REFERENCES

Ackroyd, S., Batt, R. and Thompson, P. (eds) (2005) *The Oxford Handbook of Work and Organization*. New York: Oxford University Press.

Adler, P.S. (2009) 'Marx and Organization Studies Today', in Adler (ed.) *The Oxford Handbook of Sociology and Organization Studies: Classical Foundations*, pp. 62–91. New York: Oxford University Press.

Adler, P.S. (forthcoming) 'Marxist Philosophy and Organization Studies: Marxist Contributions to the Understanding of Some Important Organizational Forms', in H. Tsoukas and R. Chia (eds) *Research in the Sociology of Organizations: Philosophy and Organization Theory*. Greenwich: JAI Press.

Banerjee, S.B. (2009) *Corporate Social Responsibility: The Good, The Bad, and the Ugly*. Cheltenham: Edward Elgar.

Burawoy, M. (1979) *Manufacturing Consent*. Chicago: University of Chicago Press.

Caporaso, J. and Levine, D. (1992) *Theories of Political Economy*. Cambridge: Cambridge University Press.

Hassard, J., Hogan, J. and Rowlinson, M. (2001) 'From Labour Process Theory to Critical Management Studies', *Administrative Theory and Praxis* 23(3): 339–62.

Jacobs, D. (1999) *Business Lobbies and the Power Structure in America: Evidence and Arguments*. Westport: Greenwood International.

Levy, D.L. and Egan, D. (2003) 'A Neo-Gramscian Approach to Corporate Political Strategy: Conflict and Accommodation in the Climate Change Negotiations', *Journal of Management Studies* 40(4): 803–29.

Marens, R. (2009) 'It's Not Just for Communists Anymore: Marxian Political Economy and Organization Theory', in P.S. Adler (ed.) *The Oxford Handbook of Sociology and Organization Studies: Classical Foundations*, pp. 92–117. New York: Oxford University Press.

Miller, R. (2008) *International Political Economy: Contrasting World Views*. London: Routledge.

Mizruchi, M.S. and Yoo, M. (2002) 'Interorganizational Power and Dependence', in J.A.C. Baum (ed.) *Blackwell Companion to Organizations*, pp. 599–620. Oxford: Blackwell.

Palmer, D. and Barber, B.M. (2001) 'Challengers, Elites, and Owning Families: A Social Class Theory of Corporate Acquisitions in the 1960s', *Administrative Science Quarterly* 46(1): 87–120.

Postmodernism

Stephen Linstead

Definition: Postmodernism is a collective term for a wide-ranging set of developments in the practice and study of culture and society in the fields of art, architecture, philosophy, literature, history, sociology, psychoanalysis, media studies, technology and critical theory, which are generally characterised as either emerging from, reacting to, interrogating or superseding modernism as epistemology; or critically reflecting on the socio-historical conditions of postmodernity as epoch.

INTRODUCTION

Postmodernism as a concept is a term that announces its need to be understood in terms of modernism – but this does not mean that it is the opposite of modernism. Indeed the sort of dualisms, oppositions and dialectical moves typical of modernism are what postmodernism tries to avoid in developing non-dialectical approaches that expose their constructed and artificial nature. Where modernism advanced spectacularly through drawing boundaries, making distinctions, establishing categories of inclusion and exclusion (logically and socially) postmodernism is interested in that which crosses or blurs boundaries, challenges distinctions, and resists representation linguistically or otherwise. Postmodern approaches are concerned that claims about what is 'true', and that therefore exists in some essential sense independent of the means of human apprehension, has been used to authorise social relations, artistic criteria, human subjectivity and even military action. Much has been written about this in the context of two Gulf Wars and their aftermath in what Jean Baudrillard has called a 'Fourth World War'. A postmodern approach is concerned to demonstrate how these 'truth effects' derive from the ways in which they are constructed and represented, and how they both derive from and subsequently enable modes of representation, representational technique, and forms of social and economic power. Its mode of engagement is therefore ironic rather than oppositional.

FROM MODERN TO POSTMODERN

Discussion of phenomena as 'modern' can be traced to the third century AD, deriving from the Latin *modo* (just now), meaning that something modern was 'of the moment'. As time is constantly in motion, so the modern is driven to constantly supersede itself, always becoming *post*modern. *Modernity* itself is thus a moving target, and depends on where one starts. Medieval historians would see modernity beginning with the Renaissance, associated with the rise of science, communication via the technology of printed word, the philosophical redefinition of the human, the first attempts at globalisation, socio-political and economic changes and challenges to the traditional authority of the church. Historians of modern Europe tend to trace its roots back to the seventeenth and eighteenth centuries – the age of reason and enlightenment – and particularly the late eighteenth century where political ideas take on effective revolutionary significances. Postmodernism is accordingly often seen as a direct attack on reason.

In art, and from the perspective of the twentieth century, the period of *modernism* as a distinctive approach, stretches from around 1880 to 1920. This period saw massive transformations in technology: the development of electricity, the automobile, powered flight, the telephone, synthetic materials and metallic alloys, news media and entertainment (radio and cinema); in science, including genetics, psychoanalysis, radioactivity, atomic structure, quantum theory and relativity; and in art where the uncertain perspectival questioning of naturalistic and realistic representational art developed in impressionism was extended into the abstractions and reductions of cubism. Where cubism, psychoanalysis, political nationalism and modernist science continued to seek a unifying character that could be abstracted from these diverse perspectives, resulting for example in the geometrical art of Mondrian and the 'machines for living' of architecture's International Style, the human was placed in question. Sociologically, across this scene two forms of modernism could be discerned – one a *systemic modernism*, that sought to put knowledge to instrumental use, applying new technology to control societies that were growing larger and more complex as social machines; the other a *critical modernism*, that sought to communicate knowledge through technology to build community and emancipate social actors from inhuman suppression by systemic logic. For the critical theorist Jürgen Habermas, modernity was always to be an unfinished project while this emancipatory human goal remained to be achieved, from which postmodernism was a distraction.

Postmodernism follows from modernism's own critiques of modernist representational and systemic practices, specifically the idea that concepts mirror reality and the ideology that social formations are similarly natural events rather than effects produced by the exercise of power. Postmodernism agrees that representations provide at best partial perspectives on their objects (perspectivism) and that cognition proceeds through representation as it is mediated by language and historicity (relativism). However, in postmodernism grand and totalising theory, including most versions of systems theory, is rejected in favour of 'local narratives' and micropolitics, unity and universality for difference and particularity. The pursuit of foundational knowledge and its manifestations in forms of structuralism, essentialism and obsessive rationalism, that require or infer a superior and determining hierarchical level outside or deeper than representation, which would guarantee truth with certainty and establish consensus, is regarded as erroneous. The extent to which postmodern thinkers might be called relativist varies and to equate postmodernism with a radical 'anything goes' relativism, or a simplistic nihilism, is a clumsy reading. As an alternative, we find narrative knowledge, in which knowledge is uncertainly formed and tentatively guaranteed between representations on the same surface level, in a play of ultimately irresolvable dissensus that includes desire, the non-rational and the irrational.

ORGANISING THE POSTMODERN AND POSTMODERN ORGANISING

Postmodernism has, perhaps ironically, been frequently typologised and Rosenau's distinction between *sceptical* (nihilist) and *affirmative* (possibilist) postmodernism was particularly influential in organisation and management studies in the USA. Although such dualisms are too simplistic, Jean-François Lyotard in identifying the conditions of postmodern knowledge warned of false postmodernisms – the reactionary *antimodernism* that called for an end to experimentation (including Francis Fukuyama's reactionary neoliberal claim that history has ended and all we need to do is fix a few minor flaws in liberal democracy and capitalism); and the image-suffused *eclectic postmodernism* that combines culture and aesthetics, kitsch and confusion, often with money as its only yardstick. The French thinker Jean Baudrillard sees this in terms of simulation and simulacra, in which he argues that the image or simulacrum has replaced the real, which is on the one hand unknowable and on the other imperceptible behind the excess of information that presents the *hyperreal* acceleration of aspects of modernity towards an implosion of meaning. The philosophers Gilles Deleuze and Félix Guattari argue that traditional root and branch or arboreal approaches to foundational knowledge (such as those of Hegel and Fukuyama) are replaced with a rhizomatic metaphor of multidirectional connections, with nomadic subjects following heterogeneous, rather than monolinear, trajectories of flight between them.

What does postmodernism entail in making a move from epistemology to organisations and organisational processes? When considering the social, ideas of convergence, coherence, evolution and notions of causality and incrementalism in societal growth and change are destabilised by concepts of multiplicity, plurality, fragmentation, immanence and indeterminacy. Power is relational and distributed throughout these relations rather than top-down or oppositional. For the individual, the modern concept of the cohesive, bounded and unified subject with a single identity (though plural roles) operating rationally is rejected in favour of a decentred, fragmented, liminally open, socially enformed, linguistically constructed, culturally nomadic, contested and multiple subject. Otherness is recognised as formative of subjectivity, which is engaged with as an ethical encounter. For the organisation, structure is teased apart by process, hierarchy by heterarchy and networking, discipline and predictability by play and novelty, system integrity by speed and responsiveness to alterity. The ability to learn is emphasised over the content of learning, as is radical change over incremental progress. For postmodernism, organising is a cultural and political process of relationality, in which aesthetics and ethics are immanent, rather than externally determined or legitimated by economic or other rationalities.

FURTHER READING

Within management and organisation studies, there are a variety of attempts to introduce postmodern ideas to the field, of equally varying quality. A reliable starting place is Cooper and Burrell's (1988) paper introducing a series of subsequent contributions that went on to explore the work of some key individual figures. Linstead and Thanem's (2007) discussion of Deleuze is a useful addition to these. Early compilations such as Parker and Hassard (1993) and Boje et al. (1996) are mixed, but Hancock and Tyler's (2001) thoughtful applied introduction is complemented by the more advanced discussion of the key thinkers and concepts by contributors to Linstead (2004).

See also: Critical Theory, Deconstruction, Marxism and Post-Marxism, Poststructuralism

REFERENCES

Boje, D., Gephart, R. and Thachenkery, T.J. (eds) (1996) *Postmodern Management and Organization Theory.* Thousand Oaks, CA: Sage.

Cooper, R. and Burrell, G. (1988) 'Modernism, Postmodernism and Organisation Studies: An Introduction', *Organization Studies* 9(1): 91–112.

Hancock, P. and Tyler, M. (2001) *Work, Postmodernism and Organization: A Critical Introduction.* London: Sage.

Linstead, S.A. (ed.) (2004) *Organization Theory and Postmodern Thought.* London: Sage.

Linstead, S.A. and Thanem, T. (2007) 'Multiplicity, Virtuality and Organization: The Contribution of Gilles Deleuze', *Organization Studies* 28(10): 1483–501.

Parker, M. and Hassard, J. (eds) (1993) *Postmodernism and Organizations.* London: Sage.

Poststructuralism

Campbell Jones

> **Definition:** Poststructuralism is a word that has been used as a shortcut to point to some of the most exciting and complex intellectual developments of the second half of the twentieth century.

Of one thing we can be quite certain: 'poststructuralism' is a word. But beyond that, things get pretty tricky. If we start with the fact that poststructuralism is a word, then we can say that indeed it is a 'signifier', that is to say, it is a sound that is spoken or a mark that is written. That is the form in which it usually first presents itself to us. But the difficult thing is to dig beneath that form of appearance and ask what is signified. This is the question of meaning, the question of what one 'means to say' when saying this word. Meaning is a question of sense, of where we are heading, of where this signifier 'poststructuralism' directs us.

To some, poststructuralism is best used to describe a particular position that someone – you, me, someone else – might hold. In this sense poststructuralism is almost like a way of seeing the world, a perspective or approach towards the world. This is quite a common way of talking about poststructuralism. We can see this in the way that both supporters and critics of poststructuralism usually have some idea of what a poststructuralist 'position' looks like.

In critical management studies the particular things that have typically been connected with this poststructuralist position are above all language, subjectivity and power. Thus when looking at management control, for example, those taking a poststructuralist position have tended to emphasise the way that management exercises control through the use of language, discourse, cultural symbols and informational codes. This observation applies both to formal bureaucratic controls but also to cultural or normative systems of control, all of which use language as a means of control. It also enables us to see the way that accounting and financial controls are precisely linguistic and that they can both be understood as 'discourses' and hence subjected to critique.

The second major focus of poststructuralism in critical management studies has been a shift in attention towards subjectivity, identity and the senses of selfhood taken up by members of organisations. Hence it has been stressed that subjection in organisations involves subjectification. That is to say, the maintenance of domination in organisations requires that both the dominant and the dominated must take on particular senses of who they are and internalise those as normal or even 'natural'. Organisation is not simply achieved by turning us into mindless 'corproids' but involves positively activating embodied subjects whose senses of themselves are subjected to influence and control.

The third central aspect that is drawn to attention by those taking a poststructuralist position is therefore power. Many, particularly those drawing on the work of Michel Foucault, have had an interest in power, although for these thinkers power is typically ultimately a matter that turns on issues of language and subjectivity (see Clegg, 1989). That is to say, these thinkers have been interested in the way that power operates not through the more obvious means of direct domination or ideological mystification, but through subtle interconnections of language, subjectivity and power. This triangle of language–subjectivity–power has therefore become, in certain parts of critical management studies, either explicitly or implicitly then taken as a matrix through which management can, and indeed must, be seen.

In addition to this focus on particular things (here we have stressed language, subjectivity and power), poststructuralism is often seen to involve a particular way of seeing. Hence it involves first of all a particular philosophy of science and with this certain ontological, epistemological and methodological commitments. This typically involves an antirealist ontology in which it is claimed that the world, and in particular the social relations of management, are socially constructed and hence are contingent, open and at least potentially negotiable (Chia, 1995; cf. Fleetwood, 2005). Second, it involves a subjectivist epistemology according to which different ideas of the truth of management are principally matters of competing representations, none of which can with certainty be judged ultimately or solidly true. Third, along with the suspicion of positivist science, there is typically a preference for interpretive research that draws on qualitative approaches, of which ethnography, case studies and discourse analysis are preferred, for the reason that they allow for more complexity and acknowledgement of competing interpretations (see Alvesson and Deetz, 2000).

All of these ideas that make up this position called poststructuralism are generally taken to be the result of the influence of thinkers that were the original inspiration of this approach. These thinkers are almost always French, and came to prominence in the late 1960s and 1970s, subsequently having a considerable impact on Anglo-American scholarship across the social sciences and humanities in the 1980s and 1990s. In critical management studies the list almost always includes Jacques Derrida and Michel Foucault, will often include Gilles Deleuze, Félix Guattari, Julia Kristeva, Jacques Lacan, Jean-François Lyotard and sometimes thinkers such as Giorgio Agamben, Judith Butler and Luce Irigaray.

As soon as we speak of poststructuralism as a signifier that points us to a set of thinkers, however, it should be noted that some of what we have said above, in particular about the idea that there is one unified 'poststructuralist position' starts to look rather questionable. First of all, what is clear is that these thinkers have written many different things and have often violently opposed and criticised each other. Some of the more extreme claims regarding the philosophy of science imputed to these thinkers is more an invention of commentators than something that can be found in their work. This process of filtering is something that has marked the reception of French theory more generally (Cusset, 2008). Indeed, the 'poststructuralist position' that is described above is a fiction that has been created in Critical Management Studies, sometimes based on commentaries but often at the expense of the original authors' writings, even though these authors are still appealed to in an effort to legitimise claims about this position (see Jones, 2002, 2003).

The second notable issue that is raised when we think of poststructuralism as a set of thinkers is that we move away from the abstract notion of a perspective, of a 'position', that comes almost from nowhere. Instead the emphasis is put back on particular thinkers who advanced particular thoughts, and above all they made *arguments* for them. One of the unfortunate aspects of the reception of poststructuralism in management studies has been the lack of willingness to argue for particular claims made by these thinkers. It often looks as if a thinker such as Derrida merely dreamt up his ideas, in isolation, in the absence of quite specific arguments for his specific claims.

The third problem is that although the term poststructuralism is often used to cover the production of authors from around the late 1960s until the present day, in discussions in critical management studies there is often a sense that time stopped at some point shortly after the death of Foucault in 1984. Time stopped in two senses: firstly, thinkers of the first generation of poststructuralist writings (Deleuze, Derrida, Foucault) are very rarely subjected to careful, specific or sustained criticism, and secondly, thinkers of the generation following them – in France and beyond – are often not given their due. Indeed, even if we restrict our focus to France then we see a distinct and quite different set of arguments in the more recent work of Alain Badiou or Jacques Rancière. The point is that the word poststructuralism has often been used to claim a final and solid position, when it might better be used to refer to a moment that has now been passed.

For these three reasons, then, although the term 'poststructuralism' ushered a break of fresh air into critical management studies, there is a danger that it acts today as a defensive closure and consolidation rather than an invitation to think and to explore. If we conceive of poststructuralism as a placeholder that points to something elsewhere then we might today be tempted to erase this word and venture into that 'elsewhere'.

FURTHER READING

Jones, C. (2009) 'Poststructuralism in Critical Management Studies', in M. Alvesson, T. Bridgman and H. Willmott (eds) *Handbook of Critical Management Studies*, pp. 76–98. Oxford: Oxford University Press.

Jones, C. and ten Bos, R. (eds) (2007) *Philosophy and Organization*. Oxford: Routledge.

Linstead, S. (ed.) (2004) *Organization Theory and Postmodern Thought*. London: Sage.

See also: *Deconstruction, Discourse, Identity, Paradigm, Postmodernism, Power, Subjectivity and Subjectivation*

REFERENCES

Alvesson, M. and Deetz, S. (2000) *Doing Critical Management Research*. London: Sage.

Chia, R. (1995) 'From Modern to Postmodern Organizational Analysis', *Organization Studies* 16(4): 579–604.

Clegg, S. (1989) *Frameworks of Power*. London: Sage.

Cusset, F. (2008) *French Theory: How Foucault, Derrida, Deleuze, & Co. Transformed the Intellectual Life of the United States*, trans. J. Fort. Minneapolis: University of Minnesota Press.

poststructuralism

Fleetwood, S. (2005) 'Ontology in Organization and Management Studies: A Critical Realist Perspective', *Organization* 12(2): 197–222.

Jones, C. (2002) 'Foucault's Inheritance/Inheriting Foucault', *Culture and Organization* 8(3): 225–38.

Jones, C. (2003) 'Theory After the Postmodern Condition', *Organization* 10(3): 503–25.

Power

Stewart Clegg

Definition: Power is embedded in the relational shaping of the world.

The concept of power is probably *the* most contested term in social theory. The key contemporary literature that uses the term can be traced back to the early writings of Niccolò Machiavelli and Thomas Hobbes. Hobbes saw power as equivalent to a causal relation, whereby, mechanically, some action causes another as a reaction, while Machiavelli was more inclined to discuss power in terms of strategy. Hobbes' influence has been most marked in debates about power in which the conception of it as a causal relation has been predominant. Hobbes has been more influential in discussions of power that see the concept in terms of a capacity that causes things to happen, while Machiavelli has been more influential on approaches to power that see it in terms of the overall structuring of social relations as a field of complex forces, strategies and tactics.

Within management studies, the major works that use the concept of power have been split between these two approaches. In the Hobbesian tradition is work by authors such as Pfeffer and Salancik, which sees power in terms of resource dependencies, whereby those who have most resources are more likely to secure outcomes that they desire. On balance, most mainstream organisation theory and organisation behaviour approaches to power use an underlying model of power as a causal relation in which things happen because of some control over resources or capacity that some actor(s) possess compared to others and whose effects can be seen in terms of the distribution of resources. However, the distribution of resources that are embedded in overall structures of power relations defined in terms of variable control over means of production, communication and administration are generally not regarded as a part of power; instead, these are seen as 'authority'. Authority is regarded as the normal shape of things in terms of structured social relations of command and obedience that are not questioned.

Writers influenced by the French poststructuralist Michel Foucault are more inclined to see power in terms of forces, strategies, and tactics, in a view of the world more Machiavellian than Hobbesian. These writers are less likely to accept authority as something naturalised or normalised and instead are interested in how what is taken-for-granted as natural and normal has been constituted. Their remit is much broader than that of the writers concerned with causality and rather than focus on people observably doing things to others that have immediate consequences, in terms of causes and effects, they will be interested in how the meaningful relations of people at work, and in and between organisations, are constructed and reproduced.

POWER AND POLITICS

The management and organisation theory of the 1950s barely had any conceptions of power in it. In the 1960s, influenced profoundly by Michel Crozier's (1964) account of how maintenance workers in a French tobacco monopoly were able to use the dependency of other members of the organisation on their capacity to resolve the only source of uncertainty – machine breakdowns – in which the smooth functioning of all other elements of the system depended, a limited conception of power emerged as a mainstream part of analysis that saw power as something that was exercised illegitimately by actors in a system to gain some advantage they would not otherwise have. Authors such as Mintzberg (1983) popularised these views in the 1980s.

From the mid-1970s a Marxist account of power that saw power defined in terms of relations of production and exploitation came into focus after the publication of Braverman's (1974) work, that led to a lively debate about power and resistance that has been maintained to the present day (Fleming and Spicer, 2007). Joining this debate from the later 1970s was a focus on power as essentially a matter of discipline embedded in discourses as a result of the influence of Foucault's work. Both Braverman and Foucault's influence oriented researchers to more ethnographic accounts of organisations while the more causally inclined researchers tended to rely on survey methods to 'measure' power and influence. Foucauldian studies have come to centre on the twin foci of how issues of identity are constituted discursively and organisationally, thus making a bridge with studies of gender, ethnicity and postcolonialism, and with how organisations constitute surveillance over their members. Typically, the focus on hierarchical and surveillance elements in power relations has been more emphasised by labour process theorists influenced by Braverman, than discourse analysts, who have been more influenced by Foucault.

There are still quite distinct traditions of work established in the field. Mainstream work continues to survey bases of power and to propose that power is an essentially causal concept. Some of the debates from broader social theory, especially around Lukes' (2005) three-dimensional conception of power, have crept in and modified the rather restricted conception of causality at work in a limited number of mainstream theories. Ideas from Foucault have largely been a no-go zone for the mainstream. Labour process studies have become largely reiterations of cases of power and resistance, often emphasising more subtle and individual forms of resistance, given the decline in industrial relations struggles as a result of the dominance of neoliberal ideas. There are occasional calls from the margins of the mainstream for more attention to be paid to structural matters of power, inequality and control (Greenwood and Hinings, 2002) but these go largely unheeded. The current fashion for institutional theory in management and organisation analysis, despite some of its auspices in well-regarded approaches to power in social theory (in Bourdieu, 1977) seems largely to have neglected issues of power. Recently there has been a resurgence of interest in the neglected but important work of Goffman (1961) on total institutions, such as prisons and religious foundations, as extreme examples of the practices of power that can be seen clearly therein but which are also evident in less extreme organisations.

FURTHER READING

Clegg's work (Clegg, 1989; Clegg et al., 2006) is a starting point for students interested in this concept. Fleming and Spicer (2007) provide a good review of the current field and Badham and Buchanan (2008) provide a useful overview of the uses of power and politics in organisations and management.

See also: Bureaucracy, Critical Realism, Critical Theory, Gender, Labour Process Theory, Marxism and Post-Marxism, Postmodernism, Poststructuralism, Surveillance

REFERENCES

Badham, R. and Buchanan, D. (2008) *Power, Politics and Organizational Change: Winning the Turf Game.* London: Sage.

Bourdieu, P. (1977) *Outline of a Theory of Practice.* Cambridge: Cambridge University Press.

Braverman, H. (1974) *Labor and Monopoly Capital: The Degradation of Work in the Twentieth Century.* New York: Monthly Review Press.

Clegg, S.R. (1989) *Frameworks of Power.* London: Sage.

Clegg, S.R., Courpasson, D. and Phillips, N. (2006) *Power and Organizations.* London: Sage.

Crozier, M. (1964) *The Bureaucratic Phenomenon.* Chicago: University of Chicago Press.

Fleming, P. and Spicer, A. (2007) *Contesting the Corporation: Struggle, Power and Resistance in Organizations.* Cambridge: Cambridge University Press.

Goffman, E. (1961) *Asylums.* Harmondsworth: Penguin.

Greenwood, R. and Hinings, C.R. (2002) 'Disconnects and Consequences in Organization Theory', *Administrative Science Quarterly* 47: 411–21.

Lukes, S. (2005) *Power: A Radical View,* 2nd edn. London: Palgrave Macmillan.

Mintzberg, H. (1983) *Power in and Around Organizations.* Englewood Cliffs: Prentice-Hall.

power

Queer Theory

Nancy Harding

> **Definition:** Queer Theory (QT) is both theory and political action. Definition is impossible, but QT can be summarised as exploring the oppressive power of dominant norms, particularly those relating to sexuality, and the immiseration they cause to those who cannot, or do not wish to, live according to those norms. In analysing the power of 'the normal', QT contributes to a politics and ethics of difference. It challenges dominant norms, especially those of sexuality.

Its predecessors are feminist theories and lesbian/gay studies, but its strongest influence is the work of Michel Foucault. Sedgwick's *Epistemology of the Closet* (1991) and Butler's *Gender Trouble* (1990) are regarded as QT's foundational texts, even though they were written before the term was coined in 1990. These books question the essentialist, given nature of grounding categorisations such as heterosexual/homosexual and why one category is regarded as inferior to the superior other. They also perhaps allow challenge to ontologies other than sex and gender, including manager/employee.

Feminism showed how gender is socially constructed upon a biological base, Butler showed that biology, too, is constructed. Butler argues that what is constructed is not identities such as male/female, straight/gay, but *regulatory fictions* that both govern identities and order the 'taken-for-granted' through which identities emerge. There is no 'core' or essential 'centre' producing an authentic identity: rather it is the performance of identity which produces that identity. Sex, sexuality and gender are achieved through work, through the very *doing* of practices governed by the norms of how a person with the relevant genitalia *should* behave. This is what Butler means by 'performativity', in contrast to its use in management studies where it refers to the productive capacities of organisations.

Failure to conform to dominant norms renders a person abject. Dominant norms are heteronormative. Heteronormativity is:

the institutions, structures of understanding, and practical orientations that make heterosexuality seem not only coherent – that is, organized as a sexuality – but also privileged. Its coherence is always provisional, and its privilege can take several (sometimes contradictory) forms: unmarked, as the basic idiom of the personal and the social; or marked as a natural state; or projected as an ideal or moral accomplishment. It consists less of norms that could be summarized as a body of doctrine than of a sense of rightness produced in contradictory manifestations – often unconscious, immanent to practice or to institutions. Contexts that have little visible relation to sex practice ... can be heteronormative in this sense, while in other contexts forms of sex between men and women might *not* be heteronormative. Heteronormativity is thus a concept distinct from heterosexuality. (Berlant and Warner, 2003: 179/80 ff)

QT therefore shows that we are born into heteronormative cultures in which rules of gender and other identities already exist. To exist as a person, as an 'I', requires conforming to those rules and norms. Refusal or inability to conform leaves only an unrecognisable 'I', an 'I' with no place and no identity, an 'I' regarded as so strange, subordinate, inferior, 'queer' it is infused with shame. Crucially, the dominant requires the despised subordinate in order to know itself as dominant: heterosexuality *requires* homosexuality, queer makes straight.

Proponents of QT are often radical social constructionists who use the theory's insights to develop a politics of change.

QT IN ORGANISATION STUDIES (OS)

QT's influence in OS is developing slowly. Current literature in OS can be divided into three types: (1) explorations of workplace gender/sexualities; (2) theorising from the working lives of non-heterosexual people to explore organisations more generally; and (3) using QT to explore other forms of immiseration. The first paper in OS that could be called 'queer', although it does not use the term, is by Brewis, Hampton and Linstead (1997) who aim to destabilise concepts of gender in workplaces. Bowring (2004) shares that aim, wishing to make leadership theory queer through doing away with 'the presuppositions and expectations at the heart of the binary distinctions that are so prevalent in positivist research' (402). A strong strand in this category explores the working lives of LGBT (lesbian, gay, bisexual and transsexual) people (e.g. Rumens, 2008).

queer theory

199

Authors attempting to develop broader theory about organisations based on the lives of gay men include Lee (2004) who analyses the heteronormativity of management through exploring gay managers who adopt a 'straight' subject position, and Steyeart (2010) who uses Derek Jarman's late work to call for heterotopic organisational spaces in which the rigidity of workplace identities is shattered. Papers using QT to develop understanding of various forms of workplace oppression include: Parker (2002) who turns QT back upon management theory more generally; Tyler and Cohen (2008) who 'undo' managerial claims through analysing the BBC television series *The Office* using Butler's work; and Lee, Harding and Learmonth (2008) who reread interview transcripts to open new ways of understanding public-sector organisations.

Queer theorists working in OS thus aim to explore sex, sexuality and gender in organisations, and/or to identify ways in which organisations render working lives more or less unliveable. This summary disguises uncertainty about the ethics of broadening QT's focus beyond sex, sexuality and gender.

Should QT analyse only sex and gender, or can it be used to challenge other ontologies? Sedgwick and Butler have differing views. Sedgwick (quoted in Halle, 2004: 10) writes 'Given the historical and contemporary force of the prohibitions against *every* same-sex sexual expression, for anyone to disavow those meanings, or to displace them from the term's definitional center, would be to dematerialize any possibility of queerness itself.' So, to extend QT's arguments to issues other than sex/gender could lessen its political impact in relation to sexualities. Butler, meanwhile, has written that although her focus is on gender her theories can be applied in other domains, including that of work. Halle (2004: 10) supports Butler's stance, writing that 'queer knowledge was never a property of the homosexual. Queer knowledge adhered to and often accrued to the homosexual, but it never belonged to the homosexual'.

CONCLUSION: USING QT IN OS?

Organisation theorists' use of QT is still evolving. Some prefer to limit its use to issues surrounding sex, sexuality and gender, whereas others argue it offers potential for understanding the abjection which organisations impose upon working lives. This needs debate within OS. On the one hand: what disservice would be done if issues regarding sexualities in organisations were side-lined by a heteronormative impetus to colonise queer theory? On the other hand: what disservice would be done if the emancipatory potential of QT was not used to develop a politics of workplace change more generally? There can be no easy answers to these questions, but the debate itself could facilitate understanding of the impact of organisations upon the people who work in them in the twenty-first century.

FURTHER READING

The works of Butler and Sedgwick are challenging to read but vital and repay the effort. Foucault's *History of Sexuality* is indispensable reading. A useful introductory text is Jagose's (1997) and Parker (2002) is vital reading in OS. Generally, however, an interest in queer theory requires reading texts in disciplines other than management and organisation studies, including philosophy, sociology and cultural studies.

See also: Feminism, Gender, Postmodernism, Poststructuralism, Sexuality

REFERENCES

Berlant, L. and Warner, M. (2003) 'Sex in Public', in R.J. Corber and S. Valocchi (eds) *Queer Studies*, pp. 170–83. Oxford: Blackwell.

Bowring, M.A. (2004) 'Resistance is Not Futile: Liberating Captain Janeway from the Masculine–Feminine Dualism of Leadership', *Gender, Work and Organization* 11: 381–405.

Brewis, J., Hampton, M.P. and Linstead, S. (1997) 'Unpacking Priscilla: Subjectivity and Identity in the Organization of Gendered Appearance', *Human Relations* 50: 1275–1304.

Butler, J. (1990) *Gender Trouble.* London: Routledge.

Halle, R. (2004) *Queer Social Philosophy.* Chicago: University of Chicago Press.

Jagose, A. (1997) *Queer Theory: An Introduction.* New York: New York University Press.

Lee, H. (2004) 'Queer(y)ing Health Management', in M. Learmonth and N. Harding (eds) *Unmasking Health Management*, pp. 129–42. New York: Nova Publishers.

Lee, H., Harding, N. and Learmonth, M. (2008) 'Queer(y)ing Public Administration', *Public Administration* 86(1): 1–19.

Parker, M. (2002) 'Queering Management and Organization', *Gender, Work and Organization* 9: 146–66.

Rumens, N. (2008) 'Working at Intimacy: Gay Men's Workplace Friendships', *Gender, Work and Organization* 15(1): 9–30.

Sedgwick, E.K. (1991) *Epistemology of the Closet.* New York: Harvester.

Steyeart, C. (2010) 'Queering Space: Heterotopic Life in Derek Jarman's Garden', *Gender, Work and Organization* 17(1): 45–68.

Tyler, M. and Cohen, L. (2008) 'Management in/as Comic Relief: Queer Theory and Gender Performativity in *The Office*', *Gender, Work and Organization* 15(2): 113–32.

Reflexivity

Carl Rhodes and Edward Wray-Bliss

> **Definition:** Reflexivity refers to the idea that people are actively involved in the process of producing their own sense of reality, on account of the cultural dispositions, personal biases and ideological expectations that they use to interpret their experiences. In critical management studies (CMS) this has been especially taken up in terms of methodological reflexivity and the call for researchers to account for the ways that, rather than passively reporting on what they research, they are active in the construction of its meaning.

Reflexivity has become a major methodological preoccupation for researchers and writers of organisational research. Contemporary organisational theorists have struggled with the question of how to conduct and write reflexive research (Cunliffe, 2003) to such an extent that reflexivity is named by some as one of the core identifying features that unites critical approaches to the study of management (Fournier and Grey, 2000). Emerging through debates over methodology leading up to the 1990s, reflexivity marks a critique of the assumed scientism of positivist organisational research and, in CMS, its complicity with functionalism and managerialism. With reflexivity researchers are understood as active in their rendering of organisational realities, rather than being passive transmitters of an observable and externalised world accessed through the application of an assumedly neutral suite of established methods.

Reflexive researchers see the social world as being constructed rather than discovered by research (Alvesson et al., 2008). For them language constitutes and constructs, rather than represents, organisation and organised meaning, both on account of the particularities of individual researchers, and the habits and dispositions they inherit from the research community of which they are a part (Hardy et al., 2001). Research writing is no more just concerned with the epistemological function as the medium of knowledge, but is recognised in terms of its ontological function of constituting that which it commonly professes to represent (Johnson and Duberley, 2003). The methodological onus is to acknowledge research as being the production of subjective and cultural knowledge, rather than the production of 'truth' independent of people and culture.

In response to reflexivity researchers have been called to account for their own entanglement in the knowledge they produce and the power that is implicit in it. Researchers are asked to engage in research practices that enable them to reflect back on their own relationship to the research process and to research subjects. The emphasis is on processes of self-accounting within research texts themselves. Attending to 'textual practices used by researchers to present their work reflexively' (Alvesson et al., 2008: 481) commonly manifests in researchers including in their writing a meta-commentary on their own work that explicitly acknowledges, and tries to account for, their role in the construction of the meaning of that writing. Reflexive researchers are implored to question how they 'make truth claims and construct meaning' so as to make the nature of those claims 'more transparent' (Cunliffe, 2003: 985). Other textual responses to reflexivity include the reporting of research from multiple perspectives, the inclusion of diverse 'voices' from the field in research, the questioning of the privileged position of research knowledge, and the theoretical destabilisation of research itself.

With reflexivity the identity of the researcher and of those researched are implicated and involved in the character of the research text. In the more extreme variant of radical reflexivity (Cunliffe, 2003), subjectivity and knowledge are regarded in terms of text, and their hierarchy disrupted such that 'the prized self-conception of intellectuals as underdetermined and autonomous' is undermined (Johnson and Duberley, 2003: 1294). Reflexivity points to a certain desirability for research to recognise itself as a creative practice that can delegitimise the common sense of reality and render that reality malleable rather than immutable – this possibility of the reconstruction of oppressive social arrangements being an appeal to CMS's broader project (Fournier and Grey, 2000).

CRITICS OF REFLEXIVITY

Reflexivity has not been without its critics in organisation studies. Czarniawska (in Weick 2002) has it that reflexivity can become narcissistic when researchers, in recognising themselves in the mirrors of their own text, fall in love with themselves and forsake those people and organisations that they are researching. Weick sums up that there needs to be a constant reminder that 'we are *not* the point'. He adds that 'in the name of reflexivity, many of us tend to be more interested in our own practices than in those of anybody else' (Weick, 2002: 898). This is so because reflexivity can become manifest in researchers writing extensively about themselves at the expense of attending to that which they are researching. There is also the danger of reflexivity becoming a machinery of moral judgements over other researchers who might be accused of failing to be adequately reflexive (cf. Alvesson et al., 2008).

Reflexivity intimates the demand to highlight the problematic power effects of the elevation of the expert academic voice over that of the researched. This ethos can work against itself, however, when reflexivity is responded to from a position that researchers can and should 'reveal' themselves in their research (Rhodes, 2009). Reflexive researchers are asked to 'make their assumptions *explicit*', '*expose* their situated nature', '*uncover* taken-for-granted practices', as well as '*revealing* how our research is a narrative construction with its own discursive rules and conventions' (Cunliffe, 2003: 985, 995, 1000 and 993, italics added). Reflexivity is thus concerned with rendering a researcher's biases 'visible through personal disclosure' (Hardy et al., 2001: 535).

The irony in reflexivity is that while it questions the authorial authority to know, it has been practised through the institution of an additional and more far-reaching knowledge and self-authority. This is the presumed ability of researchers to be able to be self-present in their writing by revealing themselves, as if a cloak of mystery and deceit can be removed to reveal the real goings on behind the artifice of the written account. When reflexivity means that researchers feel required to add their own meta-commentary about themselves in their work there is a significant danger of enhancing, rather than questioning, the authorial authority that spurred the turn to reflexivity in the first place. In such cases the author is not just claiming to 'know' their field in an authoritative manner, but also gesturing to knowing themselves in the same way (Rhodes, 2009).

ETHICS AND REFLEXIVITY

Latterly there is growing interest in explicitly shifting reflexivity from a preoccupation with the researcher's self, and the textual academic products of self, to the ethico-political relationship with the other. There has been a call for 'a more critical and ethical basis for constructing meaning, identities and the taken-for-granted workings of our institutions and language communities' (Cunliffe, 2003: 990). In relation to this Brewis and Wray-Bliss (2008) argue that reflexivity has been richly conceptualised, but poorly realised or embodied, by CMS in its research practices. Much greater attentiveness to, and reflexivity around, research ethics – to the possibilities and complexities of attempting to practically redraw the relationships between researcher and researched – is necessary, they argue, if the field wishes to explore the possibilities of what a *critical* management studies could be. As Rhodes (2009) has argued, such an exploration goes beyond a desire to know both self and other, and attends instead to the ways that research might be moved by an ethical openness to the other, and the experimentation with ways of writing that seek engagement with those people researched, rather than with pinning them down in structures and categories of one's own knowledge.

FURTHER READING

Reviews of reflexivity in organisation studies can be found in Alvesson et al. (2008), Johnson and Duberley (2003) and Cunliffe (2003). The implications of this for CMS in particular are considered by Brewis and Wray-Bliss (2008) who, together with Rhodes (2009), extend debates over reflexivity in terms of ethics and responsibility.

See also: Discourse, Paradigm, Postmodernism, Poststructuralism

REFERENCES

Alvesson, M., Hardy, C. and Harley, B. (2008) 'Reflecting on Reflexivity: Reflexive Textual Practices in Organization and Management Theory', *Journal of Management Studies* 45(3): 480–501.
Brewis, J. and Wray-Bliss, E. (2008) 'Re-searching Ethics: Towards a More Reflexive Critical Management Studies', *Organization Studies* 29(12): 1521–40.
Cunliffe, A. (2003) 'Reflexive Inquiry in Organizational Research: Questions and Possibilities', *Human Relations* 56(8): 983–1003.
Fournier, V. and Grey, C. (2000) 'At the Critical Moment: Conditions and Prospects for Critical Management Studies', *Human Relations* 53(1): 7–32.
Hardy, C., Phillips, N. and Clegg, S. (2001) 'Reflexivity in Organization and Management Theory: A Study of the Production of the Research "Subject"', *Human Relations* 54(5): 531–60.
Johnson, P. and Duberley, J. (2003) 'Reflexivity in Management Research', *Journal of Management Studies* 40(5): 1279–303.

reflexivity

Rhodes, C. (2009) 'After Reflexivity: Ethics, Freedom and the Writing of Organization Studies', *Organization Studies* 30(6): 653–72.

Weick, K. (2002) 'Real Time Reflexivity: Prods to Reflection', *Organization Studies* 23(6): 893–8.

Sexuality

Albert J. Mills

Definition: Sexuality refers to an individual's sexual self; those aspects of a person that are thought to relate to their interest and ability to engage in some form of sexual activity.

Sexuality centres on, but is not restricted to, such things as sexual attractiveness, sexual preference, sexual relationships, sexual fantasies, and a person's reproductive capacities. Anything, in fact, felt to deal with sexual feelings, thoughts, behaviours and relationships. However, as will be discussed below, definitions of sexuality cannot be entirely separated from the discourse of sexuality in which they are embedded. In other words, sexuality is the *focus* but also the *outcome* of various discourses of sexuality.

In one form or another essentialist notions of sexuality have played a dominant role in society over time. At the heart of this view sexuality is an inherent quality in people, a *natural* tendency, or drive, to seek out sexual pleasure and/or biological reproduction. Nonetheless, whether, how, and when such tendencies should be expressed is a contested area of debate. Such debates range from antigay pronouncements through to feminist accounts of the way that female sexuality has been characterised through patriarchal lenses. In such debates reference to the essential character of sexuality is often used to convince people of the unassailable evidence of the argument. When, for example, some marketers argue

key concepts in critical management studies

that 'sex sells' they act in the belief that they are appealing to some base instinct in their target audience. In some feminist accounts there is an implicit (if not explicit) argument that patriarchy masks women's 'real' sexuality or scope to express their own sexuality. At the other end of the spectrum, anti-gay arguments reference the unnatural character of 'homosexuality' as a reason for prohibiting gays from certain areas of social life. One of the more extreme examples in recent years have been the anti-gay regulations of the United States Armed Forces. Until quite recently US Army regulations referred to homosexuality as 'a severe personality defect', while the US Navy Regulations characterised 'homosexuals' as 'sexual deviates'.

Although covering widely differing opinions about the appropriate use and character of sexuality the essentialist view has arguably served to locate sexuality within the realm of the natural, with study – including feminist studies – focused on *its* representation and control. In contrast, a number of feminist and gender studies have sought to move the debate towards sexuality as an *outcome* of social interaction. Alternative perspectives include interactionist, psychoanalytic, and discursive approaches (Weeks, 1990).

The interactionist perspective views sexuality as an outcome of the interplay of language whereby, depending on the interactions between people, nothing or anything can be sexualised. From this perspective there is not anything that is intrinsically sexual but what is sexual depends on the labelling process whereby aspects of behaviour are understood through a lexicon of symbols. In a nod to biological explanation some symbolic interactionists speak of the 'bodily potentialities' that are experienced through the meanings ascribed to them (Weeks, 1990). It should be noted that this focus on the relationship between the body, sexuality and language moves away from the simple notion that language either describes and/or characterises the function of the body. Instead, language should be seen as the medium through which aspects of the body are constituted. It is through symbolic interaction that certain bodily potentialities come to be viewed as sexual/not sexual, normal/abnormal expressions of sexuality.

The psychoanalytic perspective – in particular the work of Lacan (1978) and Mitchell (1974) – also views sexuality as constituted in language, but not so much through symbolic interaction as a relatively fixed, pre-existing, symbolic order into which the child enters life. Within this perspective the focus is on the creation of sexual desire through a number of psychological processes that result from a person's trajectory from birth through adulthood. As Weeks (1990: 3–4) describes it, sexual desire is rooted in the 'pained entry of the child into the "symbolic order" . . . at the Oedipal moment, which instigates "desire"'. From this perspective language and meaning are seen as giving order to 'component instincts'.

The discursive perspective – specifically the work of Foucault (1980) – views sexuality as that which is produced through an interrelated process of thought, talk, behaviour and evaluation in regard to activities deemed sexual; in other words, the outcome of discourse. What this means in practice is that some things are viewed as characteristics of sexuality (e.g., certain types of attractiveness) and in the process are acted on in terms of their supposed qualities of sexuality. Thus, sexuality consists of selected human experiences (such as feelings, thoughts, discussions, emotions, and activities) that have come to be labelled as sexuality through discursive processes.

For example, to gossip about a supposed relationship between two co-workers observed in intimate discussion can have the effect of sexualising the observation by inviting people to think of the sexual consequences. The gossip is about sexuality because it serves to surface and evaluate the (suspected sexual) behaviours of those involved. In the process, people produce and reproduce sexuality.

The discursive perspective differs from the interactionist approach not only through its focus on the ordering processes of discourses that (re)produce and structure interactions but on its tracing of discourses over time. In the latter regard, Foucault (1980) views modern understandings of sexuality as rooted in manifestations of power, that 'sexuality' as we have come to know it is the associative outcome of a 'slowly developed discursive practice' which constitutes a (modern) science of sexuality: 'the essential features of the sexuality are not the expression of a representation that is more or less distorted by ideology, or a misunderstanding caused by taboos; they correspond to the functional requirements of a discourse that must produce its truth' (Foucault, 1980: 68). In material terms, the discursive approach views sexuality as working on 'bodies, organs, somatic localizations, functions, anatomophysiological systems, sensations, and pleasures' which have no internal or natural logics of their own (Foucault, 1980: 153).

SEXUALITY AT WORK

Each of the various perspectives and viewpoints can be found in play in one form or another in the management and organisational literature. One of the earliest attempts to understand the relationship between sexuality and work can be found in the studies of the Frankfurt School. Reich (1927/1968) in particular sought to fuse Marxism with Freudianism to develop a theory of sexuality. He argued that capitalism acted as a repressive system in which sexuality is subordinated to the supposed needs of capital accumulation and productivity. In the process sexuality is increasingly controlled, objectified, manipulated, and commodified by the agents of a system overly focused on the profit motive. Sexual energy is viewed as a distraction from the productive needs of capitalism. We can note here that this perspective reproduces the notion of an essential sexuality that is repressed. Variants of this approach can be found in the later work of Marcuse (Marcuse, 1970).

In the field of management and organisational studies, the work of Acker and van Houten (1974) represents an early attempt to understand the role of sexuality in workplace dynamics and research outcomes. Revisiting the Hawthorne Studies from a feminist perspective, Acker and van Houten argued that male supervisors and male researchers, respectively, used sexual dynamics or 'sex-differentiated power strategies' to control and study young female employees. Focusing on paternalism and control of female sexuality, Acker and van Houten (1974) went on to note that the Hawthorne researchers failed to recognise the impact of sexuality on the research outcomes.

In the ensuing decades a number of feminist, gender and poststructuralist organisational studies have focused on issues such as the eroticisation of female sexuality; sexual harassment; repression and desexualisation; men, masculinity and management; resistance; performativity; sexuality, organisational life, and bureaucratisation; the organisational construction of sexuality; violence; and a number of other studies that focus on the relationship between management, organisation and the social construction of sexuality and impact on relations at work.

FURTHER READING

One of the best overviews of sexuality at work is Hearn and Parkin's (2001) *Gender, Sexuality and Violence in Organizations: The Unspoken Forces of Organization Violations*.

See also: *Feminism, Gender, Poststructuralism*

REFERENCES

Acker, J. and van Houten, D.R. (1974) 'Differential Recruitment and Control: The Sex Structuring of Organizations', *Administrative Science Quarterly* 9(2): 152–63.

Foucault, M. (1980) *The History of Sexuality, Vol. 1*. New York: Vintage Books.

Hearn, J. and Parkin, W. (2001) *Gender, Sexuality and Violence in Organizations: The Unspoken Forces of Organization Violations*. Thousand Oaks, CA: Sage.

Lacan, J. (1978) *The Four Fundamental Concepts of Psycho-analysis*. New York: Norton.

Marcuse, H. (1970) *Eros & Civilization*. London: Sphere.

Mitchell, J. (1974) *Psychoanalysis and Feminism*. New York: Pantheon Books.

Reich, W. (1927/1968) *The Function of the Orgasm: Sex-economic Problems of Biological Energy*. London: Panther.

Weeks, J. (1990) *Sex, Politics & Society*. London: Longman.

Subjectivity and Subjectivation

Nick Butler

> **Definition:** Subjectivity is the experience of being a human subject. Subjectivation is the process by which one becomes a subject.

Subjectivity is a central concept in modern Continental philosophy, but its meaning is complex and variable. The philosophical idea of an individualised self-consciousness dates back to Descartes, for whom the thinking subject provides an indubitable foundation for truth in the world. Over the last fifty years, thinkers have challenged this essentialist notion of the subject. It is argued that, contrary to Descartes, the subject is not universally given, but is in fact socially constructed by forms of knowledge and techniques of power. The historical fabrication of subjectivity has come to be known as 'subjectivation'.

The word 'subject' has a number of meanings: it can refer to a unit of grammar (subject of a sentence), a disciplinary field (academic subject), and a legal status (British subject). It is typically used philosophically to describe an individual who is endowed with consciousness and capable of thought. It is worth noting that this definition of the subject is so broad and inclusive that it potentially encompasses almost everyone, barring only the most irrational or completely deranged. This was certainly part of its appeal for seventeenth century thinkers such as Descartes. The subject was important in philosophy at this time because it alone was thought to be able to ground knowledge upon a secure and stable basis. Although our senses may well deceive us, Descartes argued, a degree of absolute certainty can be attained by the very fact of thinking. This led to his famous assertion, *cogito ergo sum* ('I am thinking, therefore I exist'). Although Descartes did not speak about 'subjectivity' in its contemporary sense, he certainly helped to establish the primacy of human consciousness in philosophy over the next three centuries, from Kant's transcendental idealism to Husserl's phenomenology.

The privileged standpoint accorded to the subject has been an important focus of critique for structuralist and poststructuralist thought beginning in the mid-twentieth century. The target of these attacks is the assumption that human subjectivity is universal, rational, and non-gendered. The subject, as it is conceptualised from Descartes onwards, is now seen by many as a highly partial, Western European and male-oriented construct. This draws our attention to the fact that subjectivity is no longer considered as belonging intrinsically to the individual, existing outside of history. Rather, subjectivity is understood as something that comes to be attached to the individual at a particular time and in a particular place, and is therefore overlaid with social and political meanings.

An important early contribution to this debate is the French Marxist philosopher Louis Althusser's concept of interpellation, which he derives from the psychoanalyst Lacan's analysis of the mirror stage. The subject, for Althusser, is nothing more than the effect of ideology or, to be precise, ideological state apparatuses (ISAs) such as education, mass media and the family. Interpellation occurs when ISAs address the individual and compel them to identify with capitalist society as a free and autonomous subject. As Althusser explains, ISAs interpellate the individual in the same way that a policeman hails to a passerby, 'Hey, you there!': '[T]he hailed individual will turn round. By this mere one-hundred-and-eighty-degree physical conversion, he becomes a *subject*. Why? Because he has recognised that the hail was "really" addressed to him, and that "it was *really him* who was hailed" (and not someone else)' (2008: 48). The individual is transformed into a subject because he or she recognises him or herself in this hailing, for example, when a student responds to the teacher's call or a child to their parent's call. The process of interpellation is obscured when the individual mistakenly believes that they are, innately, a 'good student' or an 'obedient child'. But our sense of self, Althusser contends, is in fact determined by our everyday association with ISAs.

The critique of the universal humanist subject has since been extended by contemporary feminism, psychoanalysis, deconstruction and anthropology. Despite their theoretical disparity, what these approaches have in common is their explicit challenge to the notion of a freely-acting, freely-thinking subject. While this anti-subjectivist perspective is common to many structuralist and poststructuralist approaches, it is the work of Michel Foucault that has had most impact on how we understand subjectivity and subjectivation in critical management studies.

Broadly speaking, Foucault's work is concerned with the relation between knowledge and power in its constitution of the human subject. Knowledge, here, is understood as forms of expertise that are developed and applied by authorities such as doctors, psychiatrists and judges. Of particular interest to Foucault is how this knowledge characterises individuals in specific ways (e.g. as 'sick', 'mad', or 'criminal') and how this, in turn, allows their conduct to be governed according to certain criteria (e.g. to be diagnosed and cured, to be evaluated and confined, to be judged and punished). Medical, psychiatric, and judicial expertise targets the individual at the level of their will, inclinations and aptitudes, and in so doing renders them knowable and manageable as a particular type of subject. This departs from the conventional view of subjectivity as an unalterable ontological essence, our innermost core. For Foucault, subjectivity is manufactured by the nexus between knowledge and power at a given historical moment. As Nikolas Rose (1998: 37) puts it, processes of subjectivation can be understood as 'a kind of infolding of exteriority' whereby forces outside of us come to determine the way we intimately relate to ourselves and so constitute us as subjects.

Organisation studies has drawn extensively on the work of Foucault to examine modes of subjectivation in the contemporary workplace, although more recent work has begun to examine the contribution of Althusser, Lacan, Slavoj Žižek and Judith Butler to issues of subjectivity in organisational life. What is at stake for critical management scholars is the way in which subjects are produced at work by an interplay between authorities, expertise, techniques and institutions. On this view, we become who we are in organisations because our subjectivities are made there; our sense of self is not 'ours', strictly speaking, but the result of a complex set of relations.

FURTHER READING

The literature on subjectivity and subjectivation is extensive and diffuse. The best place to begin, in terms of a critique of the humanist subject, would be Foucault's own work. *The Order of Things* (1966/2002) provides an influential discussion of the construction of 'human nature' in modern scientific discourse; *Discipline and Punish* (1975/1991) extends this analysis by describing the role of disciplinary mechanisms in the formation of the modern subject; and *The Use of Pleasure* (1984/1992) recasts the debate by turning to the question of subjectivity and self-conduct in ancient Greece. Drawing on Foucault's ideas, Rose's *Governing the Soul* (1999) presents a detailed account of modes of subjectivation in the twentieth century.

See also: *Feminism, Governmentality, Identity, Ideology, Marxism and Post-Marxism, Postmodernism, Poststructuralism, Power*

REFERENCES

Althusser, L. (2008) *On Ideology*. London and New York: Verso.

Foucault, M. (1966/2002) *The Order of Things: An Archaeology of the Human Sciences*, trans. Alan Sheridan. London and New York: Routledge.

Foucault, M. (1975/1991) *Discipline and Punish: The Birth of the Prison*, trans. Alan Sheridan. London: Penguin.

Foucault, M. (1984/1992) *The Use of Pleasure: The History of Sexuality, Vol. 2*, trans. Robert Hurley. London: Penguin.

Rose, N. (1998) *Inventing Our Selves: Psychology, Power, and Personhood*. Cambridge: Cambridge University Press.

Rose, N. (1999) *Governing the Soul: The Shaping of the Private Self*, 2nd edn. London and New York: Free Association Books.

subjectivity and subjectivation

Surveillance

Rick Iedema and Carl Rhodes

> **Definition:** Surveillance refers to ways that employees are observed by their managers, peers and even themselves in workplace settings as a means through which their behaviour, performance and identity are monitored and disciplined.

Surveillance has performed a prominent role in critical management and organisation studies since the early 1990s. The central idea, adapted from Michel Foucault's panoptic theory (pan = everywhere; optic = see), is that when employees are placed under direct or indirect surveillance they will enact the behaviours desired by those watching them (Foucault, 1977). Panoptic theory was based on the design principle inscribed into Jeremy Bentham's 1785 fan-shaped prison, isolating prisoners and arranging their cells so as to make a large number of them observable to a single warden. This principle was applied in workplace design, subjecting people at work to similar forms of surveillance. The theory underpinning Bentham's design is that surveillance, and even merely the suspicion of being watched, leads people to identify with the norms and values embedded in the surveilling gaze.

Panoptic theory regards surveillance as a pervasive, potent and sometimes even dangerous expression of power in contemporary organisations. It extends supervisory control beyond traditional command-and-control relationships and mechanisms. In what Collinson (2003) refers to as the 'surveillance-based organization', employee monitoring by management is further extended by embedding surveillance over what workers do to themselves and each other. Here, surveillance is a matter of not just being physically watched by superiors, but also becoming entwined in a range of 'horizontal' practices through which employees render each others' behaviour the target of normative judgement. Such practices include team work, performance management, and corporate culture programmes. Surveillance then can be potentially productive, engendering in employees a 'natural need' to show initiative, commitment and organisational identification.

While traditional forms of monitoring focus on managing what people do, surveillance is seen to extend the ambit of managerial power to who people are, and how they speak and behave in each others' presence. Surveillance thereby offers management forms of 'power and discipline [that] actively construct conformist selves' (Collinson, 2003: 536) thanks to the strength of the employee's pervasive suspicion that s/he is being observed by those in power. Through this suspicion, the worker 'inscribes in himself [*sic*] the power relation in which he simultaneously plays both roles [of observer and observed]; he becomes the principle of his own subjection' (Foucault, 1977: 202–3).

'Becoming the principle of one's own subjection' is given a key explanatory function in surveillance theory. Surveillance therefore is a psychological technology: it comes to manage the 'subjectivity' of workers by inviting them to internalise supervisory monitoring, scrutiny, assessment and evaluation. An important concern is that this internalisation is a form of self/other discipline whose norms and values are determined without involving workers or acknowledging their interests. Construed as 'soft power' due to being surreptitiously exacted by the self on the self and neighbouring others, the surveillant gaze is therefore regarded as ethically and politically dubious (Sewell and Barker, 2006).

Central to the meaning and effect of surveillance in organisations is a historical shift in power from overt and direct control to covert forms of discipline that operate through workers' involvement, engagement, commitment and mutual attention. Regarding these practices as prototypical of management-instilled self-surveillance, surveillance theory furnishes organisational scholars with a psychologised explanation as to how workers in contemporary organisations are led to acquiesce to, as well as help accomplish, management control. Here however, the line between organisational surveillance and social interaction begins to blur. Workers' identity performances are not necessarily limited to what they do and say within the organisation, or as part of their organisational tasks, raising questions about the psychological depth and reach of surveillance.

In response, surveillance theorising has moved out from Foucault's panoptic explanation towards what is termed a 'postpanoptic view'. Postpanoptic power stretches further and wider than direct (embodied) surveillance by engaging with how surveillance is now operationalised

surveillance

'from a distance', targeting and enlisting people in spaces other than organisational ones. Surveillance here is no longer contingent on (the suspicion of) 'being seen' by an identifiable supervisor or colleague. Instead, postpanopticism highlights how becoming a surveillance-aware person is contingent on everyday dialogic practices whose norms and values are congruent with those of the original panoptic gaze by being 'purposive and productive' in essence. This everyday self- and peer-surveillance is reinforced further by technologised types of surveillance, constituted by an expansive grid of electronic multidirectional informational traces, biometric measurement, satellite-enabled and telecommunication surveillance.

Besides pointing to the ubiquity of surveillance in contemporary society, this postpanoptic theorising also addresses one of the main limitations of conventional surveillance theory: the view that traditional power relations and surveillance practices are fully efficacious for 'objectifying the subject'. As Townley (2005) points out, surveillance theory regards organisational discipline as producing comprehensive control, give or take some resistance. Submitting to the internalisation of surveillance leaves the person 'imprisoned' unless their resistance salvages them. This pairing of surveillance with resistance creates a 'control/resistance dualism' that evidences 'a totalitarian vision' (Townley, 2005: 645). But organisational relationships cannot be fully explained on the basis of compliance and resistance. Subject making, or *subjectivisation*, exceeds whatever organisations might seek to do with, or demand from, people. Indeed, an 'overly deterministic and omnipotent conception of power effectively rule[s] out the active subject' (Knights and McCabe, 2003: 427). Because subjects harbour their own vitality, they may comply or resist, but, because they are each a unique and constantly changing assemblage of affects (Thrift, 2004), they will inevitably also lapse in the face of the subjectifying forces that envelop them.

A key limitation of surveillance theory, then, is that it fails to explore employees' responses to, or uses of, surveillance that exceed control, compliance and resistance. An alternative perspective reveals that surveillance is constituted in and through complex interactive dynamics among employees from various ranks and roles. Studying these interactive dynamics reveals that people's seeing and being seen exceed surveillance as organisational control mechanism. Alongside the panoptic and the postpanoptic understandings of surveillance, this third rendering takes surveillance away from necessarily exploitative readings of power and control, towards a paradigm that also acknowledges the significance of interactive complexity and emergent conduct. Indeed, what is retrieved here is the potential for 'sur-veillance' (Fr. 'watch/guard over') to instil or harbour an ethic of care. This reading regards the meanings, feelings and effects produced by organisational practices in general, and surveillance in particular, as uncertain, open-ended and sometimes even contradictory, but never entirely circumscribed by compliance and/or resistance (Iedema and Rhodes, 2010).

Originally seen as a relational technology turned on workers to exact their submission to managerial prerogatives, then, surveillance can now also be recognised as potentially enabling caring conduct by underwriting values that are congruent with, or of benefit to, those of the worker. On grounds that 'being seen' does not necessarily constitute a form of control that translates into subjection, surveillance can equally well produce vigilance or observance of agreed or sensible forms of action and interaction.

On a broader front, surveillance can now also be read as one of the means through which workers respond to, and link in to, constantly changing organisational directions and social coalitions. This mode of surveillance harbours the potential of accounting for how workers enter new modalities of co-operation and competition. This surveillance ensnares everyone equally, managers, supervisors and workers, in a constant monitoring of situational change, interpersonal realignment and productive movement. Here, surveillance assumes a much broader spectrum of meanings than allowed for in 'surveillance theory'. From accounting for organisational power and worker subjection in psychologised terms, this more expansive concept of surveillance encompasses employees' attentiveness to the ongoing play of shifting priorities and orientations that increasingly define organisational participation and identity.

FURTHER READING

Given the reliance on the work of Michel Foucault to theorise surveillance in organisations, the best starting point for further reading is *Discipline and Punish* (1977). Within critical management and organisation studies, key authors who have applied Foucault's ideas include David Collinson, David Knights, Darren McCabe, Graham Sewell and Barbara Townley.

See also: *Discourse, Governmentality, Identity, Power, Subjectivity and Subjectivation*

REFERENCES

Collinson, D. (2003) 'Identities and Insecurities: Selves at Work', *Organization* 10(3): 527–47.

Foucault, M. (1977) *Discipline & Punish: The Birth of the Prison*. Harmondsworth: Penguin.

Iedema, R. and Rhodes, C. (2010) The Undecided Space of Ethics in Organizational Surveillance, *Organization Studies*, 31(2): 199-217.

Knights, D. and McCabe, D. (2003) *Organization and Innovation: Guru Schemes and American Dreams*. Maidenhead: Open University Press.

Sewell, G. and Barker, J.R. (2006) 'Coercion Versus Care: Using Irony to Make Sense of Organizational Surveillance', *Academy of Management Review* 31(4): 934–61.

Thrift, N. (2004) 'Intensities of Feeling: Towards a Spatial Politics of Affect', *Geografiska Annaler* 86B(1): 57–78.

Townley, B. (2005) 'Controlling Foucault', *Organization* 12(5): 643–8.

Utopia and Utopianism

Pauline Maclaran

Definition: Utopia is a name for an ideal society; utopianism refers to social theory that envisages schemes of perfection. The terms are used in a colloquial sense to imply wishful fantasising.

The concept of 'utopia' was originally introduced into English society by Sir Thomas More in 1516 in his book that first described the ideal land of Utopia where people lived in harmony and happiness. Etymologically the word is a mixture of the Greek words 'outopia' (nowhere) and 'eutopia' (a good place), resulting in the intended pun of 'nowhere being a good place'. As a literary form, More's book was designed not only to entertain, but also to create a context in which More could offer a critique of existing society in a Tudor England where neither freedom of speech nor freedom of thought existed.

key concepts in
critical management studies

This seminal work by More gave birth to a whole literary genre that has spawned many diverse and imaginative visions of what the ideal society might be, a genre that has been traced back as far as Plato's *Republic* (Manuel and Manuel, 1979). Being frequently visualised in terms of planning the ideal city, the concept of utopia has also permeated architectural theory and design. In particular, visions for urban reorganisation detailed by utopian socialists in the nineteenth century, such as Charles Fourier, Etienne Cabet and Robert Owen, have had a lasting impact on city planning. Fourier's design of phalansteries (systems of communal living) had a direct influence on retail planning from the design of early arcades and department stores, through to the contemporary shopping mall.

Although it is the literary genre that people tend to associate most readily with the word utopia, there is another, rather less familiar body of utopian scholarship inspired by these early socialist thinkers, a vein of scholarship that is sometimes described as 'emancipatory'. This places more emphasis on critical function and less on the literary form. In other words, rather than containing a comprehensive prescription for the ideal life with the minutiae of day-to-day living spelt out in their imaginary domains (e.g More's Utopia), the emancipatory writings stipulate more abstract goals for which to universally strive (e.g. Ernst Bloch's *The Principle of Hope* in which he explores the human potential to envisage a better world). Other famous neo-Marxist thinkers such as Herbert Marcuse and Karl Mannheim have also contributed to this latter body of writing that has influenced much political and social theory. The essence of the utopian in this context is its transformative quality in questioning the limitations of human existence and anticipating a better future. This utopianism envisions alternatives that challenge the status quo with a focus on utopia's function as social or critical theory, as opposed to its literary form and the detailed specification of a perfect society.

In general, whether of the literary or emancipatory variety, the utopian concept itself has been heavily criticised, primarily on account of its association with the universalising explanatory schemes of the modern era. Essentially this explains why scepticism towards utopia characterises much of twentieth-century thinking on the subject. The paradox of utopianism is that, instead of bringing about a system of peace and stability, it has so often, in its attempted realisation, brought about totalitarian coercion. Major world wars, mass bombings, figures such as Hitler and Stalin, the tarnished images of America and the former Soviet Union have all contributed to these anti-utopian feelings in the twentieth century.

Over the last two decades, however, there has been an increasing resurgence of interest in the concept of utopia, particularly driven by feminist writers (Sargisson, 1996). This has come alongside the acknowledgement that utopian thinking is more than just an escapist dream or a pejorative term for impossible imaginings. It is a significant part of western culture that provides a crucial critical function to question taken-for-granted assumptions and norms about the world around us (Levitas, 1990). Utopian thinking is a process that draws attention to the gap between what is, and what could be, thus opening up new conceptual spaces for the imagination to explore (Sargisson, 1996). The nature of this gap changes with a society's evolving consciousness. An increasing emphasis in the twentieth century on the function of utopia with its more broadly defined boundaries has also led to a change in the forms that the utopian impulse is seen to take. This thinking has been particularly influenced by Bloch (1988) who finds a utopian function in daydreams, myths, fairy-tales, travellers' tales, circuses, fairs, art, film, theatre, the sea voyages of medieval Irish monks and even the alchemists' attempts to synthesise gold.

Accordingly, many argue that utopia is not dead but rather transformed. In keeping with its historical and socio-cultural basis, utopia now mirrors the characteristics of a postmodern era where heterogeneity and pluralism are celebrated. In other words, utopia has become fragmented and individualised, traceable in many other cultural forms apart from the written text such as film, art, photography, music and many other forms of entertainment, and, ultimately, now deeply embedded in global consumer culture. For example, Maclaran and Brown's (2005) study of a refurbished festival marketplace showed how utopian meanings were created in a dyadic relationship between marketers and consumers, and how the festival marketplace provided consumers with a way of critiquing other forms of high street shopping.

As a way to express possible alternative ways of organising, utopianism is also very relevant to contemporary organisational theory (Parker et al., 2007), particularly in relation to the intersection between commerce as, for example, Henry Ford who set up churches and established a welfare education programme to provide moral guidance. Henry Ford was, of course, also the source of Huxley's 'our Ford' in *Brave New World*. The Oneida community, founded on utopian communal principles by John Humphrey Noyes in 1848, became the Oneida joint-stock company in 1881. In their 'gallery of utopians' Neville-Sington and Sington (1993: 257) list John Harvey Kellogg (1852–1945) who, to support his utopian ideals on good dietary habits, created and marketed cornflakes and branflakes, as 'part of a good breakfast'; and William Lever (1851–1925) who, as the soap magnate and philanthropist, tore down a slum in Liverpool to make way for a model estate, Port Sunlight, to house his workers. The creation of an ideal working community is also the philosophy underlying the paternalism of the early department store owners and Quaker enterprises such as Cadbury's at Bournville and the Rowntree empire. It is perhaps epitomised in present times by Walt Disney's EPCOT (Experimental Prototype Community of Tomorrow) Center and his Disney ideals. Bryman (1995) comments that by idealising aspects of America's past, present and future, the Disney parks celebrate America as a utopian space.

FURTHER READING

Frank and Fritzie Manuel's *Utopian Thought in the Western World* (1979) is the largest and most comprehensive overview of utopian thought. Most relevant to CMS is Martin Parker, Valerie Fournier and Patrick Reedy's *Dictionary of Alternatives: Utopianism & Organization* (2007) that gives an excellent summary of many fictional, political and social utopias as organisational counterpoints to market managerialism.

See also: *Alternative Organisation, Critical Theory, Feminism, Ideology, Marxism and Post-Marxism, McDonaldisation, Postmodernism*

REFERENCES

Bloch, E. (1988) *The Utopian Function of Art and Literature: Selected Essays*. trans. J. Zipes and F. Mecklenburg, Cambridge, MA: MIT Press.
Bryman, A. (1995) *Disney and His Worlds*. London: Routledge.
Levitas, R. (1990) *The Concept of Utopia*. New York: Philip Allan.
Maclaran, P. and Brown, S. (2005) 'The Center Cannot Hold: Consuming the Utopian Marketplace', *Journal of Consumer Research*, 32(September): 311–23.
Manuel, Frank E. and Manuel, Fritzie P. (1979) *Utopian Thought in the Western World*. Oxford: Basil Blackwell.
Neville-Sington, P. and Sington, D. (1993) *Paradise Dreamed: How Utopian Thinkers Have Changed the Modern World*. London: Bloomsbury.
Parker, M., Fournier, V. and Reedy, P. (2007) *Dictionary of Alternatives: Utopianism & Organization*. London and New York: Zed Books.
Sargisson, L. (1996) *Contemporary Feminist Utopianism*. London: Routledge.

index

key concepts in

critical management studies

index

key concepts in
critical management studies

index